D0205747

THE TRIUMPH OF PRACTICE OVER THEORY IN ETHICS

THE TRIUMPH OF PRACTICE OVER THEORY IN ETHICS

James P. Sterba

University of Notre Dame

New York   Oxford
OXFORD UNIVERSITY PRESS
2005

170
S83t

Oxford University Press

Oxford   New York
Auckland   Bangkok   Buenos Aires   Cape Town   Chennai
Dar es Salaam   Delhi   Hong Kong   Istanbul   Karachi   Kolkata
Kuala Lumpur   Madrid   Melbourne   Mexico City   Mumbai
Nairobi   São Paulo   Shanghai   Taipei   Tokyo   Toronto

Published by Oxford University Press, Inc.
198 Madison Avenue, New York, New York 10016
www.oup.com

Oxford is a registered trademark of Oxford University Press

Library of Congress Cataloging-in-Publication Data

M|L

Sterba, James P.
    The triumph of practice over theory in ethics / James P. Sterba.
       p. cm.
    Includes bibliographical references and index.
    ISBN 0-19-513284-X -- ISBN 0-19-513285-8 (pbk.)
       1. Ethics--History. I. Title.

  BJ71.S69 2004
  170--dc22

                                                    2004049530

Printing number: 9 8 7 6 5 4 3 2 1

Printed in the United States of America
on acid-free paper

This book is dedicated to all the people
who helped me in so many ways to write it.

CONTENTS

PREFACE

This book has been six long years in the making. At the beginning, it was not clear how to work out its central idea now captured in the title. Then, other book projects intervened (*Terrorism and International Justice* (Oxford, 2003) and *Affirmative Action and Racial Preference* with Carl Cohen (Oxford, 2003). As it turns out, the time it took the book to develop proved to be very useful. My ideas and arguments actually got better over the years, as I was able to run them by so many different people.

In its penultimate version, a good part of the book was read and commented on by our Ethics Discussion Group here at Notre Dame whose members at the time included, Julia Annas, Robert Audi, Lynn Joy, Alasdair MacIntyre, Kristin Shrader-Frechette, David Solomon, Fritz Warfield, Paul Weithman, and Nicholas Wolterstorff. A better group of commentators/critics an author cannot hope to find. Very special thanks also go to Carl Cohen, Janet Kourany, Terry Pell, Peter Singer, and Paul Taylor for extended discussion of the arguments of particular chapters of the book.

I also benefited from an earlier conference that was organized on my work at the University of Notre Dame. Those who contributed to the conference and/or to the volume of published essays that drew upon the conference included Michael Boylan, Claudia Card, Chung-Ying Cheng, Eve Browning Cole, John Corvino, John Deigh, C.F. Delaney, Bernard Gert, Alan Gewirth, Carol Gould, Denis Goulet, Karen Hanson, Alison Jaggar, Eva Kittay, Tibor Machan, Alistair Macleod, Charles Mills, Jan Narveson, Kai Nielsen, Holmes Rolston, Lilly Russow, Ruth Sample, Robert C. Solomon, Laurence Thomas, Rosemarie Tong, Mary Ann Warren, and Catherine Zuckert.

Earlier versions of the chapters of the book were presented at the American Philosophical Association, Eastern, Central, and Pacific Division Meetings on numerous occasions, the Australasian National University, Gustavus Adolphus College, Indiana State University, Kent State University, Lewis University, Loyola University of Chicago, the Mary Lou Williams Center for Black Culture at Duke University, Marymount University, McMaster University, Miami University of Ohio, Murray State University, the Research Triangle Ethics Discussion Circle, Santa Clara University, Southern Methodist University, the University of California at Irvine, the University of Cape Town, the University of Colorado at Boulder, the University of Edinbourgh, the University of Florence, the University of Illinois at Chicago, the University of Melbourne, the University of Missouri at Columbia, the University of North Carolina at Charlotte, the University of Notre Dame on numerous occasions, the University of Oregon, the University of Waterloo, the University of Witwatersrand, Utah Valley State College, Vanderbilt University, Walsh College, Washington University, the World Bank, the World Congress of Philosophy, the World Congress on Philosophy of Law and Social Philosophy, and Youngstown State University.

On these and other occasions, I benefited from the comments of so many people. In particular, I want to thank Kurt Baier, Tista Bagchi, David Benatar, Bernard Boxill, Jan Boxill, Allen Buchanan, Thomas Bushnell, Leon Dunkley, Gerald Early, Don Garrett, Bill Gay, Michael Goldman, Robert Goodin, Gary Gutting, Virginia Held, Vittorio Hosle, Aaron James, Robert Johanson, Philip Kain, Matthew Kennedy, Bonnie Kent, Christopher Kulp, Scott LaBarge, Anthony Laden, Linda LeMoncheck, Mark Levine, Douglas MacLean, Deborah Marble, Terry McConnell, Michelle Moody-Adams, Albert Mosley, Alan Nelson, Lawrence Nelson, James Nickel, Alasdair Norcross, Ernest Partridge, Glen Pettigure, Roger Pilon, Louis Pojman, Gerald Postema, Philip Quinn, Paul Quirk, Elizabeth Radcliffe, James Rakowski, David Reeve, Tom Regan, Jeffrey Reiman, John Robinson, Geoffrey Sayre-McCord, George Sher, Michael Smith, Cynthia Stark, Michael Walzer, Karen Warren, Peter Wenz, David Wong, and Iris Young.

I especially want to thank Robert Miller, Executive Editor at Oxford University Press, who persevered with me over the years it took to complete this book, the Institute for Scholarship in the Liberal Arts at the

University of Notre Dame and the National Humanities Center in North Carolina for financial support, and in the case of the center, an ideal environment in which to do much of the writing. Special thanks also go to Christine D'Antonio, Senior Project Editor, and to Douglas Puchowski for their help in the production of the book.

Material from previous publications is used with permission of Oxford University Press and Cambridge University Press.

THE TRIUMPH OF PRACTICE
OVER THEORY IN ETHICS

CHAPTER ONE

~

Introduction

Ethics appears to be unlike other areas of inquiry. After all, we cannot find contemporary defenders of Ptolemy (c.100–c.170 CE), Copernicus (1473–1543), or even Isaac Newton (1642–1727), all claiming to have the best theory of the physics of celestial motion. Nor are there contemporary mercantilists or physiocrats, as there were in the eighteenth century, all claiming to have the best theory of economics. But we can find contemporary defenders of Aristotle (384–322 BCE), Immanuel Kant (1724–1804), and John Stuart Mill (1806–1873), for example, all claiming to have the best theory of ethics. Of course, significant disagreements remain in other areas of inquiry, but the extent of disagreement appears to be much greater in ethics.

One explanation for this seemingly greater disagreement in ethics is that there is little or nothing that can really be established in ethics. This would explain why so many of the ethical theories that have been proposed in the past continue to have their contemporary defenders. According to this account, ethics simply lacks the resources to defeat any of the contending theories, and so they all remain live options. Obviously, this explanation does not put ethics in a very favorable light.

Another explanation, the one I defend in this book, is that traditional theories of ethics, be they Aristotelian, Kantian, Millian, or whatever, have come to be revised and reformed in such a way that, at least in their most morally defensible formulations, they no longer differ in the practical requirements they endorse. This explains how

1

contemporary philosophers can claim allegiance to the various figures in the history of ethics, while rejecting many of the substantive requirements these figures endorsed. In searching for what is morally defensible in these traditional theories, contemporary defenders have jettisoned much of what had distinguished these traditional theories from each other.

Consider, for example, the extent to which contemporary Aristotelians reject the views that Aristotle himself defended. Aristotle, in his *Nicomachean Ethics* and his *Politics,* defended a hierarchical society in which women were regarded as naturally inferior to men, and some men and women were regarded as natural slaves. Contemporary Aristotelians, however, reject both of these aspects of Aristotle's view. Alasdair MacIntyre, for example—probably the most well-known contemporary Aristotelian—explicitly rejects Aristotle's "indefensible defense of slavery," and at least implicitly rejects Aristotle's sexism as well. And Martha Nussbaum, another contemporary Aristotelian, further rejects all of the hierarchy in Aristotle's account as well.

Contemporary Aristotelians, moreover, disagree with each other as to whose account is best. Nussbaum, for example, has strongly criticized MacIntyre's views.[1] But their differences and disagreements do not preclude them from regarding each other as Aristotelians. What they share with Aristotle and with other contemporary Aristotelians, however, are only a few relatively formal tenets that distinguish them from their opponents, such as the priority of the good and the centrality of virtues to a good life.

What holds of Aristotle and his contemporary defenders, holds as well of Kant and Mill and other figures in the history of ethics and their contemporary defenders. Contemporary Kantians reject Kant's endorsement of the subordination of wives to their husbands and the exclusion of women from intellectual pursuits and political rights. They also reject Kant's racism. Kant held that "the Negroes of Africa have by nature no feeling that rises about the trifling . . . so fundamental is the difference between the two races of man [blacks and whites] and it appears to be as great in regard to mental capacities as in color."[2] Similarly, contemporary defenders of Mill reject Mill's colonialism. Mill wrote:

> Perhaps the English are the fittest people to rule over barbarous or semi-barbarous nations like those of the East, precisely because they are the stiffest, and most wedded to their own customs, of all civilized

people. All former conquerors of the East have been absorbed into it, and have adopted its ways, instead of communicating to it their own. So do the Portuguese; so would the French have done. Not so John Bull; if he has one foot in India he will always have another on the English shore.[3]

In addition, contemporary feminists, while praising Mill's defense of women's rights, note his failure to see any need to compensate women for the work they do in the home. Interestingly, Harriet Taylor, Mill's spouse and acknowledged inspiration, recognized such a need. She contended that it would be preferable "if women both earned and had a right to possess a part of the income of the family."[4] Accordingly, after all the corrections and modifications are made, all these major figures in the history of ethics share with their contemporary defenders only a few relatively formal tenets that distinguish them from their opponents. Indeed, what is frequently most interesting about the work of major figures in ethics and their contemporary defenders are the practical arguments offered for those claims that go beyond the relatively formal tenets that now differentiate them from their opponents. It is these practical arguments, not the relatively formal tenets that distinguish their views, which are primarily designed to support their conclusions about how we should act and be.

Yet important though these practical arguments are to the views defended by philosophers, unfortunately, they are not always very cogent. Take, for example, Aristotle's practical arguments for natural slaves and the domination of women. Concerning natural slavery, Aristotle remarks, "There are others . . . who regard the control of a slave by a master as contrary to nature. In their view the distinction of master and slave is due to law or convention; there is no natural difference between them: the relation of master and slave is based on force, and being so based has no warrant in justice."[5] Aristotle himself, however, rejects this view. A slaveowner himself, Aristotle held that slavery is justified by the inferior rationality of slaves, which enables them to recognize and obey commands but not to deliberate. Because of this deficiency, Aristotle argues that a slave needs to be ruled by a master.[6] Yet, at the same time, Aristotle supported the manumission of slaves. "It is wise to offer all slaves the eventual reward of emancipation," he said, and in his will, he freed his own slaves.[7] Thus, the overall argument that Aristotle offered for natural slavery is both inconsistent and weak.

Aristotle's argument for the subordination of women is even weaker. Aristotle judged women to be inferior to men because, although unlike slaves they can deliberate, the rational element in them lacks authority, that is, it is easily overruled by irrational impulses.[8] The explanation that Aristotle gives for this deficiency in women is that semen is warmer than menstrual discharge, heat being a principle of perfection in his biology.[9] Aristotle further argues that lack of heat in the reproductive process leads to the generation of females rather than males.[10] To back up his claim, Aristotle cites as evidence that young parents produce more female offspring and that more female offspring are conceived when the wind is in the north.[11] But this practical argument for the subordination of women clearly looks more like a conclusion in search of premises, especially since Aristotle provided no comparable explanation for the generation of natural slaves.

There are similar problems with some of Kant's practical arguments. In Kant's "What Is Enlightenment?" he calls on everyone to "have courage to use your own reason" and notes disapprovingly that:

> The guardians . . . will see to it that by far the largest part of mankind, including the entire "beautiful sex" should consider the step into maturity, not only as difficult, but as very dangerous.[12]

At the same time, Kant himself mocks women who take steps toward enlightenment. He writes:

> A women who . . . carries on fundamental controversies about mechanics, like the Marquise du Chatelet might as well even have a beard, for perhaps that would express more obviously the mien of profundity for which she strives.[13]

Yet by the time of her premature death in 1749 the Marquise du Chatelet was well known in French intellectual circles and had been elected to the Bologna Academy of Sciences.[14] She had published a book on the metaphysics of natural science, completed the first translation into French of Newton's *Principia Mathematica* (with commentary), as well as anonymously coauthored with Voltaire a popularization of Newtonian physics. Despite these accomplishments, she was unable to carry out anything like a long-term research program. Her responsibilities for family and household, with her husband absent on military service throughout most of their married life, made it impossible for her to lead the life of a full-time scientist. Indeed, she was able to achieve as much as she did only by functioning on four or five hours of sleep a night. Sometimes, she even survived on less by dipping her arms in ice water to stay awake. So we can see that the discipline that Marquise du Chatelet required to complete her scientific work somewhat matched the stern regimen that Kant imposed on his own life. Nevertheless, Kant himself, despite these facts of the Marquise du Chatelet's life, and despite his universal call to enlightenment, still argued that she and other women like her were unsuitable by nature for real intellectual achievement.[15]

Yet while it is sometimes useful to draw attention to the inadequate practical arguments of major figures in the history of ethics and their contemporary defenders, my main goal in this book is to set out practical arguments that should work for contemporary Aristotelians, Kantians, and Millians who are concerned to provide the most morally defensible formulations of their views.

In this book, I argue that the relatively formal tenets shared by Aristotelians, Kantians, and Millians respectively, when correctly understood, do little to divide these groups from one another, at least at the practical level, with regard to the most morally defensible formulations of their views. Take for example, the tenet of the priority of the good shared by Aristotelians and compare it with the tenet of the priority of the right over the good shared by Kantians. Surely these tenets appear to be opposed, but, in fact, when correctly understood, they're not. What needs to be understood here is that Aristotelians are using "the good" in a more inclusive sense than are Kantians. As a result, the Kantian good and right are included within the notion of "the good" as Aristotelians are employing the concept.[16] So Aristotelians can agree to the priority of the right over the good as Kantians are using these concepts, and Kantians can agree to the priority of the good as Aristotelians are using this concept. In short, there need not even be any theoretical conflict between Aristotelians and Kantians with regard to this issue, let alone any conflict at the level of practice. But obviously I need to do more to establish that there is this practical coincidence.

PREVIEW OF WHAT IS TO COME

In chapter 2, I take up the question of whether Kantian and Aristotelian ethical theories, suitably refurbished by their contemporary defenders, can be practically reconciled, and also whether they can provide an adequate justification for morality. I examine three ethical issues that have been thought to divide Aristotelians from Kantians: the ideal of a morally good or virtuous person, whether moral assessment requires a decision-procedure like Kant's categorical imperative, and the importance of rules to morality. I argue that these issues need not divide Aristotelians from Kantians under the most morally defensible interpretations of their respective views. I further argue that it is possible to provide a justification for morality that both Aristotelians and Kantians can accept, one that is grounded in a rational standard of non-question-beggingness.

In chapter 3, I take up the question of whether both Aristotelian and Kantian ethical theories, suitably refurbished, are in serious conflict with utilitarian ethical theories, suitably refurbished. I argue that they are not. First, I take up the presumed conflict between welfare liberal Kantian ethical theories, as exemplified in the work of John Rawls and utilitarianism. Then I examine the even greater presumed conflict between libertarian Kantian ethical theories and utilitarianism. With respect to the presumed conflict between welfare liberalism and utilitarianism, I argue that once utilitarianism is given its most morally defensible interpretation and so recognized to be constrained by the "ought" implies "can" principle that is common to all moral and political perspectives, it can be seen as practically reconcilable with Rawlsian welfare liberalism. Similarly, with respect to the even greater presumed conflict between libertarianism and utilitarianism, I argue that once libertarianism is also given its most morally defensible interpretation and so recognized to be constrained by the "ought" implies "can" principle, it too can be seen as practically reconcilable with utilitarianism.

In chapter 4, I attempt to extend the reconciliation at the practical level between Kantian and utilitarian ethics to reach agreement on the moral status of nonhuman life. I defend a form of nonanthropocentrism that gives moral status to all living beings against anthropocentrism that holds that all or only human beings have moral status. The nonanthropocentrism I defend is captured in principles of defense, self-preservation, disproportionality, and restitution. These principles attempt to strike the right balance between concerns of human welfare and the welfare of nonhuman nature in a way that should be acceptable to both Kantians and utilitarians alike. To provide an even more complete defense of this form of nonanthropocentrism, the perspectives of extraterrestrial invaders and radical Earth Firsters are also taken into account.

There follows a "Philosophical Interlude" in which I discuss how the practical reconciliation of Aristotelian, Kantian, and utilitarian ethics generally relates to the solutions of moral problems and how it specifically relates to the solutions of the moral problems discussed in the three chapters of the book that follow.

In chapter 5, I review the developments in sexual harassment law, hoping thereby to increase our understanding of what is, or better yet what should be considered sexual harassment. I offer a partial explanation of the high incidence of sexual harassment in both military and civilian life. I then suggest what positive norms we need to focus on in order to make progress toward reducing the frequency of sexual harassment.

In chapter 6, I discuss affirmative action. Affirmative action is a policy of favoring qualified women and minority candidates over qualified men or nonminority candidates with the immediate goals of outreach, remedying discrimination, or achieving diversity, and with the ultimate goals of attaining a color-blind (racially just) and a gender-free (sexually just) society. I examine each of these forms of affirmative action in order to determine when specifically they can be justified. I focus particularly on diversity affirmative action because of the U.S. Supreme Court's two recent very important decisions in this area: *Grutter v. Bollinger* (2003) and *Gratz v. Bollinger* (2003).

In chapter 7, I approach the question of how we should think about international terrorism from the perspective of just-war pacifism. Just-war pacifism, as I defend it, does not impose an absolute prohibition on intentionally harming innocents. In fact, using both hypothetical and historical examples as analogies, I argue that suicide bombing can be morally justified under certain conditions. I then consider whether Iraqi War II was morally justified. I argue that there was adequate evidence available before the war that Iraq was no longer attempting to develop nuclear weapons, nor had stockpiles of chemical or biological weapons, nor was linked to Osama bin Laden's Al Qaeda network. I further argue that there is also considerable evidence available that President Bush and members of his administration deliberately lied to the American people about whether Iraq presented such a threat, undercutting U.S. democracy in a way that merits impeachment. Finally, I contend that recent attempts to justify Iraqi War II on grounds other than a threat of weapons of mass destruction simply will not work.

Clearly, there will always be moral problems to resolve, but if we can achieve a practical reconciliation of Aristotelian, Kantian, and utilitarian ethics, the task of resolving such problems should be far easier.

CHAPTER TWO

Aristotelians and Kantians and the Justification for Morality

After contemporary Aristotelians and Kantians are finished cleaning up their respective ethical theories, making them as morally defensible as possible, can these theories be practically reconciled? Even more importantly, can these theories, so refurbished, tell us why we should be moral?

THEORETICAL DIFFERENCES

Now some moral philosophers have thought that even the most refurbished Kantian and Aristotelian ethical theories will still be radically opposed over the ideal of a morally good or virtuous person, over whether moral assessment requires a decision-procedure like Kant's Categorical Imperative, and over the importance of rules to morality.[1] Let's take up each of these issues in turn before turning to the question of the justification for morality.

In his *Groundwork of a Metaphysics of Morals,* Kant uses two examples to help elucidate his ideal of a morally good or virtuous person. The first example is that of a person, let's call her Angel, who finds it very easy and attractive to act according to duty but whose actions, Kant claims, are not fully virtuous because she does not act from a sense of duty. The second example is that of a person, let's call her Stoa, who is naturally cold-hearted, but whose actions, Kant claims, are virtuous because she manages to help others out of a sense of duty. By contrast, Aristotle in the *Nicomachean Ethics* draws a distinction between a "fully virtuous" person, let's call her Angelina, who acts virtuously and in accordance with her desires, and a "self-controlled" person, let's call her Stoalina, who also acts virtuously but against her desires. Now although Angel is similar to Angelina and Stoa is similar to Stoalina, Kant clearly prefers Stoa to Angel, while Aristotle clearly prefers Angelina to Stoalina. So it appears that Kant and Aristotle radically disagree over who is a morally good or virtuous person. What Kant takes to be the more virtuous person seems to be the less virtuous person for Aristotle, and what Aristotle take to be the more virtuous person seems to be the less virtuous person for Kant.

As some contemporary Aristotelians and Kantians have shown, however, there are good reasons to both agree and disagree with Kant's and Aristotle's views in this regard.[2] First, in support of Kant's view but not Aristotle's, there surely are cases where the harder it is for a person to act virtuously the more virtuous the person is. For example, a person may have to overcome a tremendous fear in order to risk her life to rescue a small child from a burning building.[3] Similarly, soldiers may have to struggle against great odds to defend a city from attack. In these cases, the harder it is for the person to act virtuously, the greater the virtue. Second, in support of Aristotle's view but not Kant's, there are also cases where the harder it is for a person to be virtuous the less virtuous the person is. For example, rich people who are disinclined to help those in need but still manage to do so are not as virtuous as those who readily provide the same assistance. Third, in support of Kant's view but not Aristotle's, there are cases where people find it easy to act according to duty but where their actions are not virtuous at all, as when shopkeepers treat their customers honestly but only because it is good for business. Fourth, in support of Aristotle's view but not Kant's, failing to be naturally inclined to perform certain virtuous acts can tell against one's virtue. The naturally cold-hearted person in Kant's example who helps the poor but only from duty is clearly not as virtuous as someone who helps the poor motivated both by duty and by a heartfelt sympathy for the poor. So it turns out that not only are the best elements of Aristotle's and Kant's accounts of a morally good or virtuous person not radically opposed, but they need to be combined into one unified account, if we want to have the most morally defensible view.

But are Kant's and Aristotle's refurbished theories similarly reconcilable over the use of Kant's Categorical Imperative as a tool of moral assessment? The first formulation of Kant's Categorical Imperative is: Act only on that maxim which you can at the same time will to be a universal law. In Aristotle's ethical theory, there is clearly nothing like Kant's Categorical Imperative to serve as a test of right action. We can, of course, specify a comparable Aristotelian Imperative: Act only from a concern to do what it is virtuous to do. But this imperative would not purport to do what Kant's Categorical Imperative purports to do. To apply the Aristotelian Imperative, you already have to know which actions are virtuous, whereas Kant's Categorical Imperative attempts to further specify right or virtuous actions in terms of what can be consistently willed to be a universal law. The problem for Kant, and for Kantians, is that this further specification has not served to pick out right or virtuous actions.

Consider the maxim not to steal whenever favorable opportunities arise. Surely this is the sort of maxim we assume can be consistently willed to be a universal law that everyone abides by. But suppose a person wants to further his or her overall self-interest by stealing whenever favorable opportunities arise. Would it, then, not be inconsistent for such a person to will it to be a universal law that everybody not steal whenever favorable opportunities arise? Obviously, willing this maxim to be a universal law that *everyone* abides by conflicts with the person's self-interest in just the same way that willing the maxim to steal whenever favorable opportunities arise to be a universal law that *everyone* abides by conflicts with the person's self-interest. Willing either maxim results in a conflict of will. So neither passes the Kantian test of right or virtuous action. In fact, whenever important moral questions are at issue, such conflicts inevitably arise, rendering it impossible for any maxim to be consistently willed to be a universal law.

Aware of the difficulties of using Kant's Categorical Imperative as a test of right or virtuous action, some contemporary Kantians have favored Kant's fourth formulation of the Categorical Imperative, the Kingdom of Ends formula, which is: Act as if you were by your maxims in every case a legislating member of a universal Kingdom of Ends.[4] The main problem with this formulation of Kant's Categorical Imperative is that it is no more useful than what I have called the Aristotelian Imperative; you cannot apply either of these imperatives without presupposing a substantial account of morality. So, in this regard, Kant's ethical theory is no better off than Aristotle's; the usefulness of the Categorical Imperative as a decision procedure in Kant's ethical theory turns out to be illusory.[5]

Another area of opposition between Aristotelians and Kantians has been over the importance of rules to morality. Some Aristotelians have noted how difficult it is to devise relevant rules with respect to many of the virtues of ordinary life.[6] For example, consider the virtues of gratitude and self-respect. It is difficult to know how we can specify rules relevant to these virtues except by using the uninformative admonitions "Be grateful" and "Respect yourself." We surely cannot specify what is required in such a way, for example, that an ungrateful person can still obey the relevant rule with respect to gratitude while lacking the appropriate motives and beliefs required for exercising that virtue. Obeying rules of this sort requires more than just some external conduct; it requires having certain relevant intentions and beliefs as well. So, for many of the virtues of ordinary life, rules turn out not to be very useful for communicating what should be done. Stories or paradigm cases of virtuous action, such as the story of the Good Samaritan, are generally more helpful to communicate what should be done.

Now while it is usually Aristotelians who make these points about the limitations of rules, it is not clear why Kantians need deny anything that Aristotelians are claiming here. Kantians can grant that with respect to many of the virtues of ordinary life there is no corresponding rule that is useful in communicating what should be done. At the same time, they can point out that with respect to other virtues of ordinary life there are more useful, more informative rules, for example, for truthfulness "Don't lie," for honesty "Don't steal," and for respect for innocent life "Don't kill." The reason these rules are a bit more useful and more informative is that they provide an alternative way of characterizing what their respective virtues require. Of course, Aristotelians need not deny that this is the case, and this should lead to considerable agreement between Kantians and Aristotelians concerning both the limitations and the usefulness of moral rules.[7]

Are there, then, any other issues of ethical theory over which Kantians and Aristotelians are radically opposed? It is not clear that there are. Speaking for Aristotelians, Rosalind Hursthouse claims that any difference between the two theories that remains today is simply a "historical accident," nothing that either theory cannot remedy if need be.[8] Speaking for Kantians, Marcia Baron makes a similar point:

> Contemporary Kantians can utilize the work of virtue ethicists to enrich Kant's account of virtue. We do well to add to the Kantian account both what is suggested by his remarks . . . and ideas gleaned from virtue theorists and others . . . .[9]

Thus, for example, if Aristotelians turn out to have a better account of friendship than Kantians, there appears to be no reason why Kantians can't modify their account to make it more acceptable, or, if necessary, simply graft on the entire Aristotelian account into their refurbished ethical theory.[10]

Let us assume, then, that we can virtually eliminate the differences between the most morally defensible Aristotelian and Kantian ethical theories in this way.[11] Having done this, there remains the question of whether either sort of theory can provide us with a justification of morality.

A JUSTIFICATION FOR MORALITY

Now to defend morality, it would be helpful to show that morality is grounded in rationality. This requires not simply showing that morality is rationally permissible, because that would imply egoism and immorality were rationally permissible as well. Rather, what needs to be shown is that morality is rationally required, thus excluding egoism and immorality as rationally permissible.[12] Unfortunately, the goal of showing that morality is rationally required has been abandoned by most contemporary moral philosophers, including virtually all contemporary Aristotelians and Kantians, who seem content to show that morality is simply rationally permissible.[13] No doubt most contemporary moral philosophers would like to have an argument showing that morality is rationally required, but given the history of past failures to provide a convincing argument of this sort, most contemporary moral philosophers have simply given up hope of defending morality in this way.[14] Fortunately, it is possible to provide just such a defense of morality. Let me first sketch this defense of morality in a more Kantian framework that presupposes a conflict between morality and self-interest and then show how the same defense can be reformulated in a more Aristotelian framework without that presupposition. In light of the success that contemporary moral philosophers have had in breaking down the theoretical differences between Aristotelians and Kantians, it would surely be useful to now also have a justification for morality that both Aristotelians and Kantians can endorse.

Let us begin by imagining that each of us is capable of entertaining and acting upon both self-interested and moral reasons and that the question we are seeking to answer is what sort of reasons for action it is rational for us to accept.[15] This question is not about what sort of reasons we should publicly affirm, since people will sometimes publicly affirm reasons that are quite different from those they are prepared to act upon. Rather, it is a question about what reasons it is rational for us to accept at the deepest level–in our heart of hearts.

Of course, there are people who are incapable of acting upon moral reasons. For such people, there is no question about their being required to act morally or altruistically. Yet the interesting philosophical question is not about such people but about people, like ourselves, who are capable of acting morally as well as self-interestedly and are seeking a rational justification for following a particular course of action.

In trying to determine how we should act, let us assume that we would like to be able to construct a *good* argument favoring morality over egoism, and given that good arguments are non-question-begging, we accordingly would like to construct an argument that, as far as possible, does not beg the question. The question at issue here is what reasons each of us should take as supreme, and this question would be begged against egoism if we proposed to answer it simply by assuming from the start that moral reasons are the reasons that each of us should take as supreme. But the question would be begged against morality as well if we proposed to answer the question simply by assuming from the start that self-interested reasons are the reasons that each of us should take as supreme. This means, of course, that we cannot answer the question of what reasons we should take as supreme simply by assuming the general principle of egoism:

> Each person ought to do what best serves his or her overall self-interest.

We can no more argue for egoism simply by denying the relevance of moral reasons to rational choice than we can argue for pure altruism simply by denying the relevance of self-interested reasons to rational choice and assuming the following general principle of pure altruism:

Each person ought to do what best serves the overall interest of others.[16]

Consequently, in order not to beg the question, we have no other alternative but to grant the prima facie relevance of both self-interested and moral reasons to rational choice and then try to determine which reasons we would be rationally required to act upon, all things considered. Notice that in order not to beg the question, it is necessary to back off both from the general principle of egoism and from the general principle of pure altruism, thus granting the prima facie relevance of both self-interested and altruistic reasons to rational choice.[17] From this standpoint, it is still an open question, whether egoism or pure altruism will be rationally preferable, all things considered.

Here it might be objected that we *do* have non-question-begging grounds for favoring self-interested reasons over moral reasons, if not egoism over altruism. From observing ourselves and others, don't we find that self-interested reasons are better motivators than are moral reasons, as evidenced by the seemingly greater number of egoistically inclined people in the world than altruistically inclined people? It might be argued that because of this difference in motivational capacity, self-interested and moral (or altruistic) reasons should not *both* be regarded as prima facie relevant to rational choice.

But is there really this difference in motivational capacity? Do human beings really have a greater capacity for self-interested behavior than for moral (or altruistic) behavior? If we focus, for a change, on the behavior of women, I think we are likely to observe considerably more altruism than egoism among women, particularly with respect to the care of their families.[18] Of course, if we look to men, given the prevailing patriarchal social structures, we may tend to find more egoism than altruism.[19] But most likely any differences that exist between men and women in this regard, irrespective of whether we consider them to be good or bad, are primarily due to the dominant patterns of socialization—nurture rather than nature.[20] In any case, it is beyond dispute that we humans are capable of both self-interested and altruistic behavior, and given that we have these capabilities, it seems reasonable to ask which ones should have priority.[21]

Our situation is that we find ourselves with some capacity to move along a spectrum from pure altruism to egoism, with someone like Mother Teresa of Calcutta representing the paradigm of pure altruism and someone like Thrasymachus of Plato's *Republic* representing the paradigm of egoism. Obviously, our ability to move along this spectrum will depend on our starting point, the strength of our habits, and the social circumstances in which we happen to live. But at the outset, it is reasonable to abstract from these individual variations and simply focus on the general capacity virtually all of us have to act on both self-interested and altruistic reasons. From this, we should conclude that both sorts of reasons are relevant to rational choice and then ask the question which reasons should have priority. Later, with this question answered, we can take into account individual differences and the effects of socialization to adjust our expectations and requirements for particular individuals and groups. Initially, however, all we need to recognize is the relevance of both self-interested and altruistic reasons to rational choice.

In this regard, there are two kinds of cases that must be considered: cases in which there is no conflict between the relevant self-interested and moral reasons, and cases in which there is such conflict.[22]

No Conflict Cases

It seems obvious that where there is no conflict and both reasons are conclusive reasons of their kind, both reasons should be acted upon. In such contexts, we should do what is favored both by morality and by self-interest.

Consider the following example. Suppose you accepted a job marketing a baby formula in a developing country, where the formula was improperly used, leading to increased infant mortality.[23] Imagine that you could just as well have accepted an equally attractive and rewarding job marketing a similar formula in a developed country, where the misuse does not occur, so that a rational weighing of the relevant self-interested reasons alone would not have favored your acceptance of one of these jobs over the other.[24] At the same time, there were obviously moral reasons that condemned your acceptance of the first job—reasons that you presumably are or were able to acquire. Moreover, by assumption in this case, the moral reasons do not clash with the relevant self-interested reasons; they simply made a recommendation where the relevant self-interested reasons were silent. Consequently, a rational weighing of all the relevant reasons in this case could not but favor acting in accord with the relevant moral reasons.[25]

Needless to say, defenders of egoism will be disconcerted with this result, since it shows that actions in accord with egoism are contrary to reason at least when there are two equally good ways of pursuing one's self-interest, only one of which does not conflict with the basic requirements of morality. Notice also that in cases where there are two equally good ways of fulfilling the basic requirements of morality, only one of which does not conflict with what is in a person's overall self-interest, it is not at all disconcerting for defenders of morality to admit that we are rationally required to choose the way that does not conflict with what is in our overall self-interest. Nevertheless, exposing this defect in egoism for cases where moral reasons and self-interested reasons do not conflict would be but a small victory for defenders of morality if it were not also possible to show that in cases where such reasons do conflict, moral reasons have priority over self-interested reasons.

Conflict Cases

Now when we rationally assess the relevant reasons in conflict cases, it is best to cast the conflict not as a conflict between self-interested reasons and moral reasons but instead as a conflict between self-interested reasons and altruistic reasons.[26] Viewed in this way, three solutions are possible. First, we can say that self-interested reasons always have priority over conflicting altruistic reasons. Second, we can say, just the opposite, that altruistic reasons always have priority over conflicting self-interested reasons. Third, we can say that some kind of compromise is rationally required. In this compromise, sometimes self-interested reasons will have priority over altruistic reasons, and sometimes altruistic reasons will have priority over self-interested reasons.

Once the conflict is described in this manner, the third solution can be seen as the one that is rationally required. This is because the first and second solutions give exclusive priority to one class of relevant reasons over the other, and only a completely question-begging justification can be given for such an exclusive priority. Only by employing the third solution, and sometimes giving priority to self-interested reasons, and sometimes giving priority to altruistic reasons, can we avoid a question-begging resolution.[27]

For example, suppose that you are in the waste disposal business and you have decided to dispose of toxic wastes in a manner that is cost-efficient for you but predictably causes significant harm to future generations. Imagine that there are alternative methods available for disposing of the waste that cost only slightly more and will not cause any significant harm to future generations.[28] In this case, you are to weigh your self-interested reasons favoring the most cost-efficient disposal of the toxic wastes against the relevant altruistic reasons favoring the avoidance of significant harm to future generations. If we suppose that the projected loss of benefit to yourself is ever so slight and the projected harm to future generations is ever so great, then a nonarbitrary compromise between the relevant self-interested and altruistic reasons has to favor the altruistic reasons in this case. Hence, as judged by a non-question-begging standard of rationality, your method of waste disposal was contrary to the relevant reasons.

Notice also that this standard of rationality will not support just any compromise between the relevant self-interested and altruistic reasons. The compromise must be a nonarbitrary one, for otherwise it begs the question with respect to the opposing egoistic and altruistic perspectives.[29] Such a compromise has to respect the rankings of self-interested and altruistic reasons imposed by the egoistic and altruistic perspectives, respectively. Since for each individual there is a separate ranking of that individual's relevant self-interested and altruistic reasons (which will vary, of course, depending on the individual's capabilities and circumstances), we can represent these rankings from the most important reasons to the least important reasons as follows:

INDIVIDUAL A		INDIVIDUAL B	
Self-Interested Reasons	Altruistic Reasons	Self-Interested Reasons	Altruistic Reasons
1	1	1	1
2	2	2	2
3	3	3	3
.	.	.	.
.	.	.	.
.	.	.	.
N	N	N	N

Accordingly, any nonarbitrary compromise among such reasons in seeking not to beg the question against either egoism or pure altruism has to give priority to those reasons that rank highest in each category. Failure to give priority to the highest-ranking altruistic or self-interested reasons is, other things being equal, contrary to reason.

Now it might be objected here that my argument just assumes that we can provide an objective ranking of both a person's self-interested and altruistic reasons.[30] This is correct. But it is difficult to see how any defender of egoism could deny this assumption. Egoism claims that each person ought to do what best serves his or her overall self-interest, and this clearly assumes that each person can know what that is. Nor is it plausible to interpret egoism as maintaining that, while we can each know what best serves his or her own self-interest, we cannot know what best serves the interest of others, and that is why we should be egoists. Rather, the standard defense of egoism assumes that we can each know what is good for ourselves and what is good for others and then claims that, even with this knowledge, we still always ought to do what is good for ourselves. Nor is the idea of providing a relatively precise ranking of one's self-interested reasons from an egoistic perspective or a relatively precise rankings of one's altruistic reasons from an altruistic perspective something to which an egoist would reasonably object.[31] Difficult though such rankings may be to arrive at in practice, the egoist's objection is that even when such relatively precise rankings of our self-interested and altruistic reasons are known, we should still always favor our self-interested reasons over our altruistic ones.

Accordingly, the egoist's objection to morality must be distinguished from the relativist's or the skeptic's objection. Although it is important to defeat each of these foes of morality, it is best to take them one at a time.[32] Here we are simply concerned with the egoist, who does not deny what I have assumed for the sake of argument—a relatively precise ranking of self-interested reasons from an egoistic perspective and a relatively precise ranking of one's altruistic reasons from an altruistic perspective.

Lifeboat Cases

Of course, there will be cases in which the only way to avoid doing what is contrary to your highest-ranking reasons is by forcing someone else to do what is contrary to her highest-ranking reasons. Some of these cases will be "lifeboat cases," as, for example, where you and two others are stranded on a lifeboat that has only enough resources for two of you to survive before your being rescued. But although such cases are surely difficult to resolve (maybe only a chance mechanism, like flipping a coin, can offer a reasonable resolution), they surely do not reflect the typical conflict between the relevant self-interested and altruistic reasons that we are or were able to acquire. At least among humans, typically one or the other of the conflicting reasons will rank significantly higher on its respective scale, thus permitting a clear resolution.[33]

Now we can see how morality can be viewed as just such a nonarbitrary compromise between self-interested reasons and altruistic ones. First, a certain amount of self-regard is morally required or at least morally acceptable. Where this is the case, high-ranking self-interested reasons have priority over low-ranking altruistic reasons, other things being equal. Second, morality obviously places limits on the extent to which people should pursue their own self-interest. Where this is the case, high-ranking altruistic reasons have priority over low-ranking self-interested reasons, other things being equal. In this way, morality can be seen as a nonarbitrary compromise between self-interested and altruistic reasons, and the "moral reasons" that constitute this compromise can be seen as having priority over the self-interested or altruistic reasons that conflict with them, other things being equal.

It is also important to see how this compromise view has been supported by a two-step argument that is not question-begging at all. In the first step, our goal was to determine what sort of reasons for action it would be rational for us to accept on the basis of a good argument, and this required a non-question-begging starting point. Noting that both egoism, which favored exclusively self-interested reasons, and altruism, which favored exclusively altruistic reasons, offered only question-begging starting points, we took as our non-question-begging starting point the prima facie relevance of both self-interested and altruistic reasons to rational choice. The logical inference here is analogous to the inference of equal probability sanctioned in decision theory when we have no evidence that one alternative is more likely than another.[34] Here we had no non-question-begging justification for excluding either self-interested or altruistic reasons as relevant to rational choice, so we accepted both kinds of reasons as prima facie relevant to rational choice. The conclusion of this first step of the argument for the compromise view does not beg the question against egoism or altruism because if defenders of either view had any hope of providing a good, and, hence, a non-question-begging argument for their views, they too would have to grant this very conclusion as the only non-question-begging alternative. In accepting this step of the argument, therefore, the compromise view does not beg the question against a possible defense of these other two perspectives, and that is all that should concern us.

Once, however, both self-interested and altruistic reasons are recognized as prima facie relevant to rational choice, the second step of the argument for the compromise offers a nonarbitrary ordering of those reasons on the basis of rankings of self-interested and altruistic reasons imposed by the egoistic and altruistic perspectives respectively, other things being equal. According to this ordering, high-ranking self-interested reasons have priority over low-ranking altruistic reasons, other things being equal, and high-ranking altruistic reasons have priority over low-ranking self-interested reasons, other things being equal. There is no other plausible nonarbitrary ordering of these reasons. Hence, it certainly does not beg the question against either the egoistic or altruistic perspective, once we imagine these perspectives (or their defenders) to be suitably reformed so that they too are committed to a standard of non-question-beggingness. In the end, if one is committed to a standard of non-question-beggingness, one has to be concerned only with how one's claims and arguments stake up against others who are also committed to such a standard. If you yourself are committed to the standard of non-question-beggingness, you don't beg the question by simply coming into conflict with the requirements of other perspectives, unless those other perspectives (or their defenders) are also committed to the same standard of non-question-beggingness. In arguing for one's view, when one comes into conflict with bigots, one does not beg the question against them unless one is a bigot oneself.

Suppose, for example, we are trying to decide who are the two greatest moral and political philosophers of the twentieth century. Suppose some of us assume from the start that the two must belong to the British/American tradition and proceed to nominate John Rawls and R. M. Hare, while others assume from the start that the two must belong to the continental tradition and proceed to nominate Jurgen Habermas and Jean-Paul Sartre.[35] By contrast, a compromise view, in order not to beg the question, would start by assuming that the two greatest moral and political philosophers of the twentieth century could belong to either the British/American or the continental tradition, or, for that matter, to any philosophical tradition, and it might well then proceed to nominate John Rawls and Jurgen Habermas. This would put the compromise view partly in conflict and partly in agreement with the other two views in this discussion, but it would not show that it begged the question against them because they did not approach the discussion in a non-question-begging manner. Again, being in conflict with bigots does not necessarily make one a bigot; to be a bigot, you yourself must also be arguing from a question-begging standpoint.

Accordingly, it would be a mistake to think that the conflicts existing between the compromise view and either an unreformed egoistic or an unreformed altruistic perspective are grounds for thinking the compromise view begs the question against those perspectives. Thus, we can imagine an unreformed altruistic perspective as holding that:

1. All high-ranking altruistic reasons have priority over conflicting lower-ranking self-interested reasons, other things being equal.
2. All low-ranking altruistic reasons have priority over conflicting higher-ranking self-interested reasons, other things being equal.

And we can also imagine an unreformed egoistic perspective as holding that:

1'. All high-ranking self-interested reasons have priority over conflicting lower-ranking altruistic reasons, other things being equal.
2'. All low-ranking self-interested reasons have priority over conflicting higher-ranking altruistic reasons, other things being equal.[36]

By contrast, the compromise view holds (1) and (1'). Now one might think that part of what the compromise view holds about the priority of reasons, that is, (1) begs the question against an unreformed egoistic perspective, and another part, that is, (1') begs the question against an unreformed altruistic perspective; hence, to that extent, one might conclude the compromise view does beg the question against each view.[37] But there is no reason to view the conflicts between the compromise view and an unreformed egoistic perspective or an unreformed altruistic perspective as begging the question against those perspectives. To beg the question, it is not enough that one is in complete or partial conflict with someone else's view; you, or both you and the other person, must also be proceeding from a question-begging standpoint. And this is clearly not the case with respect to the compromise view.[38]

An analogy might help here. Suppose a judge is trying to decide how to distribute resources between two claimants, each with an equal prima facie claim to the use of those resources. Suppose further that the two claimants have conflicting plans for the use of the disputed resources, yet within each plan it is possible to rank their proposed uses on a scale of importance. Now if the judge is trying to decide how to distribute the resources in the way that would be most justified to both claimants, then surely a distribution that equally supports the high-ranking uses of both plans is required, other things being equal. Similarly, I claim, a compromise that favors high-ranking self-interested reasons over low-ranking altruistic reasons and high-ranking altruistic reasons over low-ranking self-interested reasons is required, other things being equal.[39]

A Weaker Egoist View

Notice, too, that this defense of morality succeeds not only against the view that egoism is rationally preferable to morality but also against the view that egoism is only rationally on a par with morality. The "weaker view" does not claim that we all ought to be egoists. Rather, it claims that there is just as good reason for us to be egoists as there is for us to be pure altruists or anything in between. Kai Nielsen summarizes this view:

> We have not been able to show that reason requires the moral point of view or that all really rational persons not be individual egoists. Reason doesn't decide here.[40]

Yet because the above defense of morality shows morality to be the only nonarbitrary resolution of the conflict between self-interested and altruistic reasons, it is not the case that there is just as good reason for us to endorse morality as there is for us to endorse egoism or altruism. Thus, the above defense of morality succeeds against the weaker as well as against the stronger interpretation of egoism.

In addition, this defense of morality works against the partial egoism that is frequently found in the world in which we live if not in our very own hearts. This partial egoism would allow low-ranking self-interested reasons to *sometimes* trump high-ranking moral or altruistic reasons that clearly outweigh them. Fortunately, this defense of morality works here because partial egoism, unlike morality, cannot be given a non-question-begging defense. This shows the real-life usefulness of this defense of morality.

Now it might be objected that even if morality is required by a standard of question-beggingness, that does not provide us with the right kind of reason to be moral. It might be argued that avoiding question-beggingness is too formal a reason to be moral and that we need a more substantive reason.[41] Happily, the need for a substantive reason to be moral can be met, because in this case the relatively formal reason to be moral—namely, avoiding non-question-beggingness—itself entails a substantive reason to be moral—namely, to give high-ranking altruistic reasons priority over conflicting lower-ranking self-interested reasons, other things being equal and to give high-ranking self-interested reasons priority over conflicting lower-ranking altruistic reasons, other things being equal, or to put the reason more substantively still, to avoid inflicting basic harm on others for the sake of nonbasic benefit to oneself, other things being equal. So, as it turns out, morality as compromise can be shown to provide both relatively formal and substantive reasons to be moral.

Of course, this defense of morality can be undercut in the debate over egoism, altruism, and morality, if we simply give up any attempt to show that any one of these views is rationally preferable to the others. But we cannot rationally do this. For we are engaged in this debate as people who can act self-interestedly, can act altruistically, can act morally; and we are trying to discover which of these ways of acting is rationally justified. To rationally resolve this question, we must be committed to finding out whether one of these views is more rationally defensible than the others. So as far as I can tell, there is no escaping the conclusion that morality is more rationally defensible than either egoism or altruism.

A Neglected Defense

Unfortunately, this approach to defending morality has been generally neglected by previous moral theorists. The reason is that such theorists have tended to cast the basic conflict with egoism as a conflict between morality and self-interest. For example, according to Kurt Baier:

> The very *raison d'etre* of a morality is to yield reasons which overrule the reasons of self-interest in those cases when everyone's following self-interest would be harmful to everyone.[42]

Viewed in this light, it did not seem possible for the defender of morality to be supporting a compromise view, for how could such a defender say that, when morality and self-interest conflict, morality should sometimes be sacrificed for the sake of self-interest? Thus, Henry Sidgwick, at the end of his *Methods of Ethics,* unable to find a rational reconciliation between egoism and utilitarian morality, entertained the possibility of a omnipotent and benevolent deity who guaranteed their reconciliation in an afterlife.[43] But while previous theorists, including Sidgwick, understood correctly that moral reasons can not be compromised in favor of self-interested reasons, they failed to recognize that this is because moral reasons, including the reasons that constitute a utilitarian morality, are already the result of a purportedly nonarbitrary compromise between self-interested and altruistic reasons. Thus, unable to see how morality can be represented as a compromise solution, previous theorists have generally failed to recognize this approach to defending morality.

This failure to recognize that morality can be represented as a compromise between self-interested and altruistic reasons also helps explain Thomas Nagel's inability to find a solution to the problem of the design of just institutions.[44] According to Nagel, to solve the problem of the design of just institutions, we need a morally acceptable resolution of the conflict between the personal and the impersonal standpoints, which Nagel thinks is unattainable. But while Nagel may be right that a morally acceptable resolution of the conflict between these two standpoints is unattainable, the reason this may be the case is that these two standpoints already represent different resolutions of the conflict between self and others. The personal standpoint represents the personally chosen resolution of this conflict, while the impersonal standpoint represents a completely impartial resolution of this conflict, which may not be identical with the personally chosen resolution.[45] Since each of these standpoints already represents a resolution of the conflict between oneself and others, any further resolution of the conflict between the two standpoints seems to violate the earlier resolutions either by favoring oneself or others too much or not enough in light of the earlier resolutions.[46] It is no wonder, then, that an acceptable resolution of the two standpoints seems unattainable. By contrast, if we recast the underlying conflict between oneself and others, as I have suggested, in terms of a conflict between egoism and altruism, self-interested reasons and altruistic reasons, then happily a rationally defensible resolution can be seen to emerge.

Individual Variations in the Ability to Be Moral

In setting out this defense of morality, I assumed that we humans have the capacity to move along a spectrum from egoism to altruism. I granted that our ability to move along this spectrum will depend on our starting point, the strength of our habits, and the social circumstances under which we happen to be living. But I argued that, at the outset, it is reasonable to abstract from these individual variations and simply focus on the general capacity virtually all of us have to act on both self-interested and moral reasons. Now, however, that I have argued that both self-interested and altruistic reasons are relevant to rational choice and assigned priorities in cases of conflict, it is appropriate to return to the question of how individual differences and the effects of socialization should adjust our expectations and requirements for particular individuals and groups.

Here two kinds of cases seem particularly relevant. In one case, certain people by nature lack, to some degree, the capacity to act on high-ranking altruistic reasons when they conflict with low-ranking self-interested reasons. In the other case, certain people due to socialization lack, to some degree, the capacity to act on high-ranking altruistic reasons when they conflict with low-ranking self-interested reasons. Obviously, people who have the capacity for altruism will have to try to work around, and, if necessary, protect themselves from those who, to varying degrees, lack this capacity. In cases in which those who lack this capacity are themselves at least partially responsible for this lack, blame and censure is also appropriate.[47] In other cases, some people will rightly be regarded as incapable of moral behavior. Nevertheless, as long as the greater majority of people have, by nature and/or by nurture, the capacity to act on high-ranking altruistic reasons when they conflict with low-ranking self-interested reasons, it should be possible to set up a social order that corresponds with the requirements of morality. Moreover, once we take into account the capacities of *both* men and women, there is good reason to think that the greater majority of humankind do have this capacity for altruism.[48]

The Reasons We Have and the Reasons We Could Have

Now it might be objected that we should not take into account people's capacities but simply whatever reasons they just happen to have at the present moment, whether these reasons are just self-interested reasons, or just altruistic reasons, or a combination of self-interested and altruistic reasons. As a matter of fact, however, we rarely limit our evaluations of other people to reasons they just happen to have at the present moment. In imputing moral responsibility, for example, it is not necessary to show that people have the relevant moral reasons for acting otherwise, as we hold people morally responsible even when they lack such reasons, provided they are morally responsible for the lack. Thus, if political leaders have the capabilities and opportunities to become aware of their society's racist and sexist practices, but in fact fail to do so, with the consequence that they presently lack any moral reasons to oppose such practices, we still hold them morally responsible, because their lack of moral reasons in this regard is something for which they are morally responsible. Similarly, if parents have the capacities and opportunities to become more sensitive to their children's needs but in fact fail to do so, with the consequence that they presently lack the moral reasons to respond effectively to those needs, they are still held morally responsible, because their lack of moral reasons in this regard is something for which they are morally responsible.[49] As these examples indicate, having moral reasons to act otherwise is not necessary for imputing moral responsibility. Rather, what is necessary is that people are or were able to acquire the relevant moral reasons. What is not so generally recognized, however, is that the reasons a person could have acquired can also be relevant when assessing a person's conduct from a self-interest point of view.

Consider the following example. An acquaintance of mine bought a house on the last day it was being offered for sale, when it was too late to have the house inspected. The house was found to have such a termite infestation that it cost several thousands of dollars to correct the structural damage. Apparently, the previous owners did not know about the termites, and my acquaintance, having inspected the house on her own, did not think she needed to have the house professionally inspected. My acquaintance now admits, I think rightly, that she acted unreasonably in purchasing the house without a professional inspection. I think it is plausible to say that her action was not unreasonable in terms of any reasons she had at the time of purchase, because at that time she didn't know or have reason to believe that the house had termites, and the opportunity to have the house inspected no longer existed. Rather, her action is best seen as unreasonable in terms of the reasons she could have had at the time of purchase if only she had arranged to have the house professionally inspected. What these examples show is that not just the reasons people have but also the reasons they could have acquired are relevant to a rational evaluation of their conduct. Accordingly, we do need to take into account people's capacity for both egoism and altruism when providing a rational assessment of their conduct.[50]

AN ARISTOTELIAN FRAMEWORK

Let's call this defense of morality, "Morality as Compromise." Now it might be objected that framing the justification of morality as requiring a response to the egoist presupposes a Kantian understanding of a morality of obligations rather than an Aristotelian understanding of a morality of personal flourishing or eudaimonia.

In response to this objection, it should be noted that dealing with the egoist has venerable Platonic roots (recall Thrasymachus), and so this concern should not be alien to an Aristotelian understanding of morality. Nevertheless, the claim that Morality as Compromise favors a Kantian conception of a morality of obligations over an Aristotelian conception of a morality of personal flourishing seems correct. Accordingly, to provide an adequate defense of morality, it must be possible to recast its central argument of Morality as Compromise into an Aristotelian framework. That is what I propose to do.

Of course, among Aristotelians, while morality is conceived in terms of personal flourishing, there is considerable debate over how personal flourishing is to be understood.[51] According to views that draw heavily on book X of the *Nicomachean Ethics,* personal flourishing is understood in terms of just one activity: contemplation. According to other views, personal flourishing includes a range of different (virtuous) activities in addition to contemplation. Fortunately, I don't need to enter this debate here. What I want to argue is that however this debate is resolved, it is possible to construct an argument within an Aristotelian framework that parallels the argument of Morality as Compromise.

Let us begin by considering all the viable Aristotelian accounts of personal flourishing.[52] Let us ask of each account the question: Should people always seek personal flourishing? For the moment, set aside those accounts for which the answer is yes and consider just those accounts for which the answer is no.[53] Richard Kraut's Aristotelian account of personal flourishing is one such account.[54] Kraut claims that people should not pursue their personal flourishing when it conflicts significantly with the good of others. He gives the example of the son of a king who would be happiest by pursuing philosophical contemplation, but for the good of others should pursue a political life instead. Another example is that of a man who curtails his pursuit of philosophical contemplation to care for an ailing parent. Now I contend that the balancing of the pursuit of personal flourishing against the pursuit of the good of others that is required here parallels the balancing of self-interested and altruistic reasons in Morality as Compromise. In both cases, the goal is to pursue a reasonable balance or compromise between self and others. Moreover, this will hold true of all viable Aristotelian accounts of personal flourishing that require its pursuit be limited when it conflicts significantly with the good of others.

Next consider all those viable Aristotelian accounts of personal flourishing that we previously set aside which answered yes to the question of whether people should always pursue their personal flourishing. Now ask of these accounts of human flourishing how we are to explain our experience of self-sacrifice. I suggest that these accounts will try to explain how pursuing personal flourishing is compatible with self-sacrifice, either by distinguishing between conflicting interests of the self, or by distinguishing between conflicting selves or conflicting virtues, or by making some comparable move. A reasonable resolution of the recognized conflict will then be defended. Personal flourishing for such accounts is thus constituted by a compromise between conflicting interests of the self (for example, self-regarding interests and other-regarding interests) or by a compromise between a more self-regarding (lower?) self and a more other-regarding (higher?) self, or by some similar compromise. Again, the parallel with the compromise in Morality as Compromise is evident. It follows, then, that for any viable Aristotelian account of personal fulfillment, it is possible to construct a defense of morality that parallels the defense of morality offered by Morality as Compromise. This shows that the Kantian-inspired argument of Morality as Compromise can be further defended by being recast into an Aristotelian framework.

Of course, I am not denying that there will be considerable debate about what are the relevant interests or relevant selves or relevant virtues that need to be compromised. What I am claiming is that the debate will have to take a certain form if it is to be reasonable. That form, I claim, is captured in the Kantian-inspired Morality as Compromise as a compromise between self-interested reasons and altruistic reasons, but it can also be found in Aristotelian accounts as a compromise between personal flourishing and the good of others, or as a compromise within the account of personal flourishing itself between conflicting interests of the self or between conflicting selves or something similar.[55] In this way, it is possible to show that Morality as Compromise can be interpreted to provide a justification of morality that is also acceptable within an Aristotelian framework.

Still, it might be objected that the Aristotelian ideal of personal flourishing or eudaimonia should be understood as providing common goods or goods of mutual benefit that transcend conflict, and so there is no need for Morality as Compromise. Of course, no one denies there are common goods that equally or abundantly benefit all as well as goods of mutual benefit that also equally or abundantly benefit all. And if all our relationships with others involve just such goods, then getting along with others would be quite easy because there would be no real conflicts between self and others, or between conflicting interests of the self, or differing selves, or anything similar. But we do have real conflicts. Even when we are dealing with mutual benefit schemes, there can be conflicts over how the benefits should be divided, as well as conflicts over how the burdens of producing common goods should be shared. Such conflicts are at the heart of morality, and they in turn ground the need for Morality as Compromise.

OBJECTIONS

Now that we can see how the argument for Morality as Compromise can be formulated in both Kantian and Aristotelian frameworks, let us now consider three objections to the argument that have been raised by Jeffrey Reiman, Charles Pigden, and Bernard Gert respectively.

Reiman's Objections

In responding to an earlier version of Morality as Compromise, Jeffrey Reiman questions whether my argument suffices to show that altruistic reasons should be regarded as prima facie relevant to rational choice. Reiman claims that to regard them as prima facie relevant, it is not enough to show that a person does not have any non-question-begging grounds for *rejecting* altruistic reasons. Before regarding them as relevant, Reiman thinks that a person who already regards self-interested reasons as obviously relevant must be given a non-question-begging reason for *accepting* altruistic reasons as prima facie relevant. Presumably, Reiman also thinks that a person who already regards altruistic reasons as obviously relevant must be given a non-question-begging reason for *accepting* self-interested reasons as well.

But why is it reasonable to demand non-question-begging grounds for accepting reasons to which I am not already committed when I don't require non-question-begging grounds for continuing to accept the reasons to which I am already committed? Why is it reasonable to demand a higher standard of acceptability of reasons that I might come to accept than I demand of reasons I have already accepted?

The situation is even worse because by allowing ourselves to retain our old reasons on lesser grounds than we require of ourselves for accepting new reasons, we may effectively block the acquisition of new reasons which are better grounded than our old reasons simply because these new reasons happen to conflict with our old reasons. Clearly, a more reasonable strategy would be to evaluate both new and old reasons by the same standard. If we were to proceed in this fashion, then, both self-interested and altruistic reasons would have to be regarded as prima facie relevant since we lack non-question-begging grounds to reject reasons of either kind.

It is also the case that we all find ourselves somewhere on the spectrum between egoism and altruism with some capacity and opportunity to move toward one or the other, and with a strong interest in resolving the question of how we should act in this regard in a reasonable manner.

Reiman goes on to suggest that regarding both self-interested and altruistic reasons as prima facie relevant on these grounds is analogous to naturalists and supernaturalists splitting the difference between their views and counting supernatural reasons as valid half the time. But as I understand the debate between naturalism and supernaturalism, many naturalists claim to have non-question-begging reasons for rejecting supernaturalism, and some supernaturalists claim to have non-question-begging grounds for rejecting naturalism. So this example does not parallel the case of egoism and altruism.

But suppose there were equally good reasons for naturalism as for supernaturalism, would we be rationally required to act on naturalism half the time and supernaturalism the other half the time, as Reiman suggests? In this case, a far more reasonable resolution is to continue to lead the life of a naturalist or a supernaturalist at the practical level while periodically reevaluating the relevant reasons with the hope of some day resolving this issue. This interim solution is preferable because there is no way to compromise the issue between naturalism and supernaturalism that respects the most important elements of each view. This is why the conflict between naturalism and supernaturalism differs from the conflict between egoism and altruism because in the latter case there is a way to compromise the issue between the two views that respects the most important elements of each: favor high-ranking self-interested reasons over low-ranking altruistic reasons, other things being equal, and favor high-ranking altruistic reasons over low-ranking self-interested reasons, other things being equal.

This illustrates how the requirement of non-question-beggingness favors different solutions in different contexts. Thus, in contexts where action can be deferred, it favors deferring action until compelling reasons favoring one course of action can be found, for example, putting off your choice of a vacation spot until you have good reasons for going to a particular spot. However, in contexts where action cannot be deferred, either it is or it is not possible to combine the best parts of the existing alternatives into a single course of action. If it is not possible to combine the best parts of the existing alternatives, as in the case of naturalism and supernaturalism, the requirement of non-question-beggingness favors arbitrarily choosing between them, while periodically reexamining the situation to determine whether compelling reasons can be found favoring one alternative over the others. If it is possible to combine existing alternatives, as in the case of egoism and altruism, the requirement of non-question-beggingness favors this course of action. It is on this account that I argue that Morality as Compromise is rationally preferable to either egoism or altruism.

Pigden's Objection

Another specific objection to Morality as Compromise raised by Charles Pigden is that it violates the conservativeness of logic, according to which you cannot get out of a valid inference what you don't put in.[56] Stated formally, this thesis about logic maintains that "a predicate or propositional variable cannot occur non-vacuously in the conclusion of a valid inference unless it appears among the premises."[57] David Hume's famous thesis that you cannot derive an "ought" from an "is" turns out to be just a special case of this general thesis about the conservativeness of logic. The particular form of the thesis that is relevant to Morality as Compromise simply claims that moral conclusions cannot be derived from nonmoral premises.

For some reason, this sort of challenge to a defense of morality has not been taken very seriously throughout the history of ethics. When Kant sought to show that morality was grounded in rationality, most attacked the validity of his argument. To my knowledge, no one argued that he was trying to do something that was impossible. Similarly, among contemporary philosophers, attempts by Alan Gewirth, Kurt Baier, Christine Korsgaard, myself, and others to ground morality in rationality have not been greeted with claims of impossibility, but rather with specific objections to the derivations we provided.[58] To my knowledge, no one has challenged Gewirth's claim to derive morality from logical consistency on the grounds that it just can not be done because the premises of Gewirth's argument were non-moral.[59] All the criticisms were directed at the particular steps of Gewirth's argument, which seem to imply that what he was trying to do was at least logically possible. Nor when Korsgaard argues that morality is the product of a certain type of constitutive unity of the self or self-reflectiveness, critics have not replied that you cannot derive the moral from the nonmoral, but rather they have tried to show that even immoral people have that same unity or self-reflectiveness and so that it cannot be the grounds for our moral life.[60]

Still, I do think that there is something to this thesis about logic.[61] Consider how it applies to my argument for Morality as Compromise. The basic premise in my argument for Morality as Compromise is the principle of non-question-beggingness, which is a rational requirement for a good argument. So my argument is an attempt to derive morality from this principle of rationality. Accordingly, it moves not from an "is" to an "ought," but from an "ought" to an "ought." In fact, I agree with Hume that you cannot derive an "ought" from an "is," unless, that is, the "is" already has a "ought" built into it. At the same time, I take the ought-ought gap to be bridgeable in a way that the is-ought gap is not.

Nevertheless, the conservativeness of logic thesis maintains that my argument from "ought" to "ought" can only succeed in defending morality if its premises are moral. The principle of non-question-beggingness, however, doesn't look like a moral premise. It looks like a rational principle for good arguments, which would make it a rational "ought" not a moral "ought." But there is a sense in which it can also be regarded as moral. What the principle of non-question-beggingness requires is that we be fair or unbiased in our use of premises in deriving conclusions. It is a requirement of fair argumentation. It proscribes arguments, irrespective of their validity, where the conclusion is explicitly or blatantly in the premises, but not arguments where the conclusion is implicitly or subtlety contained in the premises. In my argument for Morality as Compromise, the requirement of fair argumentation leads to a fair standard for leading one's life, which is recognizably a moral standard. So in my argument there is a sense in which the morality of the conclusion is contained in my premises as well.

Even so, the argument for Morality as Compromises remains interesting and important, even with the admission that its moral conclusion is contained in its premises, because the sense that morality is in its premises is neither obvious nor well understood. It definitely takes some doing to show how the protomorality of fair argumentation supports the morality of ordinary life. This explains why there are many people who accept the premise of my argument (the principle of non-question-beggingness) without thinking that they are thereby bound to accept its conclusion (the endorsement of morality in ordinary life). Hence, my argument does serve an important function of helping to bring people to endorse the requirements of morality, even if, as the thesis of the conservation of logic maintains, its moral conclusion is contained in its premises.

Gert's Objection

In two of his recent articles, Bernard Gert objects to Morality as Compromise on the grounds that it is difficult to read off from it what we are required to do in certain troublesome cases.[62] This is true. Yet an account of morality that is useful for some purposes may not be useful for others, and Morality as Compromise is not intended to be useful as a decision-procedure for churning out the particular requirements of morality, especially for troublesome cases. Of course, once we have reached a resolution concerning what is morally required in a troublesome case, we may be able to read that resolution back into my account of morality by showing that it implies some particular altruistic reason is higher-ranking than some particular self-interested reason or vice versa, other things being equal. But even that may not always be possible to do because it may not be the case that other things are equal.

Consider one of Gert's examples. In it, the benefits to oneself from cheating are said to outweigh the harms that the cheating inflicts on others. In this example, the person's self-interested reasons to cheat might be thought to outrank his or her altruistic reasons not to cheat, even when we think that cheating in this case is morally impermissible. However, Morality as Compromise might still condemn cheating in such a case because it is not committed to *always* favoring the high-ranking self-interested reasons over the low-ranking altruistic reasons, or to *always* favoring high-ranking altruistic reasons over low-ranking self-interested reasons. It only committed to doing so as long as other things are equal. And things would not be equal if such preferences violated the "ought" implies "can" principle, a principle that is common to all moral and political perspectives.[63] Now the "ought' implies "can" principle maintains, among other things, that morality "cannot" impose unreasonable requirements on people. Thus, in Gert's example it could be that cheating imposes an unreasonable burden on those who are harmed by it and so violates the "ought" implies "can" principle, thereby rendering the cheating morally impermissible. Of course, we would need to further specify Gert's example in order to determine whether it actually does violate the "ought' implies "can" principle; it surely is conceivable that cheating could be justified in such a case, for example, to save the cheater's life. Yet given that the resolution of this case depends on an appeal to the "ought" implies "can" principle, it is not possible to read it back into Morality as Compromise by showing that the resolution implies that some particular altruistic reason is higher ranking than some particular self-interested reason or vice versa. Consequently, Morality as Compromise is not a very good decision-procedure for resolving troublesome cases, and it is not always possible to read morally defensible resolutions of those cases back into the rankings of the relevant reasons when a violation of the "ought" implies "can" principle is at issue.

Nevertheless, Morality as Compromise is particularly good for the purpose for which it was designed which is to show the rational preferability of morality over egoism or altruism. For other purposes, other conceptions of morality may be more useful. In any case, we will need to do a comparable evaluation of different conceptions of morality to determine their usefulness and also to determine whether they lead to different practical recommendations.

Earlier in this chapter, I argued that once Aristotelian and Kantian ethical theories are given their most morally defensible interpretations, the differences between them can be virtually eliminated, which would presumably lead them to have the same practical requirements. But even if this is the case, it still leaves open the question of how best to determine what those practical requirements are. Although Morality as Compromise succeeds in defeating egoism and altruism and so provides a justification for morality, it leaves open the question of how best we should understand morality for the purpose of determining its practical requirements.

CHAPTER THREE

Kantians and Utilitarians and the Poor, Disadvantaged, Innocent

Assuming that we can justify morality in terms of rationality and assuming that we can reconcile the most morally defensible interpretations of Aristotelian and Kantian ethical theories—the two main conclusions of the previous chapter—it is still generally thought that both of these theories are in serious conflict with utilitarian ethical theories. Usually, that conflict is presented as a conflict between Kantian and utilitarian ethical theories. So let us examine the conflict in just those terms, focusing, as is usually done, on how these theories treat the poor, disadvantaged, innocent.

Contemporary Kantian ethical theorists generally tend to fall into two camps. One camp takes a welfare liberal (welfare and beyond) position with respect to the poor, disadvantaged, innocent and the other camp takes a libertarian (no welfare) position toward them. Despite this disagreement, both welfare liberals and libertarians claim to be in conflict with utilitarians over the treatment of the poor, disadvantaged, innocent. John Rawls, the best known contemporary Kantian welfare liberal, has always staked out his position in opposition to utilitarianism, so the presumed conflict between his welfare liberal view and utilitarianism seems to be a good place to start. Subsequently, we will take up the even starker presumed conflict between the libertarian view and utilitarianism. What I will try to do is show that both these conflicts can be resolved.

WELFARE LIBERALISM AND UTILITARIANISM

In *A Theory of Justice,* John Rawls, like Immanuel Kant before him, argues that principles of justice are those principles that free and rational persons who are concerned with advancing their own interests would accept in an initial position of equality. Yet Rawls goes beyond Kant by interpreting the conditions of his "original position" to explicitly require a "veil of ignorance." This veil of ignorance, Rawls claims, requires that we discount certain knowledge about ourselves in order to reach fair agreements. A good example of what is at issue here is the practice of withholding information from juries. As we know, judges sometimes refuse to allow juries to hear certain testimony. The rationale behind this practice is that certain information is highly prejudicial or irrelevant to the case at hand. The hope is that without this information, juries will be more likely to reach fair verdicts. Similarly, when prejudicial or irrelevant information is blurted out in the courtroom, intentionally or unintentionally, judges will usually instruct juries to discount this information to increase the likelihood that juries will reach fair verdicts. Of course, whether judges and juries in fact carry out their responsibilities in this regard is beside the point. What is crucial is that it is recognized in these contexts that justice demands that we discount certain information in order to achieve just results.

Rawls's ideal of justice can be seen as simply a generalization of this practice. It maintains that if we are to achieve a fair system of rights and duties in general, then we must discount certain information about ourselves when choosing our system of rights and duties. In particular, we must discount our knowledge of whether we are rich or poor, talented or untalented, male or female. In general, this ideal of justice requires that we should choose as though we were standing behind an imaginary "veil of ignorance" with respect to most particular facts about ourselves, anything that would bias our choice or stand in the way of unanimous agreement. Rawls calls this choice situation "the original position" because it is the position we should start from when determining what fundamental rights and duties people should have.

But what rights and duties would be chosen in the original position? In *A Theory of Justice,* Rawls argues that a system of rights and duties that maximizes benefit to the least-advantaged position would be chosen.[1] This would be the result of using the *maximin* strategy, which requires that we *maxi*mize benefit to those who have the *min*imum. Rawls argues that persons in the original position would use the maximin strategy because:

I. Persons so situated would have no reliable basis for estimating the probabilities of outcomes that would affect them since they are choosing in ignorance of the probabilities of their occupying any particular place in society, for example, the probability of their being rich or poor, talented or untalented.

II. Persons so situated would care very little, if anything, for what might be gained above what is guaranteed by maximizing the minimum.

III. All other alternatives have outcomes that persons so situated could hardly accept.

Given that these three conditions are met, Rawls claims, it is rational to follow the maximin strategy.

To better understand what this maximin strategy requires, consider a society with just three individuals A, B, and C each facing the following alternatives:

	INDIVIDUALS			
Alternative	A	B	C	Average
I	4	7	12	7 2/3
II	3	8	14	8 1/3
III	5	6	8	6 1/3

Imagine that the numbers represent comparable social goods or utilities to the three members of this society. The maximin strategy would favor alternative III, because only this alternative maximizes the benefit to the least-advantaged member of this society, despite the fact that the other two alternatives offer a higher average expected index of social good or utility to each member of the society. According to the maximin strategy when making important choices in (imagined) ignorance of how these choices will affect one personally, it is most rational to maximize the benefit to the least-advantaged individual in order to guard against the possibility that this individual will turn out to be oneself.

Others, however, most notably John Harsanyi, have argued that persons in the original position would reject the maximin strategy in favor of a system of rights and duties that maximizes average expected benefit or utility.[2] This has been called a utilitarian strategy because it requires that we maximize average expected benefit or utility over the relevant group. In our example, this strategy would favor alternative II because this provides the highest average expected benefit or utility. According to this strategy, when making important choices in (imagined) ignorance of how they will affect one personally, it is most rational to first assign an equal probability to one's occupying each particular position and then select the alternative with the highest average expected benefit or utility.

According to Rawls, the principles of justice that would be derived from the original position are the following:

I. Special Conception of Justice	II. General Conception of Justice
1. Each person is to have an equal right to the most extensive basic liberty compatible with a similar system of liberty for others.	All social goods—liberty and opportunity, income and wealth, and the bases of self-respect—are to be distributed equally unless an unequal distribution of any or all of these goods is to the advantage of the least favored.
2. Social and economic inequalities are to be arranged so that they are (a) to the greatest benefit of the least advantaged, consistent with the just savings principle and (b) attached to offices and position open to all under conditions of fair equality of opportunity.	

The general conception of justice differs from the special conception of justice by allowing trade-offs between liberty and other social goods. According to Rawls, people in the original position would want the special conception of justice to be applied in place of the general conception of justice whenever social conditions allowed all representative people to exercise their basic liberties.

In his later work, *Justice as Fairness: A Restatement,* Rawls reformulated his principles of justice somewhat differently:

1. Each person has the same indefeasible claim to a fully adequate scheme of equal basic liberties, which scheme is compatible with the same scheme of liberties for all; and
2. Social and economic inequalities are to satisfy two conditions: first they are to be attached to offices and positions open to all

under conditions of fair equality of opportunity; second, they are to be to the greatest benefit of the least-advantaged members of society (the difference principle).[3]

In this formulation, there is no longer a general conception of justice, and except for dropping a reference to liberty in general in his first principle, the only remaining changes are stylistic.

Thoughout his work, Rawls has always argued that his principles of justice would be preferred to utilitarian principles of justice because, he claims, utilitarian principles will always justify imposing harm on a few (innocent individuals) to secure a greater benefit for others. Yet actually this cannot be what makes utilitarianism objectionable because any defensible moral theory will justify imposing harm on a few (innocent individuals) for the sake of greater benefit for others, at least in certain circumstances. For example, suppose that the only way a doctor can get out of a crowded subway in an emergency situation is by stepping on a few people's toes. Surely, the harm that the doctor inflicts on these innocent individuals would be justified by any defensible moral theory by the greater benefit the doctor is able to do in an emergency situation. In this case, the harm inflicted for the sake of the greater benefit is trivial. In other cases, however, the harm inflicted is not trivial, but it is still reparable, as when one might lie to a temporarily depressed friend to keep her from committing suicide. Here too any defensible moral theory would hold that the harm inflicted on an innocent person in this case is justified by the greater benefit that results.

Clearly, the most difficult cases of this sort are when the harm inflicted is not trivial, nor reparable, but is still arguably justified by the good consequences that result. A widely discussed case of this sort is provided by Bernard Williams. In Williams's case, an explorer, let us call her Sonya, arrives in a South American village just as Pedro, an army officer, is about to kill a group of twenty indians in retaliation for protests against the local government. In honor of Sonya's arrival, Pedro offers to spare nineteen of the twenty indians provided that Sonya will shoot one of them. For this case, even Williams, who is a critic of utilitarianism, admits that the explorer should shoot one of the indians in order to save the other nineteen. One way to see why this course of action is justified is to imagine that all twenty of the indians are behind Rawls's veil of ignorance, not knowing which of them will be killed by the explorer but knowing that if the explorer does not kill one of them, they all will be killed by Pedro. In this situation, all twenty indians would agree to have the explorer arbitrarily shoot one of them in order to save the other nineteen. If you need to be further convinced that this type of irreversible harm to innocents can be justified for the sake of achieving greater benefit for others, then just imagine that larger and larger numbers of innocents (one hundred, one thousand, one million, whatever number you want) would be lost unless one particular (innocent) individual is killed. Surely, at some point, any defensible moral theory, including Rawls's own theory, will justify such sacrifices.[4]

So what is wrong with utilitarianism cannot be that it justifies doing harm to innocents in order to secure a greater benefit for others. As I just argued, any defensible moral theory will have to do that. Rather, what must be wrong with utilitarianism is that it permits or requires harms of this sort in cases when the trade-offs cannot be justified.

The "Ought" Implies "Can" Principle

But when are such trade-offs not justified? I maintain that such trade-off are not justified when they violate one of the most fundamental principles of morality, one that is common to all moral and political perspectives, namely, the "ought" implies "can" principle. According to this principle, people are not morally required to do what they lack the power to do or what would involve so great a sacrifice that it is unreasonable to ask, and in cases of severe conflict of interest, unreasonable to require them to abide by.[5]

For example, suppose I promised to attend a departmental meeting on Friday, but on Thursday I am involved in a serious car accident that puts me into a coma. Surely it is no longer the case that I ought to attend the meeting, now that I lack the power to do so. Or suppose instead that on Thursday I develop a severe case of pneumonia for which I am hospitalized. Surely I can legitimately claim that I cannot attend the meeting on the grounds that the risk to my health involved in attending is a sacrifice it is unreasonable to ask me to bear. Or suppose the risk to my health from having pneumonia is not so serious and it is reasonable to ask me to attend the meeting (a supererogatory request); it might still be serious enough to be unreasonable to require my attendance at the meeting (a demand that is backed up by blame or coercion).

This "ought" implies "can" principle claims that reason and morality must be linked in an appropriate way, especially if we are going to be able to justifiably use blame or coercion to get people to abide by the requirements of morality. It should be noted, however, that although major figures in the history of philosophy, and most philosophers today accept this link between reason and morality, it is not usually conceived to be part of the "ought" implies "can" principle.[6] Nevertheless, I claim that there are good reasons for associating this link between reason and morality with the "ought" implies "can" principle, namely, our use of the word "can" as in the example just given, and the natural progression from logical, physical, and psychological possibility found in the traditional "ought" implies "can" principle to the notion of moral possibility found in this formulation of the "ought" implies "can" principle. In any case, the acceptability of this formulation of the "ought" implies "can" principle is determined by the virtual universal acceptance of its components and not by the manner in which I have proposed to join these components together.[7]

Now applying the "ought" implies "can" principle to the cases at hand, where the sacrifices for the sake of greater benefit to others are either trivial, reparable, or nonreparable but greatly outweigh their consequences, the principle would not be violated. In all of these cases, the sacrifices involved are not unreasonable to ask those affected to bear. Nevertheless, the "ought" implies "can" principle would be violated by cases of the sort Rawls has in mind where the least advantaged would be asked to sacrifice an acceptable minimum so that greater benefits would be enjoyed by the more advantaged. For example, Rawls envisions a case where limiting the political liberties and religious freedoms of small and weak minorities would be outweighed by the social advantages to a sizable majority.[8] This is not a sacrifice that it is reasonable to ask and/or require these minorities to bear. Accordingly, when utilitarianism is appropriately interpreted to be constrained by the "ought" implies "can" principle, it then appears not to have the practical implications to which Rawls objects.[9]

But what then becomes of utilitarianism's requirement to maximize utility overall? Since people are not morally required to make so great a sacrifice that it is unreasonable to ask, and in cases of severe conflict of interest, unreasonable to require them to abide by, then at least in some cases, the requirement to maximize utility can only be a supererogatory requirement, not something we can reasonably require of people, but something that people may choose to do in any case for the sake of the greater good that would result. Moreover, due to the declining marginal utility of goods, as utilitarians argue, it may well only rarely be the case that we can maximize utility overall by transferring benefits from the least advantaged to the more advantaged in society, and then, as I just argued, we will still have the option of understanding the requirement of maximizing utility in such cases to be morally supererogatory.[10] Alternatively, we can interpret the constraints of the "ought" implies "can" principle, which generally favor the poor, disadvantaged, innocent over the rich, advantaged, not innocent, as producing greater utility overall in the sense of producing morally greater or morally better utility overall.[11]

Of course, Rawls does not think that utilitarianism, left to its own resources, can generate an acceptable minimum. Unfortunately, in arriving at this conclusion, Rawls does not consider whether applying the "ought" implies "can" principle to utilitarianism can secure that minimum. In a way, this is surprising because Rawls is sympathetic to Thomas Scanlon's characterization of moral requirements as those to which no one could reasonably object, and this constraint is quite similar to that imposed by the "ought" implies "can" principle.[12] Unfortunately, neither Rawls nor Scanlon sees this similarity, which presumably explains why neither of them recognizes the possibility of internally reforming utilitarianism.

Warmaking and Peacemaking Ways of Doing Philosophy

Now traditionally philosophers have liked to eliminate would-be opponents in the course of defending their own views. Too often doing philosophy this way is modeled after fighting a battle or making war. Under this warmaking model of doing philosophy, philosophers have interpreted their would-be opponents so as to make them most vulnerable to serious or fatal objections.

One summer, a number of years ago I visited a major U.S. university to talk to two well-known philosophers about the differences between their views. One of these philosophers had established his reputation as a critic of the other. I talked first to the philosopher whose work had been criticized by his colleague. I asked him, bearing in mind his critic's work, whether he had any objections to interpreting his view in a way that I thought avoided his colleague's criticisms, and he said that he did not. The next day I talked to the philosopher known for his critique of his colleague (I was told that they don't talk to each other)[13] and asked him whether he had any objections to this interpretation of his colleague's work, mentioning that his colleague had just accepted this interpretation the day before. He said that he did not. Yet, it turns out that this same philosopher was hard at work on a book in which he was criticizing yet another interpretation of his colleague's work–a book in which the more favorable interpretation of his colleague's work was never mentioned.

Obviously, this warmaking way of doing philosophy does not really serve to advance our philosophical understanding. What we need is a more peaceful and cooperative way of doing philosophy, one that puts the most favorable interpretations on the views of our would-be opponents.[14] It is significant that Rawls himself explicitly endorses this more peaceful and cooperative way of doing philosophy. Rawls always started his courses in the history of moral philosophy by saying: "We are not going to criticize these thinkers, but rather to interpret their positions in ways that make the best of them. . . ."[15]

Now if we apply this peacemaking way of doing philosophy to utilitarianism, it favors an internal critique, if one is available, over an external critique of the view. An internal critique only requires that the theory be reinterpreted to be rendered acceptable, whereas an external critique usually requires that the theory be radically modified or discarded. Thus, subjecting a theory simply to an internal critique puts the theory in a much more favorable light than subjecting it to an external critique.[16] Moreover, I claim an internal critique of utilitarianism is available because the "ought" implies "can" principle is an implicit requirement of the theory, as it is of every moral and political theory. Recognizing the commitment of utilitarianism to the "ought" implies "can" principle also serves to bring the theory into practical reconciliation with Rawls's welfare liberalism.[17] This is because whenever a practical requirement would be unacceptable to those occupying the least-advantaged position behind Rawls's veil of ignorance, that same practical requirement, according to the "ought" implies "can" principle, would be unreasonable for those in the least-advantaged position in the real world to accept. Thus, following, as we should, a more peaceful, cooperative way of doing philosophy, leads to a practical reconciliation of Rawls's welfare liberalism with utilitarianism.

LIBERTARIANISM AND UTILITARIANISM

But what about that other Kantian view—libertarianism? Surely, this view will be more difficult to reconcile with utilitarianism. This is because while utilitarianism and welfare liberalism are commonly recognized to both endorse a right to welfare, libertarians are commonly thought to reject any such right at the same time as they endorse an ideal of liberty. F. A. Hayek, for example, probably the most well-known libertarian, sees his work as restating an ideal of liberty for our times. "We are concerned," says Hayek, "with that condition of men in which coercion of some by others is reduced as much as possible in society."[18] Similarly, John Hospers believes that libertarianism is "a philosophy of personal liberty—the liberty of each person to live according to his own choices, provided that he does not attempt to coerce others and thus prevent them from living according to their choices."[19] And Robert Nozick claims that if a conception of justice goes beyond libertarian "side-constraints," it cannot avoid the prospect of continually interfering with people's lives.[20] Moreover, Hayek, Hospers, and Nozick always regarded their defenses of liberty as opposed to a right to welfare. How then could it be possible to achieve a practical reconciliation between libertarianism and utilitarianism which so easily endorses a right to welfare?

To see how this can be done, let us begin by interpreting the ideal of liberty as a negative ideal in the manner favored by libertarians.[21] So understood, liberty is the absence of interference by other people from doing what one wants or is able to do. Libertarians go on to characterize their political ideal as requiring that each person should have the greatest amount of liberty commensurate with the same liberty for all.[22] Interpreting their ideal in this way, libertarians claim to derive a number of more specific requirements, in particular, a right to life; a right to freedom of speech, press, and assembly; and a right to property.

Here it is important to observe that the libertarian's right to life is not a right to receive from others the goods and resources necessary for preserving one's life; it is simply a right not to be killed unjustly.

Correspondingly, the libertarian's right to property is not a right to receive from others the goods and resources necessary for one's welfare, but rather a right to acquire goods and resources either by initial acquisition or by voluntary agreement.

Of course, libertarians allow that it would be nice of the rich to share their surplus resources with the poor. Nevertheless, they deny that government has a duty to provide for such needs. Some good things, such as providing welfare to the poor, are requirements of charity rather than justice, libertarians claim. Accordingly, failure to make such provisions is neither blameworthy nor punishable. As a consequence, such acts of charity should not be coercively required. For this reason, libertarians are opposed to coercively supported welfare programs.

Conflicting Liberties

Now in order to see why libertarians are mistaken about what their ideal requires, consider a typical conflict situation between the rich and the poor. In this conflict situation, the rich, of course, have more than enough resources to satisfy their basic needs.[23] By contrast, the poor lack the resources to meet their most basic needs even though they have tried all the means available to them that libertarians regard as legitimate for acquiring such resources. Under circumstances like these, libertarians usually maintain that the rich should have the liberty to use their resources to satisfy their luxury needs if they so wish. Libertarians recognize that this liberty might well be enjoyed at the expense of the satisfaction of the most basic needs of the poor; they just think that liberty always has priority over other political ideals, and since they assume that the liberty of the poor is not at stake in such conflict situations, it is easy for them to conclude that the rich should not be required to sacrifice their liberty so that the basic needs of the poor may be met.

Of course, libertarians allow that it would be nice of the rich to share their surplus resources with the poor. Nevertheless, according to libertarians, such acts of charity are not required because the liberty of the poor is not thought to be at stake in such conflict situations.

In fact, however, the liberty of the poor is at stake in such conflict situations. What is at stake is the liberty of the poor not to be to interfered with in taking from the surplus possessions of the rich what is necessary to satisfy their basic needs.

Needless to say, libertarians want to deny that the poor have this liberty. But how can they justify such a denial? As this liberty of the poor has been specified, it is not a positive right to receive something but a negative right of noninterference. Nor will it do for libertarians to appeal to a right to life or a right to property to rule out such a liberty, because on the libertarian view, under consideration, liberty is basic and all other rights are derived from a right to liberty. Clearly, what libertarians must do is recognize the existence of such a liberty and then claim that it conflicts with other liberties of the rich. But when libertarians see that this is the case, they are often genuinely surprised—one might even say rudely awakened—for they had not previously seen the conflict between the rich and the poor as a conflict of liberties.[24]

Now when the conflict between the rich and the poor is viewed as a conflict of liberties, we can either say that the rich should have the liberty not to be interfered with in using their surplus resources for luxury purposes, or we can say that the poor should have the liberty not to be interfered with in taking from the rich what they require to meet their basic needs. If we choose one liberty, we must reject the other. What needs to be determined, therefore, is which liberty is morally preferable: the liberty of the rich or the liberty of the poor.

The "Ought" Implies "Can" Principle Again

I submit that the liberty of the poor, which is the liberty not to be interfered with in taking from the surplus resources of others what is required to meet one's basic needs, is morally preferable to the liberty of the rich, which is the liberty not to be interfered with in using one's surplus resources for luxury purposes. To see that this is the case, we need only appeal again, as we did in interpreting utilitarianism, to the "ought" implies "can" principle, a principle common to all moral and political perspectives. According to this principle, people are not morally required to do what they lack the power to do or what would involve so great a sacrifice that it is unreasonable to ask, and/or in cases of severe conflict of interest, unreasonable to require them to abide by.

Now applying the "ought" implies "can" principle to the case at hand, it seems clear that the poor have it within their power willingly to relinquish such an important liberty as the liberty not to be interfered with in taking from the rich what they require to meet their basic needs. Nevertheless, it is unreasonable in this context to ask or require them to make so great a sacrifice. In the extreme case, it involves asking or requiring the poor to sit back and starve to death. Of course, the poor may have no real alternative to relinquishing this liberty. To do anything else may involve worse consequences for themselves and their loved ones and may invite a painful death. Accordingly, we may expect that the poor would acquiesce, albeit unwillingly, to a political system that denied them the right to welfare supported by such a liberty, at the same time we recognize that such a system imposed an unreasonable sacrifice upon the poor—a sacrifice that we could not morally blame the poor for trying to evade.[25] Analogously, we might expect that a woman whose life is threatened will submit to a rapist's demands, at the same time that we recognize the utter unreasonableness of those demands.

By contrast, it is not unreasonable to ask and require the rich in this context to sacrifice the liberty to meet some of their luxury needs so that the poor can have the liberty to meet their basic needs.[26] Naturally, we might expect that the rich, for reasons of self-interest and past contribution, might be disinclined to make such a sacrifice. We might even suppose that the past contribution of the rich provides a good reason for not sacrificing their liberty to use their surplus for luxury purposes. Yet, unlike the poor, the rich can not claim that relinquishing such a liberty involved so great a sacrifice that it is unreasonable to ask and require them to make it; unlike the poor, the rich are morally blameworthy for failing to make such a sacrifice.

Consequently, if we assume that however else we specify the requirements of morality, they cannot violate the "ought" implies "can" principle, it follows that, despite what libertarians claim, the right to liberty endorsed by them actually favors the liberty of the poor over the liberty of the rich.

This means that within the bundle of liberties allotted to each person by the basic principles of libertarianism, there must be the liberty not to be interfered with (when one is poor) in taking from the surplus possessions of the rich what is necessary to satisfy one's basic needs. This must be part of the bundle that constitutes the greatest liberty for each person because this liberty is morally superior to the liberty with which it directly conflicts, that is, the liberty not to be interfered with (when one is rich) in using one's resources to satisfy one's luxury needs if one so wishes. In this context, the "ought" implies "can" principle establishes the moral superiority of the liberty of the poor over the liberty of the rich. Here too the application of the "ought" implies "can" principle can be said to support greater liberty overall in the sense of supporting the morally greater or morally better liberty overall.

Yet couldn't libertarians object to this conclusion, claiming that it would be unreasonable to ask the rich to sacrifice the liberty to meet some of their luxury needs so that the poor can have the liberty to meet their basic needs? As I have pointed out, libertarians don't usually see the situation as a conflict of liberties, but suppose they did. How plausible would such an objection be? Not very plausible at all, I think.

For consider: what are libertarians going to say about the poor? Isn't it clearly unreasonable to require the poor to sacrifice the liberty to meet their basic needs so that the rich can have the liberty to meet their luxury needs? Isn't it clearly unreasonable to require the poor to sit back and starve to death? If it is, then, there is no resolution of this conflict that is reasonable to require both the rich and the poor to accept. But that would mean that libertarians could not be putting forth a moral resolution because a moral resolution resolves severe conflicts of interest in ways that it is reasonable to ask and require everyone affected to accept. Therefore, as long as libertarians think of themselves as putting forth a moral resolution, they cannot allow that it is unreasonable in cases of severe conflict of interest *both* to require the rich to sacrifice the liberty to meet some of their luxury needs in order to benefit the poor and to require the poor to sacrifice the liberty to meet their basic needs in order to benefit the rich. But I submit that if one of these requirements is to be judged reasonable, then, by any neutral assessment, it must be the requirement that the rich sacrifice the liberty to meet some of their luxury needs so that the poor can have the liberty to meet their basic needs; there is no other plausible resolution, if libertarians intend to put forth a moral resolution.[27]

Notice that it is not the mere size of the sacrifice required of the poor that is objectionable about the possibility of favoring the liberty of the rich over the liberty of the poor, because sometimes morality does require great sacrifices from us. Rather, what is objectionable about this possibility is the size of the sacrifice that the poor would be required to bear compared to the size of the benefit that would thereby be secured for the rich. In the conflict between the rich and the poor, the sacrifice imposed on the poor by denying them the satisfaction of their basic needs is clearly greater than the benefit the rich obtain from satisfying their nonbasic or luxury needs; hence, in this context, the unreasonableness of imposing such a sacrifice on the poor. In this case, it is more reasonable to require a certain degree of altruism from the rich than to require an even greater degree of altruism from the poor. In all such cases, the goal is to avoid imposing an unreasonable sacrifice on anyone, where the reasonableness of the sacrifice is judged by comparing the alternative possibilities. Thus, once the poor's basic needs are met, it is unreasonable to further constrain the liberty of the rich, because that would impose an unreasonable sacrifice upon them.[28]

In his book, *Individuals and Their Rights,* Tibor Machan criticizes my argument that a libertarian ideal of liberty leads to a right to welfare, accepting its theoretical thrust but denying its practical significance.[29] He appreciates the force of the argument enough to grant that if the type of conflict cases I describe between the rich and the poor actually obtained, the poor would have welfare rights.[30] But he denies that such cases—in which the poor have done all that they legitimately can to satisfy their basic needs in a libertarian society—actually obtain. "Normally," he writes, "persons do not lack the opportunities and resources to satisfy their basic needs."[31]

But this response virtually concedes everything that defenders of a right to welfare had hoped to establish. For the poor's right to welfare is not unconditional. It is conditional principally upon the poor doing all that they legitimately can to meet their own basic needs. So it is only when the poor lack sufficient opportunity to satisfy their own basic needs that a right to welfare has moral force. Accordingly, on libertarian grounds, Machan has conceded the legitimacy of just the kind of right to welfare that defenders of welfare had hoped to establish.

It should also be noted that this case for restricting the liberty of the rich depends upon the willingness of the poor to take advantage of whatever opportunities are available to them to engage in mutually beneficial work, so that failure of the poor to take advantage of such opportunities would normally cancel, or at least significantly reduce, the obligation of the rich to restrict their own liberty for the benefit of the poor.[32] In addition, the poor would be required to return the equivalent of any surplus possessions they have taken from the rich once they are able to do so and still satisfy their basic needs. Nor would the poor be required to keep the liberty to which they are entitled. They could give up part of it, or all of it, or risk losing it on the chance of gaining a greater share of liberties or other social goods.[33] Consequently, the case for restricting the liberty of the rich for the benefit of the poor is neither unconditional nor inalienable.

Of course, there will be cases in which the poor fail to satisfy their basic needs, not because of any direct restriction of liberty on the part of the rich, but because the poor are in such dire need that they are unable even to attempt to take from the rich what they require to meet their basic needs. In such cases, the rich would not be performing any act of commission that prevents the poor from taking what they require. Yet, even in such cases, the rich would normally be performing acts of commission that prevent other persons from taking part of the rich's own surplus possessions and using it to aid the poor. And when assessed from a moral point of view, restricting the liberty of these allies or agents of the poor would not be morally justified for the very same reason that restricting the liberty of the poor to meet their own basic needs would not be morally justified: It is not reasonable to require all of those affected to accept such a restriction of liberty.

It is sometimes thought that there is a different interpretation of libertarianism where rights, not the ideal of liberty, are fundamental and where an analogous argument is needed to establish the conclusion I have just established here.[34] Under this presumptively different interpretation, the rights taken as fundamental are a strong (absolute) right to property and a weak right to life. Yet given that for libertarians such rights are rights of noninterference, that is, (negative) liberty rights, the question arises of why we should accept these particular rights of noninterference (liberties) and not others—which is just the question that arises when we consider the conflicting liberties to which an ideal of liberty gives rise. What this shows is that the "rights" interpretation of libertarianism is not really distinct from the "liberty" interpretation we have been just discussing.

In brief, I have argued that a libertarian ideal of liberty can be seen to support a right to welfare by applying the "ought" implies "can" principle to conflicts between the rich and the poor. Here the principle supports such rights by favoring the liberty of the poor over the liberty of the rich. Clearly, what is crucial to the derivation of these rights is the claim that it is unreasonable to require the poor to deny their basic needs and accept anything less than these rights as the condition for their willing cooperation.

Now it might be objected that the right to welfare, which this argument establishes from libertarian premises, is not the same as the right to welfare endorsed by welfare liberals and socialists. This is correct. We can mark this difference by referring to the right that this argument establishes as "a negative welfare right" and by referring to the right endorsed by welfare liberals as "a positive welfare right." The significance of this difference is that a person's negative welfare right can be violated only when other people through acts of commission interfere with its exercise, whereas a person's positive welfare right can be violated not only by such acts of commission but by acts of omission as well. Nonetheless, this difference will have little practical import, for in recognizing the legitimacy of negative welfare rights, libertarians will come to see that virtually any use of their surplus possessions is likely to violate the negative welfare rights of the poor by preventing the poor from rightfully appropriating (some part of) their surplus goods and resources. So, in order to ensure that they will not be engaging in such wrongful actions, it will be incumbent on them to set up institutions guaranteeing adequate positive welfare rights for the poor. Only then will they be able to use legitimately any remaining surplus possessions to meet their own nonbasic needs. Furthermore, in the absence of adequate positive welfare rights, the poor, either acting by themselves or through their allies or agents, would have some discretion in determining when and how to exercise their negative welfare rights.[35] In order not to be subject to that discretion, libertarians will tend to favor the only morally legitimate way of preventing the exercise of such rights: They will set up institutions guaranteeing adequate positive welfare rights that will then take precedence over the exercise of negative welfare rights. For these reasons, recognizing the negative welfare rights of the poor will ultimately lead libertarians to endorse the same sort of welfare institutions favored by welfare liberals.[36]

Distant Peoples and Future Generations

Utilitarians will surely applaud the derivation of a right to welfare from the libertarian ideal of liberty, since they too endorse just such a right. But just as surely they want libertarians to recognize the implications of such a right for distant peoples and future generations.

Now for libertarians fundamental rights are universal rights, that is, rights possessed by all people, not just those who live in certain places or at certain times. Of course, to claim that these rights are universal rights does not mean that they are universally recognized. Obviously, the fundamental rights that flow from the libertarian ideal have not been universally recognized. Rather to claim that they are universal rights, despite their spotty recognition, implies only that they ought to be recognized because people at all times and places have or could have had good reasons to recognize these rights, not that they actually did or do so.[37] Nor need these universal rights be unconditional. This is particularly true in the case of the right to welfare, which I have argued, is conditional upon people doing all that they legitimately can do to provide for themselves. In addition, this right is conditional upon there being sufficient resources available so that everyone's welfare needs can be met. So where people do not do all that they can to provide for themselves or where there are not sufficient resources available, people simply do not have a right to welfare. Given the universal and conditional character of this libertarian right to welfare, what then are the implications of this right for distant peoples and future generations?

Consider that at present there is probably a sufficient worldwide supply of goods and resources to meet the normal costs of satisfying the basic nutritional needs of all existing persons. According to former U.S. Secretary of Agriculture Bob Bergland:

> For the past twenty years, if the available world food supply had been evenly divided and distributed, each person would have received more than the minimum number of calories.[38]

Other authorities have made similar assessments of the available world food supply.[39] Needless to say, the adoption of a policy of supporting a right to welfare for all existing persons would necessitate significant changes, especially in developed societies. For example, the large percentage of the U.S. population whose food consumption clearly exceeds even an adequately adjusted poverty index would have to substantially alter their eating habits. In particular, they would have to reduce their consumption of beef and pork so as to make more grain available for direct human consumption. (Currently, 37 percent of worldwide production of grain and 70 percent of U.S. production is fed to animals.)[40] Thus, at least the satisfaction of some of the nonbasic needs of the more advantaged in developed societies would have to be forgone, leading to greater equality, so that the basic nutritional needs of all existing persons in developing and underdeveloped societies could be met. Furthermore, to raise the standard of living in the Second and Third World will require substantial increases in the consumption of energy and other resources. But such an increase would have to be matched by a substantial decrease in the consumption of these goods in the First World, otherwise global ecological disaster would result from increased global warming, ozone depletion, and acid rain, lowering virtually everyone's standard of living.[41] For example, some type of mutually beneficial arrangement needs to be negotiated with China, which, with 50 percent of the world's coal resources, plans to double its use of coal within the next two decades yet is currently burning 85 percent of its coal without any pollution controls whatsoever.[42]

In addition, once the basic nutritional needs of future generations are also taken into account, then the satisfaction of the nonbasic needs of the more advantaged in developed societies would have to be further restricted in order to preserve the fertility of cropland and other food-related natural resources for the use of future generations. And once basic needs other than nutritional needs are taken into account as well, still further restrictions would be required. For example, it has been estimated that presently an American uses seventy-five times more resources than an Indian. This means that in terms of resource consumption the North American continent's population is the equivalent of 22.5 billion Indians.[43] So unless we assume that basic resources such as arable land, iron, coal, and oil are in unlimited supply, this unequal consumption will have to be radically altered if the basic needs of distant peoples and future generations are to be met.[44] In effect, recognizing a universal right to welfare applicable both to distant peoples and future generations will lead to an equal sharing of resources over place and time.[45]

Still, one might want to press again Machan's earlier objection to this argument, which is that it has no practical significance because "persons do not lack the opportunities and resources to satisfy their basic needs." However, this objection is even easier to refute once the libertarian ideal is seen to ground a universal right to welfare that is applicable to both distant people and future generations. This is because there is simply no denying that most of the 1.2 billion people living in conditions of absolute poverty "lack the opportunities and resources to satisfy their basic needs."[46] Yet the objection also fails when we look closely at the poor within our own society. It is estimated that some 32 million Americans live below the official poverty index, and that one fifth of American children are growing up in poverty.[47] Surely many of these Americans also "lack the opportunities and resources to satisfy their basic needs."

It might be further objected, however, that this argument falls victim to its own success. If a universal right to welfare requires an equal sharing of resources, wouldn't talented people simply lack the incentive to produce according to their ability when such a right is enforced? But what sort of incentive is needed? Surely there would be moral incentive for the talented to make the necessary sacrifices if the ideal of liberty requires such a right to welfare. Yet, except for those whose self-interest has become completely identified with morality, there clearly would not be sufficient self-interested incentive to accept the equality of resources required by a universal right to welfare. Even so, if it can be shown that morality has priority over self-interested prudence, as was argued in the previous chapter, there is no question of what ought to be done.

In brief, I have argued that when a libertarian ideal of liberty is correctly interpreted, it leads to a universal right to welfare and further that the recognition of this universal right to welfare leads to considerable equality in the shares of goods and resources over place and time. Of course, this is just the sort of outcome utilitarianism would favor given that it is committed to maximizing utility in a way that is consistent with satisfying the "ought" implies "can" principle. Since, other things equal, meeting basic needs produces greater utility than meeting nonbasic ones, utilitarianism has to be committed to a general strategy of meeting people's basic needs. This requires endorsing a right to welfare. Moreover, once that right to welfare is extended to distant peoples and future generations, as it must be, utilitarianism leads even more straightforwardly than libertarianism to considerable equality in the shares of goods and resources over place and time. What this shows is that the libertarian branch of Kantian ethics can be practically reconciled with utilitarianism in much the same way that the welfare liberal branch of Kantian ethics was so reconciled.

Moreover, if Kantian ethical theory can be reconciled with utilitarianism in this way, it stands to reason that Aristotelian ethical theory can be as well. This is because if Aristotelian and Kantian ethics can be reconciled, as I have argued in the previous chapter, and if Kantian and utilitarian ethics can be reconciled, as I have argued here, then there is no reason to think that transitivity does not hold, and that the most morally defensible Aristotelian and utilitarian theories can also be reconciled, at least at the practical level.[48] Yet another reason for thinking that this practical reconciliation holds, is that, unlike Kantian and utilitarian theories, contemporary formulations of the most morally defensible Aristotelian ethical theories have been very vague about what their practical requirements are. It should not be surprising, therefore, that once the practical requirements of these Aristotelian theories are specified and then compared with practical requirements of utilitarianism constrained, as it must be, by the "ought" implies "can" principle, there simply are no practical differences. Accordingly, it is this practical reconciliation of Aristotelian, Kantian, and utilitarian ethical theories, along with the merely formal tenets that are shared respectively by contemporary defenders of each of these theories, that constitutes the triumph of practice over theory in ethics.

Yet why not view this as the triumph of shared or common theory in ethics rather than as the triumph of practice over theory in ethics? Of course, there is some truth to this. I have allowed that competing Aristotelian, Kantian, and utilitarian ethical theories have become more alike as their contemporary defenders strive to make their theories more morally defensible by incorporating elements from each others' theories into their own. Still, what is even more significant, I have argued, is that the theoretical differences that remain, as, for example, those that distinguish Rawls's welfare liberalism from libertarianism and from utilitarianism, have little or no practical significance. In the practical argument for particular moral conclusions, it is important to recognize that the significance of these and other theoretical differences just washes away. And that is what really constitutes the triumph of practice over theory in ethics.

~

CHAPTER FOUR

Kantians and Utilitarians and the Moral Status of Nonhuman Life

If Kantian and utilitarian ethics can be reconciled at the practical level, as I have argued in the preceding chapter, it should then be possible to reach agreement on the moral status of nonhuman life. Indeed, in recent years both Kantian and utilitarian moral philosophers have surely tried to provide a defense of the moral status of at least some forms of nonhuman life. For example, Peter Singer has attempted to provide a utilitarian defense of the moral status of all sentient beings.[1] Tom Regan has proposed a Kantian defense of the moral status of all experiencing subjects of life.[2] An alternative Kantian defense of the moral status of all individual living beings has been proposed by Paul Taylor.[3] And I have extended Taylor's account to include species and ecosystems as well.[4] All of these views are versions of nonanthropocentrism because they all hold that at least some nonhuman living beings have moral status. As such, they are opposed to anthropocentrism in all its forms which holds that all or only human beings have moral status. What I propose to do in this chapter is first to try to show why my particular version of nonanthropocentrism is morally preferable to anthropocentrism, and then to try to show why it is also morally preferable to other forms of nonanthropocentrism as well. Throughout I will be looking for a defense of nonanthropocentrism that should be acceptable to both Kantians and utilitarians alike.

THE MORAL STATUS OF ALL LIVING BEINGS

Clearly what we need to defend nonanthropocentrism is a really good argument that nonhuman living beings have moral status. A really good argument, by definition, must be a non-question-begging argument. So what we need is a non-question-begging argument that nonhuman living beings have moral status, which is to say that they should count morally. Is there such an argument?

Consider: We clearly have the capacity of entertaining and acting upon both anthropocentric reasons that take only the interests of humans into account and nonanthropocentric reasons that also take the interests of nonhuman living beings into account. Given that capacity, the question we seek to answer is what sort of reasons are rational for us to accept.

Now right off, we might think that we have non-question-begging grounds for only taking the interests of humans into account, namely, the possession by human beings of the distinctive traits of rationality and moral agency. But while human beings clearly do have such distinctive traits, members of nonhuman species also have distinctive traits that humans lack, like the homing ability of pigeons, the speed of the cheetah, and the ruminative ability of sheep and cattle. Nor will it do to claim that the distinctive traits that humans possess are more valuable than the distinctive traits that members of other species possess because there is no non-question-begging standpoint from which to justify this claim. From a human standpoint, rationality and moral agency are more valuable than any of the distinctive traits found in nonhuman species, since, as humans, we would not be better off if we were to trade in those traits for the distinctive traits found in nonhuman species. Yet the same holds true of nonhuman species. Generally, pigeons, cheetahs, sheep, and cattle would not be better off if they were to trade in their distinctive traits for the distinctive traits of other species.[5]

Of course, the members of some species might be better off if they could retain the distinctive traits of their species while acquiring one or another of the distinctive traits possessed by some other species. For example, we humans might be better off if we could retain our distinctive traits while acquiring the ruminative ability of sheep and cattle.[6] But many of the distinctive traits of species cannot be even imaginatively added to the members of other species without substantially altering the original species. For example, in order for the cheetah to acquire the distinctive traits possessed by humans, presumably it would have to be so transformed that its paws became something like hands to accommodate its humanlike mental capabilities, thereby losing its distinctive speed, and ceasing to be a cheetah. So possessing distinctively human traits would not be good for the cheetah.[7] And with the possible exception of our nearest evolutionary relatives, the same holds true for the members of other species: they would not be better off having distinctively human traits. Only in fairy tales and in the world of Disney can the members of nonhuman species enjoy a full array of distinctively human traits.[8] So there appears to be no non-question-begging perspective from which to judge that distinctively human traits are more valuable than the distinctive traits possessed by other species, and so no non-question-begging justification for only taking anthropocentric reasons into account. Judged from a non-question-begging perspective, we would seemingly have to grant the prima facie relevance of both anthropocentric and nonanthropocentric reasons to rational choice and then try to determine which reasons we would be rationally required to act upon, all things considered.

In this regard, there are two kinds of cases that must be considered. First, there are cases in which there is a conflict between the relevant anthropocentric and nonanthropocentric reasons. Second, there are cases in which there is no such conflict.

It seems obvious that where there is no conflict and both reasons are conclusive reasons of their kind, both reasons should be acted upon. In such contexts, we should do what is favored both by anthropocentrism and by nonanthropocentrism.

Now when we turn to rationally assess the relevant reasons in conflict cases, three solutions are possible. First, we can say that anthropocentric reasons always have priority over conflicting nonanthropocentric ones. Second, we can say, just the opposite, that nonanthropocentric reasons always have priority over conflicting anthropocentric ones. Third, we can say that some kind of compromise is rationally required. In this compromise, sometimes anthropocentric reasons will have priority over nonanthropocentric reasons, and sometimes nonanthropocentric reasons will have priority over anthropocentric reasons.

Once the conflict is described in this manner, the third solution can be seen as the one that is rationally required. This is because the first and second solutions give exclusive priority to one class of relevant reasons over the other, and only a question-begging justification can be given for such an exclusive priority. Only by employing the third solution, and sometimes giving priority to anthropocentric reasons, and sometimes giving priority to nonanthropocentric reasons, can we avoid a question-begging resolution.[9] What we need, therefore, are conflict resolution principles that specify these priorities.

CONFLICT RESOLUTION PRINCIPLES

But how are these priorities to be specified? Now surely, even if we hold that all living beings should count morally, we can justify a preference for humans on grounds of preservation.[10] Accordingly, we have:

> A PRINCIPLE OF HUMAN PRESERVATION. Actions that are necessary for meeting one's basic needs or the basic needs of other human beings are permissible even when they require aggressing against the basic needs of individual animals and plants, or even of whole species or ecosystems.[11]

Needs, in general, if not satisfied, lead to lacks or deficiencies with respect to various standards. The basic needs of humans, if not satisfied, lead to lacks or deficiencies with respect to a standard of a decent life. The basic needs of animals and plants, if not satisfied, lead to lacks or deficiencies with respect to a standard of a healthy life. The basic needs of species and ecosystems, if not satisfied, lead to lacks or deficiencies with respect to a standard of a healthy living system. The means necessary for meeting the basic needs of humans can vary widely from society to society. By contrast, the means necessary for meeting the basic needs of particular species of animals and plants tend to be invariant.[12] Of course, while only some needs can be clearly classified as basic, and others clearly classified as nonbasic, there still are other needs that are more or less difficult to classify. Yet the fact that not every need can be clearly classified as either basic or nonbasic, as similarly holds for a whole range of dichotomous concepts like moral/immoral, legal/illegal, living/nonliving, human/nonhuman, should not immobilize us from acting at least with respect to clear cases.[13]

In human ethics, there is no principle that is strictly analogous to this Principle of Human Preservation.[14] There is a principle of self-preservation in human ethics that permits actions that are necessary for meeting one's own basic needs or the basic needs of other people, even if this requires *failing to meet* (through an act of omission) the basic needs of still other people. For example, we can use our resources to feed ourselves and our families, even if this necessitates failing to meet the basic needs of people in underdeveloped countries. But, in general, we don't have a principle that allows us to *aggress against* (through an act of commission) the basic needs of some people in order to meet our own basic needs or the basic needs of other people to whom we are committed or happen to care about. One place where we do permit aggressing against the basic needs of other people in order to meet our own basic needs or the basic needs of people to whom we are committed or happen to care about is our acceptance of the outcome of life and death struggles in lifeboat cases, where no one has an antecedent right to the available resources. For example, if you had to fight off others in order to secure the last place in a lifeboat for yourself or for a member of your family, we might say that you justifiably aggressed against the basic needs of those you fought to meet your own basic needs or the basic needs of the members of your family.[15]

Now the Principle of Human Preservation does not permit aggressing against the basic needs of humans even if it is the only way to meet our own basic needs or the basic needs of other human beings.[16] Rather this principle is directed at a different range of cases with respect to which we can meet our own basic needs and the basic needs of other humans simply by aggressing against the basic needs of nonhuman living beings. With respect to those cases, the Principle of Human Preservation permits actions that are necessary for meeting one's own basic needs or the basic needs of other human beings, even when they require aggressing against the basic needs of individual animals and plants, or even of whole species or ecosystems.

Of course, we can envision an even more permissive Principle of Human Preservation, one that would permit us to aggress against the basic needs of both humans and nonhumans to meet our own basic needs or the basic needs of other human beings. But while adopting such a principle, by permitting cannibalism, would clearly reduce the degree of predation of humans on other species, and thus be of some benefit to other species, it would clearly be counterproductive with respect to meeting basic human needs. This is because implicit nonaggression pacts based on a reasonable expectation of a comparable degree of altruistic forbearance from fellow humans have been enormously beneficial and probably were necessary for the survival of the human species. So it is difficult to see how humans could be justifiably required to forgo such benefits.

Moreover, beyond the prudential value of such implicit nonaggression pacts against fellow humans, there appears to be no morally defensible way to exclude some humans from their protection. This is because any exclusion would fail to satisfy that most basic principle of morality, the "ought" implies "can" principle, given that it would impose a sacrifice on at least some humans that is unreasonable to ask and/or require them to accept.[17]

But what about the interests of nonhuman living beings? Doesn't the Principle of Human Preservation impose a sacrifice on nonhumans that it would be unreasonable to ask and/or require any would-be human guardian of their interests to accept? Surely, we expect the animals and plants to fight us however they can to prevent being used in this fashion. Why then is it not reasonable for would-be human guardians of the interests of nonhuman living beings to also try to prevent their being used in this fashion? But this would mean that it is morally permissible for would-be human guardians of the interest of nonhumans to prevent other humans from meeting their own basic needs, or the basic needs of still other humans, when this requires aggressing against the basic needs of nonhumans. Understood as "strong permissibility," it implies that other humans are *prohibited* from interfering with such preventive actions, even if it means that their own basic needs are not met as a result. But surely, this is an unreasonable requirement for humans to impose on other humans—one that does not accord with the "ought" implies "can" principle.

But suppose we understand the permissibility involved to be that of weak permissibility according to which virtually everything is permissible and virtually nothing is morally required or prohibited. Then the Principle of Human Preservation would imply that it is permissible, in this weak sense, for humans to aggress against the basic needs of nonhumans when this was necessary for meeting their own basic needs, and at the same time imply that it is permissible, in this same weak sense, for would-be human guardians of the interests of nonhumans to prevent humans from meeting their basic needs by aggressing against the basic needs of nonhumans. Since under this interpretation of moral permissibility, virtually nothing is morally required or prohibited, what gets done will tend to depend on the relative power of the contending parties. The purpose of morality, however, is to provide resolutions in just such severe conflict-of-interest situations. Assuming then that a moral resolution must satisfy the "ought" implies "can" principle, it cannot impose moral requirements on humans that are unreasonable for them to accept.[18] This seems to suggest that the permissibility in the Principle of Human Preservation must be that of strong permissibility, which means that would-be human guardians of the interests of nonhumans are prohibited from interfering with humans who are taking the necessary action to meet their basic needs, even when this requires them to aggress against the basic needs of nonhumans.

But are there no exceptions to the Principle of Human Preservation? Consider, for example, the following real-life case.[19] Thousands of Nepalese have cleared forests, cultivated crops, and raised cattle and buffalo on land surrounding the Royal Chitwan National Park in Nepal, but they have also made incursions into the park to meet their own basic needs. In so doing, they have threatened the rhino, the Bengal tiger, and other endangered species in the park. Assume that the basic needs of no other humans are at stake.[20] For this case, then, are would-be human guardians of these nonhuman endangered species justified in preventing the Nepalese from meeting their basic needs in order to preserve these endangered species? It seems to me that before the basic needs of disadvantaged Nepalese can be sacrificed, the would-be human guardians of these endangered species are first required to use whatever surplus is available to them and to other humans to meet the basic needs of the Nepalese they propose to restrict. Yet clearly it is very difficult to have first used up all the surplus available to the whole human population for meeting basic human needs. Under present conditions, this requirement has certainly not been met. Moreover, insofar as rich people are unwilling to make the necessary transfers of resources so that poor people are not led to prey on endangered species in order to survive, then, the appropriate means of preserving endangered species should be to use force against such rich people rather than against poor people, like the Nepalese near Royal Chitwan National Park.[21] So for all present purposes, the moral permissibility in the Principle of Human Preservation remains that of strong permissibility, which means that other humans are prohibited from interfering with the aggression against nonhumans that is permitted by the principle.[22]

Nevertheless, preference for humans can still go beyond bounds, and the bounds that are required are captured by the following:

A PRINCIPLE OF DISPROPORTIONALITY. Actions that meet nonbasic or luxury needs of humans are prohibited when they aggress against the basic needs of individual animals and plants or even of whole species or ecosystems.

This principle is strictly analogous to the principle in human ethics that similarly prohibits meeting some people's nonbasic or luxury needs by aggressing against the basic needs of other people. Without a doubt, the adoption of such a principle with respect to nonhumans would significantly change the way we live our lives. Such a principle is required, however, if there is to be any substance to the claim that the members of all species count morally. We can no more consistently claim that the members of all species count morally and yet aggress against the basic needs of some animals or plants whenever this serves our own nonbasic or luxury needs than we can consistently claim that all humans count morally and then aggress against the basic needs of other human beings whenever this serves our nonbasic or luxury needs. Consequently, if saying that species count morally is to mean anything, it must be the case that the basic needs of the members of nonhuman species are protected against aggressive actions that only serve to meet the nonbasic needs of humans, as required by the Principle of Disproportionality.[23] Another way to put the central claim here is to hold that counting morally rules out domination, where domination means aggressing against the basic needs of some for the sake of satisfying the nonbasic needs of others.

To see why these limits on preference for the members of the human species are what is required for recognizing that other species and their members count morally, we need to understand the nondomination of species by analogy with the nondomination of humans. We need to see that just as we claim that humans should not be dominated but treat them differently, so too we can claim that species should not be dominated but also treat them differently. In human ethics, there are various interpretations given to human nondomination that allow for different treatment of humans. In ethical egoism, everyone is *equally at liberty* to pursue his or her own interests, but this allows us to always prefer ourselves to others, who are understood to be like opponents in a competitive game. In libertarianism, everyone has an *equal right to liberty*, but although this imposes some limits on the pursuit of self-interest, it is said to allow us to refrain from helping others in severe need.[24] In welfare liberalism, everyone has an *equal right to welfare and opportunity*, but this need not commit us to providing everyone with exactly the same resources. In socialism, everyone has an *equal right to self-development*, and although this may commit us to providing everyone with the same resources, it still sanctions some degree of self-preference. So just as there are these various ways to interpret the nondomination of humans that still allow us to treat humans differently, there are various ways that we can interpret the nondomination of species that allow us to treat species differently.

Now one might interpret the nondomination of species in a very strong sense, analogous to the interpretation of nondomination found in socialism. But the kind of nondomination of species that I have defended here is more akin to the nondomination found in welfare liberalism or in libertarianism than it is to the nondomination found in socialism.[25] In brief, this form of nondomination requires that we not aggress against the basic needs of the members of other species for the sake of the nonbasic needs of the members of our own species (the Principle of Disproportionality), but it permits us to aggress against the basic needs of the members of other species for the sake of the basic needs of the members of our own species (the Principle of Human Preservation). In this way, I have argued that we can endorse the nondomination of species, while avoiding imposing an unreasonable sacrifice on the members of our own species.

It is important to note here that the Principle of Disproportionality also imposes a limit on human reproduction. There is little doubt that the currently expanding population of six billion humans threatens the survival of many nonhuman species and possibly human survival as well, in part, simply because of its size. Consequently, human reproduction needs to be limited to the legitimate exercise of the basic human need to procreate, which means roughly one child per family.

Later, after the human population has been significantly reduced, this policy should be relaxed to one that simply serves the long-term survivability of the human species, consistent with maintaining humans within their environmental niche, where, unlike today, they would be in balance with the rest of the biotic community. This is the human reproduction policy that the Principle of Disproportionality requires. It permits human reproduction when it serves existing basic human needs and the long-term survivability of the human species, but not when it simply serves nonbasic or luxury needs at the expense of nonhuman nature. Any less restrictive policy would impose an unacceptable sacrifice on nonhuman species.

Nevertheless, in order to avoid imposing an unacceptable sacrifice on the members of our own species, we can also justify a preference for humans on grounds of defense. Thus, we have:

> A PRINCIPLE OF HUMAN DEFENSE. Actions that defend oneself and other human beings against harmful aggression are permissible even when they necessitate killing or harming individual animals or plants, or even destroying whole species or ecosystems.

This Principle of Human Defense allows us to defend ourselves and other human beings from harmful aggression first against our persons and the persons of other humans beings we are committed to or happen to care about and second against our justifiably held property and the justifiably held property of other humans beings that we are committed to or happen to care about.[26]

Here there are two sorts of cases. First, there are cases where humans are defending their own basic needs against harmful aggression from nonhumans. In cases of this sort, not only are the human defenders perfectly justified in defending themselves against aggression but also no would-be human guardians of nonhuman interests are justified on grounds of what we could reasonably require of humans in opposing that defense.

Second, there are cases where humans are defending their nonbasic needs against harmful aggression from nonhumans who, let's assume, are trying to meet their basic needs. In cases of this sort, is it justified for would-be human guardians of the interests of nonhuman living beings to assist them in their aggression against humans? In analogous cases in human ethics, we can see how just this type of aggression can be justified when the poor, who have exhausted all the other means that are legitimately available to them, take from the surplus possessions of the rich just what they require to meet their basic needs. Expressed in terms of an ideal of negative liberty endorsed by libertarians, the justification for this aggression is the priority of the liberty of the poor not to be interfered with when taking from the surplus possessions of the rich what they require to meet their basic needs over the liberty of the rich not to be interfered with when using their surplus for luxury purposes.[27] Expressed in terms of an ideal of fairness endorsed by welfare liberals, the justification for this aggression is the right to welfare that the needy have against those with a surplus. And expressed in terms of an ideal of equality endorsed by socialists, the justification for this aggression is the right that everyone has to equal self-development. Under each of these justifications, would-be guardians of the poor (for example, real or idealized Robin Hoods) are certainly justified in assisting the poor in their aggression against the rich. Are then would-be human guardians of nonhuman living beings (for example, real or idealized Earth Firsters) similarly justified in assisting plants and animals in their aggression against the nonbasic needs of humans in order to meet the basic needs of nonhumans?

There are two reasons why this is unlikely to be the case. First, as the above justifications from human ethics suggest, achieving either libertarian, welfare liberal, or socialist justice for humans requires a considerable redistribution of resources in order to meet the basic needs of humans in both existing and future generations.[28] So if justice is done in this regard, it will significantly constrain the availability of resources for legitimately meeting nonbasic human needs, and thereby limit the possibilities where humans can justifiably defend their nonbasic needs against aggression from nonhumans. Second, the Principle of Disproportionality further constrains those possibilities where humans can justifiably defend their nonbasic needs against aggression from nonhumans. This is because the principle prohibits humans from aggressing against the basic needs of nonhumans in order to meet their own nonbasic needs, and thereby significantly constrains the ways that humans can legitimately acquire resources that are used simply for meeting nonbasic human needs. For these two reasons, therefore, the possibilities for legitimately exercising the Principle of Human Defense for the sake of nonbasic needs are drastically limited, thus providing few occasions where would-be human guardians of the interests of nonhumans can have any role with regard to its exercise. Of course, some nonbasic human needs can still be legitimately met indirectly through meeting basic human needs. But any attempt by would-be human guardians of the interests of nonhumans to help nonhumans aggress against the nonbasic needs of other humans in such contexts would most likely result in aggressing against the basic needs of those humans as well, and thus would not be justified. Of course, in the nonideal societies in which we live, many humans still have access to a surplus for meeting nonbasic needs. But in these circumstances, other humans surely have a claim to a significant part of that surplus, and much of what remains has been illegitimately acquired in violation of the Principle of Disproportionality. In any case, the Principle of Defense will rarely apply because it presupposes for its application that the means for meeting the nonbasic needs of humans have been legitimately acquired.

Lastly, we need one more principle to deal with violations of the above three principles. Accordingly, we have:

A Principle of Rectification. Compensation and reparation are required when the other principles have been violated.

Obviously, this principle is somewhat vague, but for those who are willing to abide by the other three principles, it should be possible to remedy that vagueness in practice. Here too would-be human guardians of the interests of nonhumans could have a useful role figuring out what is appropriate compensation or reparation for violations of the Principle of Disproportionality, and, even more importantly, designing ways to get that compensation or reparation enacted.

Taken altogether, these four principles, I claim, constitute a defensible set of principles for resolving conflicts between human and nonhuman living beings. Of course, some may find it intuitively implausible that we should have to inconvenience ourselves at all for the sake of nonsentient living things. That some of us feel this way is certainly understandable given that virtually all of us have been socialized in the dominant anthropocentrism of our culture. But a different reaction is available to us if we begin to reflect on what we should do from a non-question-begging standpoint, as I attempted to do in this chapter. By such reflection, we can come to recognize that our dominating attitudes toward nonhuman nature cannot be given a non-question-begging justification, and we then should seek to adjust our conduct accordingly.

INDIVIDUALISM AND HOLISM

It might be objected, however, that I have not yet taken into account the conflict between holists and individualists. According to holists, the good of a species, or the good of an ecosystem, or the good of the whole biotic community can trump the good of individual living things.[29] According to individualists, the good of each individual living thing must be respected.[30]

Now one might think that holists would require us to abandon my Principle of Human Preservation. Yet consider: Assuming that people's basic needs are at stake, how can it be morally objectionable for them to try to meet these needs, even if this were to harm nonhuman individuals, or species, or whole ecosystems, or even, to some degree, the whole biotic community? Of course, we can *ask* people in such conflict cases not to meet their basic needs in order to prevent harm to nonhuman individuals or species, ecosystems, or the whole biotic community. But if people's basic needs are at stake, it will be a very unusual case where we can reasonably demand that they make such a sacrifice.

We can demand, of course, that people do all that they reasonably can to keep such conflicts from arising in the first place, for, just as in human ethics, many severe conflicts of interest can be avoided simply by doing what is morally required early on. Nevertheless, when lives or basic needs are at stake, the individualist perspective seems generally incontrovertible. We cannot normally require people to be saints.

At the same time, when people's basic needs are not at stake, we are justified in acting on holistic grounds to prevent serious harm to nonhuman individuals, or species, or ecosystems, or the whole biotic community. Obviously, it is difficult to know when our interventions will have this effect, but when we are reasonably sure that they will, such interventions (for example, culling elk herds in wolf-free ranges or preserving the habitat of endangered species) are morally permissible, and even morally required when the Principle of Rectification applies. This shows that it is possible to agree with individualists when the basic needs of human beings are at stake, and to agree with holists when they are not.[31]

Yet this combination of individualism and holism appears to conflict with recognizing that all species count morally by imposing greater sacrifices on the members of nonhuman species than it imposes on the members of the human species. Fortunately, appearances are deceiving here. Although the proposed resolution only justifies imposing holism when people's basic needs are not at stake, it does not justify imposing individualism at all. Rather, it simply permits individualism when people's basic needs *are* at stake. Of course, we could impose holism under all conditions. But given that this would, in effect, involve going to war against people who are simply striving to meet their own basic needs in the only way they can, as permitted by the Principle of Human Preservation, intervention in such cases is generally not justified.[32] It would involve taking away the means of survival from people, even when these means are not required for one's own survival.

Nevertheless, this combination of individualism and holism may leave animal liberationists wondering about the further implications of this resolution for the treatment of animals. Obviously, a good deal of work has already been done on this topic. Initially, philosophers thought that humanism could be extended to include animal liberation and eventually environmental concern.[33] Then Baird Callicott argued that animal liberation and environmental concern were as opposed to each other as they were to humanism.[34] The resulting conflict Callicott called "a triangular affair." Agreeing with Callicott, Mark Sagoff contended that any attempt to link together animal liberation and environmental concern would lead to "a bad marriage and a quick divorce."[35] Yet more recently, other philosophers, such as Mary Ann Warren, have tended to play down the opposition between animal liberation and environmental concern, and even Callicott now thinks he can bring the two back together again.[36] There are good reasons for thinking that such reconciliation is possible.

Right off, it would be good for the environment if people generally, especially people in the developed world, adopted a more vegetarian diet of the sort that animal liberationists recommend. This is because a good portion of livestock production today consumes grains that could be more effectively used for direct human consumption. For example, 90 percent of the protein, 99 percent of the carbohydrate, and 100 percent of the fiber value of grain is wasted by cycling it through livestock, and currently 64 percent of the U.S. grain crop is fed to livestock.[37] So by adopting a more vegetarian diet, people generally, and especially people in the developed world, could significantly reduce the amount of farmland that has to be kept in production to feed the human population. This, in turn, could have beneficial effects on the whole biotic community by eliminating the amount of soil erosion and environmental pollutants that result from raising livestock. For example, it has been estimated that 85 percent of U.S. topsoil lost from cropland, pasture, range land, and forest land is directly associated with raising livestock.[38] So, in addition to preventing animal suffering, there are these additional reasons to favor a more vegetarian diet.

But even though a more vegetarian diet seems in order, it is not clear that the interests of farm animals would be well served if all of us became complete vegetarians. Sagoff assumes that in a completely vegetarian human world people will continue to feed farm animals as before.[39] But it is not clear that we would have any obligation to do so. Moreover, in a completely vegetarian human world, we would probably need about half of the grain we now feed livestock to meet people's nutritional needs, particularly in underdeveloped countries. There simply would not be enough grain to go around. And then there would be the need to conserve cropland for future generations. So in a completely vegetarian human world, it seems likely that the population of farm animals would be decimated, relegating many of the farm animals that remain to zoos. But raising farm animals can be seen as mutually beneficial for humans and the farm animals involved. Surely, it would benefit farm animals to be brought into existence, maintained under healthy conditions, and hence not in the numbers sustainable only with factory farms, but then killed relatively painlessly and eaten, rather than that they not be brought into existence or maintained at all.[40] So a completely vegetarian human world would not be in the interest of farm animals.[41] Of course, no one would be morally required to bring farm animals into existence and maintain them in this manner. Morally, it would suffice just to maintain representative members of the various subspecies in zoos. Nevertheless, many will find it difficult to pass up an arrangement that is morally permissible and mutually beneficial for both humans and farm animals.

It also seems in the interest of wild species that no longer have their natural predators to be at least therapeutically hunted by humans.[42] Of course, where possible, it may be preferable to reintroduce natural predators. But this may not always be possible because of the unavoidable proximity of farm animals and human populations, and then if action is not taken to control the populations of wild species, disaster could result for the species and their environments. For example, in the absence of predators ungulates (hooved mammals such as white-tailed and mule deer, elk, and bison) as well as elephants regularly tend to exceed the carrying capacity of their environments.[43] So it may be in the interest of these wild species and their environments that humans intervene periodically to maintain a balance. Of course, there are many natural environments where it is in the interest of the environment and the wild animals that inhabit it to be left alone. But here too animal liberation and environmental concern are not in conflict. For these reasons, animal liberationists might seem to have little reason to object in this regard to the proposed combination of individualism and holism that is captured by these conflict resolution principles.

OTHER OBJECTIONS FROM ANIMAL LIBERATIONISTS

Nevertheless, animal liberationists do claim to have other reasons to object to the inclusive form of nonanthropocentrism captured by these conflict resolution principles. As we have noted, Peter Singer limits moral status to sentient beings, and Tom Regan only endorses the moral status of experiencing subjects of life. Regan differs from Singer in that he does not argue either way with respect to whether a broader class of living beings has moral status. He simply leaves the question open.[44] By contrast, Singer explicitly argues against broadening the class of beings with moral status beyond sentient beings.[45] In this respect, Singer's view is more responsible than Regan's because this is too important an issue on which to be silent.

But what are Singer's arguments against broadening the class of beings with moral status beyond sentient beings? Singer begins with a definition of intrinsic value in order to distinguish the class of living beings that have moral status.[46] According to Singer, an X is of intrinsic value if it is good or desirable *in itself;* the contrast is with being of instrumental value, where X is good as a means. Our own happiness, Singer claims, is of intrinsic value in this sense, at least to most of us, in that we desire it for its own sake.

But, as Singer's own example shows, intrinsic value in this sense is relativized to some agent or other. Thus, my happiness is typically intrinsically valuable to me, not to people generally; people generally do not regard my happiness as desirable in itself. In fact, people generally aren't concerned about my happiness at all. Rather, they are primarily concerned about their own happiness or the happiness of their family and friends. So it doesn't follow that anything that is intrinsically valuable in the sense specified by Singer is intrinsically valuable for all moral agents.[47] But we need just that kind of connection if having intrinsic value is supposed to relate to having moral status. This is because having moral status means not just having it with respect to someone or other, but having it with respect to all moral agents. All moral agents are to respect all of those who have moral status.

Fortunately, there is another sense of intrinsic value that does have the required connection to moral status. To say that X is of intrinsic value in this other sense is to say that the good of X ought to constrain the way that others use X in pursuing their own interests.[48] Thus, anything that is of intrinsic value in this second sense has it with respect to all moral agents, and so has the necessary connection to moral status. Accordingly, all moral agents are to constrain the way they use those with intrinsic value in this sense when they pursue their own interests.

Yet while this second sense of intrinsic value does exhibit the appropriate connection with moral status, Singer thinks it is too broad.[49] He wants to restrict the bearers of intrinsic value to those with interests, and to have interests, for Singer, one must be capable of suffering or experiencing pleasure.[50] Thus, for Singer, it is not enough that the good of X ought to constrain the way that others use X in pursuing their own interests in order for X to have intrinsic value. X also must be capable of suffering or experiencing pleasure.

However, this would impose an as yet unjustified requirement on what can have intrinsic value.[51] For Singer to impose this requirement, without further argument, begs the question as to whether nonsentient living beings have intrinsic value.

Singer is not, however, without further argument. In fact, he has at least two arguments against biocentrists, like Paul Taylor and myself, who would extend the class of those with intrinsic value or moral status beyond sentient beings.[52]

First, Singer argues that without sentient interests to guide them, biocentrists have no way of assessing the relative weight to be given to, say, preserving a two-thousand-year-old Huon pine compared to a tussock of grass.[53] But if this is a problem for biocentrists aren't there comparable assessment problems when we are considering just sentient living beings? For example, what is the relative weight to be given to the American bald eagle compared to an ordinary clam?[54] In both comparisons, we have aesthetic preferences that tend to distract us from the central question of why we should destroy the lives of any of these living beings. So let us focus on that question.

Surely, it is unlikely that any of these living things, a two-thousand-year-old Huon pine, a tussock of grass, an American bald eagle, or an ordinary clam will be aggressing against us, so the Principle of Human Defense does not justify our harming them. Nevertheless, their lives could conceivably be taken through the exercise of the Principle of Human Preservation. There is a presupposition here, however, that the Principle of Human Preservation should be exercised in such a way as to cause the least harm, which means that, other things being equal, we should avoid the destruction of endangered or threatened species when there are viable alternatives. The destruction of whole species causes more harm than simply killing some individual members of some species.[55] Accordingly, this would favor the preservation of the two-thousand-year-old Huon pine and the American bald eagle, other things being equal, and, of course, there are human aesthetic preferences that also favor their preservation that need to be taken into account. So it might turn out that the tussock of grass and the clam have to be sacrificed to meet basic human needs, and then again, it may turn out that there is no need to sacrifice them at all. Of course, other things being equal, it is preferable to sacrifice nonsentient than sentient beings to meet our basic needs because that avoids the suffering that sentient beings would otherwise experience. Nevertheless, if the only way that human basic needs can be met is by killing sentient beings, as is true of the Inuit in the Arctic North, then surely such killing is morally justified.[56] Hence, Singer is wrong when he claims that there is some special comparative problem if we try to take nonsentient living beings into account that we don't already have when we try to take sentient living beings into account.

However, Singer has a second argument against extending the class of those with intrinsic value or moral status beyond sentient beings. He questions how biocentrists, like Taylor and myself, can reasonably distinguish the life we claim has intrinsic value from the animate and inanimate things we claim lack intrinsic value.[57] In particular, Singer and other critics want to know how biocentrists, like Taylor and myself, can reasonably distinguish the living things we claim have intrinsic value from machines and from various other kinds of living things, like hearts and kidneys, which we claim lack intrinsic value.[58] Critics point out that machines, hearts and kidneys, can all be benefited and harmed, so why should they not also have intrinsic value? Of course, if biocentrists, like Taylor and myself, were to allow that all these things have intrinsic value that would be a reductio ad absurdum of our view. Accordingly, biocentrists need to provide some way of reasonably distinguishing what we claim has intrinsic value from what we claim lacks intrinsic value.

Nor will it do simply to point to some factual difference between what we claim has intrinsic value, and hence moral value, and what we claim lacks such value. Surely, biologists can provide a workable definition that separates living from nonliving beings.[59] And presumably we can also provide a workable definition of what life forms have "a good of their own" making them capable to an important degree of surviving on their own without human assistance. The problem that emerges here is twofold: first, how can we move from some such factual premise to the normative conclusion concerning who are bearers of intrinsic value and moral status, that is, how can we move from an "is" to an "ought"; and, second, how can we tell which factual premise (which "is") permits that inference?

The problem is not one for biocentrists alone. Animal liberationists, like Singer and Regan, who hold that only sentient beings or experiencing subjects of life have moral status, and most people, who appear to be anthropocentrists and hold that only humans or, more generally, rational beings have moral status, face the same problem. In all of these views, it looks like there is an attempt to derive an "ought" from an "is," something David Hume famously argued could not be done.[60]

So this is the problem. The question is how can the form of nonanthropocentrism I defend respond to this problem. According to the form of nonanthropocentrism I defend, our basic ethical concern is to determine what prerogatives and constraints hold for our relationship with other living beings. The prerogatives specify the ways that we can justifiably harm nonhuman living beings (the Principles of Human Defense and Human Preservation), while the constraints specify the ways that we cannot justifiably harm them (the Principle of Disproportionality). It is important to notice here that the constraints specifying ways that we should not harm other living beings are simply requirements that, under certain conditions, we should leave other living beings alone, that is, not interfere with them. They are not requirements that we do anything for them. To generally require that we do something beneficial for nonhuman living beings (except when restitution is required) would require much more of us. It would entail positive obligations to benefit nonhuman living beings, not just negative obligations not to harm them by interfering with them. In general, this demands too much from us, in effect, requiring us to be saints, and, as we have noted before, morality is usually not in the business of requiring us to be saints. Accordingly, the general obligation of noninterference that we have with respect to nonhuman living beings is fixed not so much by the nature of those other living beings as by what constraints or requirements can be reasonably imposed on us. Nevertheless, this much must be the case about the nature of the living beings who benefit from the obligations that can be reasonably imposed on us—they must have a certain independence to their lives; they must be able to get along on their own without human assistance. In other words, they must have a good of their own.[61]

Now some living things, like hearts and kidneys, don't have a good of their own in the required sense, and, therefore, they won't benefit from simply being left alone. For example, hearts and kidneys require a certain kind of sustaining environment, and to demand that moral agents provide that kind of environment, when it is contrary to their interest to do so, is to impose a significantly demanding requirement on them. Of course, there is no problem when the heart or kidney is one's own and healthy, because in this case, one almost surely wants to preserve one's own heart or kidney. But when a heart or kidney is diseased, or not one's own, one is under no positive moral obligation to preserve it as such.[62] That would be to ask too much of moral agents. As a moral agent, one's only general obligation to all living beings is simply not to interfere with them as required by the Principle of Disproportionality. But it is also assumed here that the living beings who are standardly covered by this principle would significantly benefit from such noninterference, and, hence, that they do not additionally require for their survival positive support from moral agents who have no obligation to provide it.[63] Such living beings have intrinsic value and so their good ought to constrain the way that moral agents pursue their own interests.[64]

The same holds for machines as for hearts and kidneys. It is not good for them to be left alone. They too need a sustaining environment. Yet moral agents are not under any positive obligation to provide such an environment. The only obligation moral agents have in this regard is an obligation, under certain conditions, not to interfere with beings who would benefit from such noninterference. To require that moral agents do more would be to require that moral agents do too much, and morality does not require that moral agents do more than can be reasonably expected of them.

Nevertheless, there is a further feature of machines, beyond their need for positive support, that undercuts the very possibility of moral agents having any obligations toward them. It is that, unlike living things, including hearts and kidneys, machines cannot be benefited and harmed except derivatively through their ability to serve the (instrumental) purposes of their creators or owners. Of course, we do say that a car needs an oil change or a tune-up. Yet meeting such needs doesn't really benefit the car. Rather, it usually benefits the owner of the car who is thereby provided with a more reliable means of transportation. Thus, suppose the owner of the car wants to turn it into a work of modern art by judiciously applying a sledgehammer to it. Would the car thereby be harmed? It is not clear that it would. Rather, the car would now seem to be serving the artistic needs of its owner and possibly others, and thereby benefiting them in this new way more or less. Moreover, in this new role, the car would presumably no longer need oil changes and tune-ups.[65]

Nevertheless, there are other contexts where we do speak of artifacts, if not machines, as being harmed, for example, I might say I harmed the surface of a cabinet by placing a hot cup of coffee on it. Yet here too the harm seems to be specified relative to some particular human purpose. Moreover, the artifact or machine does not have a good of its own; it cannot thrive if we just stop interfering with it and leave it alone.

Of course, it is possible machines will be constructed that are so self-sufficient and independent it makes sense to talk about them as being benefited and harmed in their own right and as having a good of their own. We clearly have already been exposed to such machines in science fiction; the creation of them in real life seems only a matter of time. At the moment, however, the machines that we actually deal with cannot be benefited or harmed except derivatively through their ability to serve the purposes of their creators or owners. As a consequence, the moral constraints of the Principle of Disproportionality does not apply to them.

Accordingly, I have specified the class of those who have intrinsic value not primarily in terms of their factual characteristics (although they must be capable of benefit and harm in a nonderivative sense and have a certain independence to their lives), but rather in terms of what constraints or requirements can reasonably be imposed on moral agents in this regard. This is not a derivation of "values" from "facts" or of "ought" from "is" where we can always ask why these facts and not some others support the derivation. But rather it is a derivation of "values" from "values" or of "ought" from "ought" where the necessity of the derivation can be displayed.

We can more clearly display this derivation by the following argument:

1. The requirements of morality are reasonable to impose on moral agents.[66]
2. The Principles of Human Preservation, Disproportionality, Human Defense, and Rectification, in contrast with the alternatives, are reasonable to impose on all moral agents.
3. The Principles of Human Preservation, Disproportionality, Human Defense, and Rectification are requirements of morality.[67]

Since the basic premise of the argument (1) is widely accepted as a fundamental characterization of morality, I think that the conclusion (3) can be seen to follow.

Singer, however, could accept this derivation of these conflict resolution principles if the Principle of Disproportionality were restricted to protecting only sentient living beings, and thus similarly avoid the Humean challenge. So my disagreement with Singer is best put in this way. We both hold:

a. Only beings that can be harmed or benefited have moral status, that is, ought to be treated by us in a certain deferential way.

b. Sentient beings can be benefited or harmed.

I also hold:

c. Nonsentient living beings can be benefited or harmed.

Singer, however, rejects (c) in favor of:

c'. Beings that are not and never will be conscious or aware of anything (nonsentient beings) cannot be benefited or harmed.

But Singer gives no reason for endorsing (c') other than the difficulties he sees arising from a biocentric view (which includes a, b, and c), all of which I think I have adequately responded to here. Singer realizes that he is going against both ordinary and scientific opinion—which endorses (b and c) without endorsing (a). Singer just thinks that he has reached a point of fundamental difference where no convincing argument is available.[68] In fact, it appears that he has adopted a fairly controversial position—a sort of ratcheted down Cartesianism—without adequate justification.

Yet what if Singer's view never departs from any of the practical recommendations that biocentrists favor? Would that render it unobjectionable? Surely, taking the interests of all sentient beings into account will promote the interests of many nonsentient living beings as well. But it is hard to believe that there will never be any conflict of interest between sentient and nonsentient living beings, and that there never will be times when biocentrists favor nonsentient living beings over sentient living beings. For example, biocentrists might surely favor the members of an endangered native nonsentient species over the members of some prolific sentient invader species when there is a conflict. Moreover, even if there are no conflicts of interest between sentient and nonsentient living beings—unlikely as that may be—Singer's indirect way of taking the interests of nonsentient living beings into account is still objectionable.

Consider an analogy. Surely, we would not be satisfied with just an economic argument against slavery—an argument that slavery didn't pay or was inefficient. Surely, we would want a human rights argument against slavery as well. So why should we be satisfied with just a practical argument against the destruction of nonsentient life? Do we not want an argument that takes harm to nonsentient living beings directly into account? However, only the biocentric view provides this sort of argument.

It is obvious that the argument for my conflict resolution principles has a distinctively Kantian favor to it. It draws upon the key ideas of Paul Taylor's Kantian biocentrism, modified in ways that Taylor now endorses.[69] But there is every reason to think that these principles are also compatible with a morally defensible utilitarian perspective as well. The rejection of Peter Singer's arguments for limiting intrinsic value and moral status to sentient beings alone is really not a rejection of utilitarianism but rather an endorsement of a broader, more defensible, utilitarianism that takes the good of all living beings, sentient and nonsentient, into account. So there is good reason to think that the most morally defensible Kantian ethics and the most morally defensible utilitarian ethics would both endorse the form of nonanthropocentrism I have defended in this chapter. While Aristotelian environmental ethics is still in its infancy, I have argued elsewhere that even here there is good reason to think that a reconciliation is both possible and desirable.[70]

AN OBJECTION FROM A SOMEWHAT ALIEN PERSPECTIVE

There remains, however, at least one serious objection to the nonanthropocentrism that I have been defending. It might be argued that from a somewhat alien perspective my view is not nonanthropocentric enough. Consider the following.

Suppose our planet were invaded by an intelligent and very powerful species of aliens who can easily impose their will upon us. Suppose these aliens have studied the life history of our planet and they have come to understand how we have wrecked havoc on our planet, driving many species into extinction, and how we still threaten many other species with extinction. In short, suppose these aliens discover that we are like a cancer on our biosphere.

Suppose further that these aliens are fully aware of the differences between us and the other species on the planet. Suppose they clearly recognize that we more closely resemble them in power and intelligence than any other species on the planet. Even so, suppose the aliens still choose to protect the very species we threaten. They begin by forcing us to use no more resources than we need for a decent life, and this significantly reduces the threat we pose to many endangered species. However, the aliens want to do more. In order to save more endangered species, they decide to exterminate a certain portion of our human population, reducing our numbers to those we had when we were more in balance with the rest of the biosphere.

Now if this were to happen, would we have moral grounds to object to these actions taken by the aliens? Of course, we could argue that it would be unreasonable for us to do more than restrict ourselves to the resources we need for a decent life, and so we are not morally required to do more. But these aliens need not deny this. They may recognize that the extermination of a certain portion of the human population is not something that humans could reasonably require of each other. What they are claiming, as champions of endangered species, is just the right to impose a still greater restriction on humans, recognizing, at the same time, a comparable right of humans to resist that imposition as best they can. Of course, in the imagined case, any resistance by humans is futile; the aliens are just too powerful.

In so acting, the aliens place themselves outside the morality captured by my conflict resolution principles. The moral permissibility to meet one's basic needs and to defend oneself guaranteed by the Principles of Human Preservation and Human Defense respectively was that of strong permissibility. It implies that any would-be guardians of the interests of nonhuman earthly species are morally prohibited from interfering with humans who are taking the necessary actions to preserve and defend themselves, even when this requires that the humans aggress against the basic needs of nonhumans. In our imaginary tale, however, the aliens have rejected this moral prohibition, claiming instead that it is morally permissible for them to ally themselves with the interests of some of the endangered species on our planet. They claim that we cannot morally blame them, or morally object to what they are doing. They say that they have a right to try to impose greater restrictions on our own species and that we have a right to resist. And they are right. How can we object to the actions of these nonhuman-species-loving aliens?

Likewise, we can not object if similar actions are undertaken by radical Earth Firsters, who, so to speak, choose to "go native" and renounce, to some extent, their membership in the human community so as to be able to take stronger steps to protect endangered species. Of course, we might argue that there are other more effective ways for these Earth Firsters to protect endangered species, but if their actions prove to be the most effective at protecting endangered species, what can our objection be? Of course, we can oppose them if they go beyond what is morally required, as we can oppose the aliens on these same grounds, but, as in the case of the aliens, we don't seem to have any moral objection against what they are doing. What this shows is that while morality cannot impose requirements that are unreasonable to accept (that is, requirements that violate the "ought" implies "can" principle), it can permit (as in this case) actions that it cannot impose, as in lifeboat cases.[71]

Even so, before these radical Earth Firsters can sacrifice the basic needs of fellow humans for the sake of endangered species, they are first required to use whatever surplus is available to them and to other humans to meet the basic needs of the humans they propose to restrict. Yet clearly it would be very difficult to have first used up all the surplus available to the whole human population for meeting basic human needs.[72] Under present conditions, this requirement has certainly not been met. So unlike our imaginary aliens who we assumed were first able to force us to use no more resources than we needed for a decent life, before they started killing us to further reduce the threat we pose to endangered species, the efforts of radical Earth Firsters will probably never get beyond that first step. All of their efforts would focus on trying to benefit endangered species by forcing humans to use no more resources than they need for a decent life. Unlike our imaginary aliens, real-life radical Earth Firsters will probably never be able to justifiably get to the second step of taking the lives of fellow humans for the benefit of endangered species.

Accordingly, even though we can envision the perspective of hypothetical aliens and radical Earth Firsters and recognize that it is a morally permissible stance to take, this still doesn't undercut the moral defensibility of the Principles of Human Preservation, Disproportionality, Human Defense, and Rectification. These principles still capture the moral requirements we can reasonably require all human beings to accept.[73] In fact, the first step of this somewhat alien perspective requires the enforcement of just these principles. It is only at the second step, simply hypothetically justified in the case of the aliens, and virtually never justifiably realized in the case of real-life radical Earth Firsters, that we depart from the principles. Hence, the mere possibility of this somewhat alien moral perspective does not undercut the real-life moral defensibility, on both Kantian and utilitarian grounds, of these conflict resolution principles.

Let me conclude by indicating the relationship between the environmental view that I have defended in this chapter with the political philosophy that I have defended in the previous chapter. In the last chapter, I argued on libertarian, welfare liberal and utilitarian grounds (all human-centered perspectives) that we are only entitled to the resources we need for a decent life—but no more. Otherwise, we would be violating the rights of distant peoples and future generations. Somewhat surprisingly, that is almost the *same conclusion* I arrived at in this chapter after also taking nonhuman living beings into account. Specifically, the Principle of Human Preservation only permits aggression against nonhuman nature for the sake of what we need for a decent life and the Principle of Disproportionality prohibits aggression against nonhuman nature for the sake of nonbasic or luxury needs.

Still, there are some ways that the more inclusive biocentrism I have defended in this chapter imposes additional obligations. First, in order to avoid unnecessary harm to nonhuman living beings, we will be required to meet our basic needs necessary for a decent life in some ways rather than others. For example, if there were no negative effects on our fellow human beings, it would be permissible for us to meet our basic needs through the consumption of meat and diary products provided by factory farming, but we can't do this once the interests of particularly farm animals are appropriately taken into account. Second, we will have additional obligations to help nonhuman living beings based on restitution. For example, where we humans have endangered nonhuman species by aggressing against them for the sake of our luxury needs, we would have an obligation to try to restore those species to a flourishing condition. Third, we have an obligation to control our population to a greater extent under a more inclusive biocentrism than we would under the human-centered political philosophy that I defended in the previous chapter. Of course, even in a human-centered political philosophy, we would need restrictions on population growth. While existing people are not required to sacrifice their basic needs for the sake of future generations, they are required to do what they can to restrict the membership of future generations so that those generations will be able to meet their basic needs.

But what does this entail? We could limit human reproduction to the legitimate exercise of the basic human need to procreate, which I think would be roughly one child per family. While it is unclear whether such a restrictive population policy would be necessary for respecting the rights of future generations of humans. Suppose it was. At some point, it would be possible to abandon such a policy because the welfare rights of future generations of humans was no longer threatened. Even at that point, however, nonhuman species could still be threatened by the size of the human population. So a more inclusive biocentrism that took all living beings into account would still want to continue this restrictive population policy. Nevertheless, at some point even a more inclusive biocentrism that took all living beings into account would favor relaxing such a population policy in favor of one that served basic human needs and the long-term survivability of the human species, consistent with maintaining humans within their environmental niche, where, unlike today, we would be in balance with the rest of the biotic community. Thus, if there were two or more ways that served basic human needs and the long-term survivability of the human species, a more inclusive biocentrism that took all living beings into account would favor the alternative that was most consistent with maintaining humans within their environmental niche, where we would be in balance with the rest of the biotic community. Of course, more would have to be said to specify more precisely this requirement of a more inclusive biocentrism.

EPILOGUE

Different versions of this chapter have been presented to a variety of audiences. Invariably, at some point in the question period, someone asks how do I distinguish basic from nonbasic needs. Usually, the questioner does not realize how widespread the use of this distinction is. While the distinction is surely important for environmental ethics, as its use in this chapter attests, it is also used widely in moral and political philosophy generally. For example, the defense of a right to welfare in chapter 3 depends on the distinction, and the distinction parallels the one between high-ranking and low-ranking interests used in the justification of morality found in chapter 2. So it would really be impossible to do much moral, political, or environmental philosophy without a distinction between basic and nonbasic needs.

Typically, I respond to the question, as I do in the text, by pointing out that the fact that not every need can be clearly classified as either basic or nonbasic, as similarly holds for a whole range of dichotomous concepts like moral/immoral, legal/illegal, living/nonliving, human/nonhuman, should not immobilize us from acting at least with respect to clear cases. This puts our use of the distinction in a still broader context suggesting that if we cannot use the basic/nonbasic distinction in moral, political, and environmental philosophy, the widespread use of other dichotomous concepts is likewise threatened. It also suggests how our inability to clearly classify every conceivable need as basic or nonbasic should not keep us from using such a distinction at least with respect to clear cases.

There is also a further point to be made here. If we begin to respond to clear cases, for example, stop aggressing against the clear basic needs of nonhuman nature for the sake of clear luxury needs of humans, we will be in an even better position to know what to do in the less clear cases. This is because sincerely attempting to live out one's practical moral commitments helps one to interpret them better, just as failing to live them out makes interpreting them all the more difficult. Consequently, we have every reason to act on the conflict resolution principles that I have defended in this chapter, at least with respect to clear cases.

Philosophical Interlude

The common ground that we have discovered among the most morally defensible interpretations of Kantian, utilitarian, and Aristotelian ethics in the preceding three chapters can be quite useful for dealing with particular moral problems. For example, the "ought" implies "can" principle can be seen as implicitly embedded in the definition of sexual harassment given in chapter 5 and the nonabsoluteness of moral constraints can be seen as relevant to terrorism and to the application of just-war theory in chapter 7.

Sometimes, however, this common ground only provides a moral framework within which a more particular discussion takes place. For example, in chapter 6, the key issue in the discussion of affirmative action is how racial or sexual preferences are compatible with or not compatible with the equality of citizens. Other times a discussion of a particular moral problem will tend to focus on the strengths and weaknesses of the legal framework within which that problem is usually discussed, as is true with respect to the discussion of sexual harassment in chapter 5 and affirmative action in chapter 6. There are also times when particular facts or the history of the problem is particularly relevant. For example, the current data about existing patterns of racial and sexual discrimination are particularly relevant to affirmative action, as is the history of the Palestinian/Israeli conflict to terrorism and the history of our past involvement in the affairs of Iraq to Iraqi War II.

There are also ways in which the solutions to particular moral problems are interconnected. For example, as the argument of chapter 3 shows, we cannot specify what would be the correct distribution of income and wealth in a given society without determining our obligations to distant peoples and future generations. In chapter 4, I argued that our obligations to nonhuman nature are also relevant. Similarly, the legitimate costs of legal enforcement must ultimately enter into any calculation of the correct distribution of income and wealth in a given society. This will require a solution to the moral problem of punishment and responsibility (who is responsible for what crimes and what should their punishment be?).

This moral problem, in turn, presupposes solutions to other moral problems as well. Thus, suppose that in a society with a just distribution of income and wealth, persons who put forth their best efforts receive a yearly income of a least $25,000. (If you think a just distribution of income would provide some other amount, plug that amount in and make the corresponding adjustments in subsequent figures.) Further suppose that the society in which you and I live has an unjust distribution of income and wealth because, although there are enough resources for a just distribution, many persons who put forth their best efforts receive no more than $10,000 a year, whereas others receive $500,000 or more. Let's say that your income is $500,000 and mine is only $10,000, even though I have tried every legal way to increase my income. Assume also that any resort to civil disobedience or armed revolution would be ineffectual and too costly for me personally. If I then rob you of $15,000, thus bringing my yearly income up to the just allotment of $25,000, what would a morally defensible system of punishment and responsibility do to me if I were caught? To require a punishment equal in severity to the $15,000 I took, simply reinforces an unjust distribution of income and wealth. So it seems that only a fairly light punishment or no punishment at all should be required.[1] This example shows that the application of a morally defensible solution to the problem of punishment and responsibility depends on a solution to the problem of the distribution of income and wealth in a society. To know, therefore, how to apply a morally defensible system of punishment and responsibility in a particular society, you must know to what degree that society incorporates a morally defensible distribution of income and wealth.

In addition, as we in the United States are painfully aware at the present time, proposed allocations for distributing income and wealth through social welfare programs can come into conflict with proposed allocations for general defense, and now a war against terrorism. Many people have argued that when this happens we must sacrifice social welfare programs to meet these military requirements, but other people have disagreed. Obviously, then, we need to know exactly how to resolve conflicts between the solutions to these interconnected problems. In sum, what is required (or permitted) by a morally defensible solution to the problem of the distribution of income and wealth within a society will depend on what is required (or permitted) by morally defensible solutions to the problems of distant peoples and future generations, the moral status of nonhuman nature, punishment and responsibility, among others. This means that any solution you might devise to one of these problems is only provisional until you can determine solutions to other problems as well. And even if you are unable at the moment to devise solutions to all these problems, you must still acknowledge that in the final analysis your solutions to them will have to be interconnected. Note, too, that acknowledging the interconnectedness of the solutions to these practical problems does not presuppose a commitment to any particular political or moral ideal. Nevertheless, for those who endorse the common ground among the most morally defensible interpretations of Kantian, utilitarian, and Aristotelian ethics defended in the previous three chapters, certain solutions to these particular moral problems are clearly favored over others.

The three moral problems to be discussed in the following chapters were chosen because of their contemporary currency and their scope and because of the way they directly draw upon, or don't directly draw upon, the common ground among the most morally defensible interpretations of Kantian, utilitarian, and Aristotelian ethics. In these respects, they serve to further illustrate the steps that we need to take in fashioning an adequate ethics for our times.

CHAPTER FIVE

～

Understanding, Explaining, and Eliminating Sexual Harassment

In 1998, the U.S. Supreme Court made four attempts to clarify sexual harassment law (*Oncale v. Sundowner Offshore Services, Inc., Burlington Industries, Inc. v. Ellerth, Faragher v. City of Boca Raton,* and *Gebser et al. v. Lago Vista Independent School District*). In 1998, as well, Judge Susan Webber Wright of the U.S. Court of Appeals for the Eighth Circuit dismissed the sexual harassment case of Paula Corbin Jones against then president Clinton on the somewhat controversial grounds that even if Clinton as governor of Arkansas had done all Jones claimed he had done (that is, summoned Jones from her convention post to his hotel suite, dropped his pants in front of her, asked her to "kiss it," touched her thigh and tried to kiss her on the neck, and despite apparently accepting her "no" for an answer, partially and momentarily blocked her exit for enough time to tell her he knew her boss and it would be best if the incident were kept between the two of them), Clinton would not have sexually harassed her because she could not demonstrate any tangible job detriment or adverse employment action for her refusal to submit to his alleged advances. Although the flurry of judicial activity in 1998 did increase the scope of sexual harassment law—sitting U.S. presidents are now liable for sexual harassment suits, as are grade school and high school teachers—unfortunately our understanding of the nature of sexual harassment has yet to achieve a comparable advance. Nor as yet do we have a very good explanation of why sexual harassment occurs as frequently as it does in our society. Accordingly, in this chapter, I will first review the developments in sexual harassment law, hoping to increase our understanding of what is, or better, what should be considered sexual harassment. My analysis here will draw upon the "ought" implies "can" principle that was defended and utilized in previous chapters of this book. Then, I will offer a partial explanation of why sexual harassment happens in both civilian and military life. Finally, I will determine what positive norms, in addition to the negative one that prohibits sexual harassment, we need to focus on in order to make progress toward reducing its frequency.

UNDERSTANDING SEXUAL HARASSMENT

Sexual harassment was not recognized by U.S. trial courts as an offense until the late 1970s, and it was only affirmed by the U.S. Supreme Court as an offense in the 1980s. The term "sexual harassment" itself was not even coined until the 1970s. So the problem of sexual harassment is one many people have only recently come to recognize. Obviously, the Senate Judiciary Committee hearings in 1991 on Anita Hill's charge that Clarence Thomas had sexually harassed her,[1] the U.S Navy's Tailhook scandal in 1992, the Bob Packwood scandal in 1995, and Paula Jones's amended sexual harassment suit against President Clinton in 1997 have all helped heighten people's awareness of this problem.

In 1976, a Federal District Judge, in the first legal case that used the term "sexual harassment," ruled that Diane Williams, a public information specialist at the U.S. Department of Justice who was dismissed after turning down her supervisor's sexual advances, had been harassed "based on sex" within the meaning of Title VII of the Civil Rights Act of 1964. Four years later, the Equal Employment Opportunity Commission (EEOC) issued guidelines finding harassment on the basis of sex to be a violation of Title VII of the Civil Rights Act of 1964, labeling sexual harassment as "unwelcome sexual advances, requests for sexual favors, and other verbal or physical conduct of a sexual nature" when such behavior occurred in any of three circumstances:

1. where submission to such conduct is made either explicitly or implicitly a term or condition of an individual's employment,
2. where submission to or rejection of such conduct by an individual is used as the basis for employment decisions affecting such individual, or

3. where such conduct has the purpose or effect of unreasonably interfering with an individual's work performance or creating an intimidating, hostile, or offensive working environment.

In 1986, the U.S. Supreme Court in *Meritor Savings Bank v. Vinson* unanimously agreed with the EEOC, ruling that there could be two types of sexual harassment: harassment that conditions concrete employment benefits on granting sexual favors (called the quid pro quo type) and harassment that creates a hostile or offensive work environment without affecting economic benefits (the hostile environment type). Nevertheless, the court made it quite difficult for a plaintiff to establish that either of these types of sexual harassment had occurred. For example, a polite verbal "no" does not suffice to show that sexual advances are unwelcome, and a woman's entire conduct both in and outside the workplace is subject to appraisal determining whether or not she welcomed the advances. For example, in the *Vinson* case, there was "voluminous testimony regarding Vinson's dress and personal fantasies," and in the Senate Judiciary Committee hearings, Anita Hill was not able to prevent intensive examination of her private life, although Clarence Thomas was able to declare key areas of his private life as off-limits, such as his practice of viewing and discussing pornographic films.

The Supreme Court also made it difficult to classify work environments as hostile to women unless the harassment is sufficiently severe or pervasive. Applying the Supreme Court's standard, a lower court, in *Christoforou v. Ryder Truck Rental* (1987), judged a supervisor's actions of fondling a plaintiff's rear end and breasts, propositioning her, and trying to force a kiss at a Christmas party to be "too sporadic and innocuous" to support a finding of a hostile work environment.[2] Similarly, in *Rabidue v. Osceola Refining Co.* (1986), a workplace where pictures of nude and scantily clad women abounded (including one, which hung on a wall for eight years, of a woman with a golf ball on her breasts and a man with his golf club standing over her yelling "Fore!") and where a coworker, never disciplined despite repeated complaints, routinely referred to women as "whores," "cunts," "pussies," and "tits," was judged by a lower court not to be a sufficiently hostile environment to constitute sexual harassment.[3] Notice, by contrast, that the U.S. Senate Arms Services Committee, in its hearings on homosexuals in the military, regarded an environment in which known homosexuals are simply doing their duty in the military to be too hostile an environment in which to ask male heterosexuals to serve.

As the Supreme Court interprets sexual harassment, a person's behavior must be unwelcome in a fairly strong sense before it constitutes sexual harassment. But why should a woman have to prove that the offer "If you don't sleep with me, you will be fired" is unwelcome before it constitutes sexual harassment?[4] Isn't such an offer objectively unwelcome? Isn't it just the kind of offer those in positions of power should not be making to their subordinates, an offer that purports to make their continuing employment conditional upon providing sexual favors? Surely, unless we are dealing with some form of legalized prostitution, and maybe not even then, such offers are objectively unwelcome.[5] And if such offers are objectively unwelcome, why is there any need to show that they are also subjectively unwelcome before regarding them as violations of Title VII of the Civil Rights Act? The requirement of subjective unwelcomeness seems to be simply a gratuitous obstacle that makes the plaintiff's case far more difficult to prove than it should be.[6]

In addition, if the plaintiff is fired after refusing such an offer, the Supreme Court requires her to prove that the firing occurred because the offer was refused, which is very difficult to do unless one is a perfect employee. Wouldn't it be fairer to require the employer to prove that the plaintiff would have been fired even if she had said "yes" to the offer?[7] Of course, employers could avoid this burden of proof simply by not making any such offers in the first place.[8] But when they do make objectively unwelcome offers, why shouldn't the burden of proof be on them to show that any subsequent firing was clearly unrelated to the plaintiff's refusal of the offer? Fairness is particularly relevant in this context because we are committed to equal opportunity in the workplace, which requires employing women and men on equal terms. Accordingly, we must guard against imposing special burdens on women in the workplace, when there are no comparable burdens imposed on men.[9]

The demand for equal opportunity in the workplace also appears to conflict with the Supreme Court's pervasiveness requirement for establishing a hostile environment. Citing a lower court, the Supreme Court contends that, to be actionable, sexual harassment "must be sufficiently severe or pervasive 'to alter the conditions of the [victim's] employment and create an abusive working environment."[10] But as this standard has been interpreted by lower courts, the pervasiveness of certain forms of harassment in the workplace has become grounds for tolerating them. In *Rabidue*, the majority argued:

> [I]t cannot seriously be disputed that in some work environments, humor and language are rough hewn and vulgar. Sexual jokes, sexual conversations and girlie magazines abound. Title VII was not meant to or can change this. Title VII is the federal court mainstay in the struggle for equal employment opportunity for the female workers of America. But it is quite different to claim that Title VII was designed to bring about a magical transformation in the social mores of American workers.[11]

The Supreme Court itself seems to sound a similar theme by emphasizing the application of Title VII to only extreme cases of sexual harassment as found in *Vinson*.

However, as the EEOC interprets Title VII, the law has a broader scope. It affords employees the right to work in an environment free from discriminatory intimidation, ridicule, and insult. According to the EEOC, sexual harassment violates Title VII where conduct creates an intimidating, hostile, or offensive environment or where it unreasonably interferes with work performance.

But how are we to determine what unreasonably interferes with work performance? In *Rabidue*, the majority looked to prevailing standards in the workplace to determine what was reasonable or unreasonable. Yet Justice Keith, in dissent, questioned this endorsement of the status quo, arguing that just as a Jewish employee can rightfully demand a change in her working environment if her employer maintains an anti-Semitic work force and tolerates a workplace in which "kike" jokes, displays of Nazi literature, and anti-Jewish conversation "may abound," surely women can rightfully demand a change in the sexist practices that prevail in their working environments.[12] In *Henson v. Dundee* (1982), the majority also drew an analogy between sexual harassment and racial harassment:

> Sexual harassment which creates a hostile or offensive environment for members of one sex is every bit the arbitrary barrier to sexual equality at the workplace that racial harassment is to racial equality. Surely, a requirement that a man or woman run a gauntlet of sexual

abuse in return for the privilege of being allowed to work and make a living can be as demeaning and disconcerting as the harshest of racial epithets.[13]

And this passage is also quoted approvingly by the Supreme Court in *Vinson*.

Moved by such arguments, the majority in *Ellison v. Brady* (1991) proposed that, rather than looking to prevailing standards to determine what is reasonable, we should look to the standard of a reasonable victim, or given that most victims of sexual harassment are women–the standard of a reasonable woman.[14] They contend that this standard may be different from the standard of a "reasonable man." For example, what male superiors think is "harmless social interaction" may be experienced by female subordinates as offensive and threatening.[15]

Nevertheless, there should be no question about what standard of reasonableness to use here. It is not that of a reasonable woman, nor that of a reasonable man for that matter, but the standard of what is reasonable for everyone affected to accept. For according to the "ought" implies "can" principle, moral requirements are those which are reasonable for everyone affected to accept. This assumes that apparent conflicts over what is reasonable to accept–for example, conflicts between the standard of a reasonable woman and that of a reasonable man–are conflicts that can and should be resolved by showing that one of these perspectives is more reasonable than the other, or that some other perspective is more reasonable still. However, at least in the context of sexual harassment, this standard of what is reasonable for everyone affected to accept will accord closely with the standard of a reasonable woman, given that once women's perspectives are adequately taken into account, the contrasting perspective of a reasonable man will be seen as not so reasonable after all.[16]

In its decision in *Harris v. Forklift Systems Inc.* (1993), the Supreme Court took an important step toward a more reasonable stance on sexual harassment. In this case, Teresa Harris worked as a rental manager at Forklift Systems. Charles Hardy, Forklift's president, said to Harris on several occasions, in the presence of other employees, "You're a woman, what do you know?" and "We need a man as the rental manager." Again in front of others, he suggested that the two of them "go to the Holiday Inn to negotiate [Harris's] raise." Hardy occasionally asked Harris and other female employees to get coins from his front pants pockets. On other occasions, he threw objects on the ground in front of Harris and other women and asked them to pick the objects up. He made sexual innuendoes about Harris's and other women's clothing. On one occasion, while Harris was arranging a deal with one of Forklift's customers, Hardy asked her in front of other employees, "What did you do, promise some [sex] Saturday night?" Soon after, Harris quit her job at Forklift.

In this case, the Supreme Court struck down the district court's requirement that in order for sexual harassment to be established Harris needed to show that Hardy's conduct had "seriously affected her psychological well-being." This was an important decision, but obviously it does not go far enough in specifying a reasonable standard for sexual harassment.

It is also important to recognize here that achieving equal opportunity in the workplace will conflict, to some degree, with freedom of speech. Consider the case of *Robinson v. Jacksonville Shipyards* (1991*)*, in which a U.S. District Court upheld claims of sexual harassment on hostile work environment grounds and issued extensive remedial orders.[17] Plaintiff Lois Robinson was one of a very small number of female skilled craftworkers employed at the Shipyards—one of 6 women of 832 craftworkers. Her allegations of sexual harassment centered around "the presence in the workplace of pictures of women in various stages of undress and in sexually suggestive or submissive poses, as well as remarks by male employees and supervisors which demean women." Although there was some evidence of several incidents in which the sexually suggestive pictures and comments were directed explicitly at Robinson, most were not.

In analyzing this case, Nadine Strossen, past president of the ACLU, argues that even sexually offensive speech should be protected unless it is explicitly directed at a particular individual or group of individuals.[18] Accordingly, Strossen endorses the ACLU's amicus brief in *Robinson v. Jacksonville Shipyards* which considered the court's ban on the public display of sexually suggestive material without regard to whether the expressive activity was explicitly directed toward any employee as too broad. However, in light of the fact that Jacksonville Shipyards had itself banned all public displays of expressive activity except sexual materials, the amicus brief went on to favor the imposition of a workplace rule that would right the balance and permit the posting of other materials as well–materials critical of such sexual expression, as well as other political and religious or social messages that are currently banned. Such a rule would implement a "more speech" approach in an effort to counter offensive speech.

But would such a rule work? Would it succeed in protecting the basic interests of women, especially their right to equal opportunity in the workplace? It is not clear that it would be effective in male-dominated workplaces like Jacksonville Shipyards, where women are a tiny minority of the work force, and likely to have their voices drowned out in the free market of expression that this rule would permit.

Nor does Strossen's distinction between offensive speech explicitly directed at a particular person or group and offensive speech that is not so directed seem all that useful, given that most sexual harassment is directed at women not because they are Jane Doe or Lois Robinson, but because they are women. So why should we distinguish between sexual harassment that is explicitly directed at a particular woman because she is a woman, and sexual harassment that is only directed at a particular woman because it is explicitly directed at all women? Of course, sexually harassing speech can be more or less offensive, and maybe its offensiveness does correlate, to some degree, with the manner in which that harassment is directed at women. Nevertheless, what is crucial here is that the offensiveness of sexually harassing speech becomes unacceptable when it undermines the equal opportunity of women in the workplace–that is, when it imposes special burdens on women in the workplace where there are no comparable burdens on men. It is at this point that justice demands that we impose whatever limitations on sexually harassing speech are needed to secure equal opportunity in the workplace.

In *Oncale v. Sundowner Offshore Services, Inc.* (1998), the Supreme Court expanded the scope of sexual harassment to include same-sex sexual harassment even when the harasser is not homosexual. In this case, Joseph Oncale was working for Sundowner Offshore Services on a Chevron U.S.A. oil platform in the Gulf of Mexico. He was employed as a roustabout on an eight-man crew, which included John Lyons, Danny Pippen, and Brandon Johnson. Lyons, the crane operator, and Pippen, the driller, had supervisory authority. On several occasions, Oncale was forcibly subjected to sex-related, humiliating actions against him by Lyons, Pippen, and Johnson in the presence of the rest of the crew. On one occasion, the men grabbed him in the company shower and forced a bar of soap between his buttocks and threatened to rape him. When he complained to the company's safety compliance clerk, Valent Hohen, about Lyons and Pippen's behavior, Hohen told Oncale that he was also being harassed by the two men himself. So Oncale quit, asking that his pink slip reflect that he "voluntarily left due to sexual harassment and verbal abuse."

The Supreme Court, seeking to end conflicting stances taken by lower courts in same-sex sexual harassment cases (some of which found sexual harassment in cases like Oncale's, while others held that same-sex sexual harassment could not be supported by Title VII of the Civil Rights Act, and still others held that same-sex sexual harassment is only actionable when the harasser is homosexual) held in a unanimous decision that nothing in Title VII necessarily bars a claim of discrimination "because of . . . sex" merely because the plaintiff and the defendant (or the person charged with acting on behalf of the defendant) are of the same sex. In these same-sex cases of sexual harassment, as in the more standard different-sex cases, special burdens are imposed on the victims of sexual harassment where there are no comparable burdens imposed on others similarly situated. In Oncale's case, sexual taunts, threats, and abuse were directed at him because his appearance and behavior was judged not to be "masculine" enough by his harassers.

It is also important to see that while sexual harassers are usually either the same-sex or different-sex harassers, they can also be what has been called "equal opportunity sexual harassers," that is, harassers who target both men and women. Moreover, some lower courts have argued that equal opportunity sexual harassment falls outside of the scope of the protection of Title VII of the Civil Rights Act because such harassers do not limit their harassment to the members of one sex, and so their victims can not claim that they would not have been harassed "but for their sex." Fortunately, in the light of the *Oncale* decision, it should be possible to reinterpret the "because of . . . sex" restriction of Title VII in such a way that all three forms of sexual harassment are prohibited. This is because what is objectionable about all three forms of sexual harassers is that they engage in degrading and abusive sexual conduct that is chosen on the basis of or "because of" the sex of their victims.

Moreover, sexual harassers, whether they be same-sex, different-sex, or equal opportunity sexual harassers typically impose special burdens on some when there are no comparable burdens imposed on others who are similarly situated, and this frequently is part of what is wrong with sexual harassment. Yet sexual harassment, understood as engaging in degrading and abusive sexual conduct that is chosen on the basis of the victim's sex, is still wrong even if it is inflicted on everyone within the harasser's reach. Thus, the comparative harm that frequently results from sexual harassment does not exhaust its offensiveness. All such burdens, however, clearly violate the "ought" implies "can" principle; they are burdens that it would be unreasonable to ask, and/or in cases of severe conflict of interest, unreasonable to require people to abide by.

Accordingly, drawing on the foregoing discussion, I offer the following:

> A DEFINITION OF SEXUAL HARASSMENT. Sexual harassment is objectively unwelcome sexual advances, requests for sexual favors, and other verbal or physical conduct of a sexual nature, which are determined to be both objectionable and actionable by the standard of what is reasonable for everyone affected to accept, and which usually, but not always, impose a special burden on some individuals when there are no comparable burdens imposed on others who are similarly situated.

Sexual harassment so defined can clearly be of the quid pro quo or the hostile environment type, but given that these two types of sexual harassment share this common definition, their features will tend to overlap in particular cases, such as in the *Burlington Industries* (1998).[19] Moreover, assuming that neither Kimberly Ellerth suffered any economic detriment from the vice president of Burlington industries who harassed her nor Paula Jones from then governor Clinton, they still could have suffered from sexual harassment according to my definition. It all depends on whether the sexual behavior to which they were allegedly exposed is both objectionable and actionable as determined by the standard of what is reasonable for everyone affected to accept. Of course, when the burdens imposed by sexual harassment are slight, they will presumably not be reasonably judged as legally actionable by everyone affected, and so will not properly fall within the scope of the law.

SEXUAL HARASSMENT IN CIVILIAN
AND MILITARY LIFE

As is well known, there is a high incidence of sexual harassment in both civilian and military life. In research conducted by psychologists, 50 percent of women questioned in the civilian workplace said they had been sexually harassed. According to the U.S. Merit Systems Protection Board, within the federal government, 56 percent of 8,500 female civilian workers surveyed claimed to have experienced sexual harassment. According to the *National Law Journal*, 64 percent of women in "pink-collar" jobs reported being sexually harassed and 60 percent of 3,000 women lawyers at 250 top law firms said that they had been harassed at some point in their careers. In a survey by *Working Women* magazine, 60 percent of high-ranking corporate women said they have been harassed; 33 percent more knew of others who had been.[20] Similarly, in a survey of 90,000 female soldiers, sailors, and pilots, 60 percent of the women said they had been sexually harassed. Only 47 percent of the army women surveyed said that they believed their leaders were serious about putting a stop to sexual harassment.[21] According to another study, 66 percent of women in the military experienced at least one form of sexual harassment in the past year.[22] Another study found that 50 percent of women at the U.S. Naval Academy, 59 percent of women at the U.S. Air Force Academy, and 76 percent of women at the U.S. Military Academy experienced some form of sexual harassment at least twice a month.[23]

Yet despite the high incidence of sexual harassment in both civilian and military life, at least in the United States, there are some important differences that suggest somewhat different explanations of why sexual harassment is taking place in these contexts. The most important difference of this sort is the still widely expressed belief that women do not belong in the military. For example, 45 percent of first-year midshipmen expressed the view that women did not belong in the military and 38 percent of fourth-year midshipmen felt the same.[24] The same view can be found among the highest commanders in the U.S. military. For example, air force Chief General Merrill McPeak testified before the Senate Arms Services Committee in 1991 that if he had to choose between a qualified woman and a less qualified man to fill a combat role, he would go with the man. "I admit it does not make much sense but that is the way I feel about it," McPeak responded.[25] Surely, it would be difficult to find a male CEO of a Fortune 500 company willing to publicly express the same feelings as General McPeak about the suitability of employing qualified women. There are, of course, some parallels in civilian life to this attitude toward women found in the military. For example, probably a significant number of the 863 craftworkers who worked along with the 6 women craftworkers at Jacksonville Shipyards in the case previously cited thought that the women did not belong there either. But what is distinctive about the U.S. military is the degree to which the belief that women do not belong there is still widely and openly held. As another general put it:

> War is a man's work. Biological convergence on the battlefield (women serving in combat) would not only be dissatisfying in terms of what women could do, but it would be an enormous psychological distraction for the male, who wants to think that he's fighting for that woman somewhere behind, not up there in the same foxhole with him. It tramples the male ego. When you get right down to it, you have to protect the manhood of war.[26]

What I am suggesting is that this widely and openly held belief that women do not belong is distinctive of military life and helps explain the prevalence of sexual harassment there.

But what then explains the prevalence of sexual harassment in civilian life? Since at present there is no comparable widely and openly held belief that women don't belong in civilian life, or even in the civilian workplace, where women now occupy 50 percent of the labor force,[27] there must be another belief supporting the sexual harassment that occurs there. I suggest it is the belief that, while women do belong in civilian life, it is still appropriate to treat them as sexual objects in ways that men are not to be treated, with the consequence that they are sexually subordinate to men. It is this belief, I think, that primarily fuels sexual harassment in civilian life. According to this belief, women are classified as having a lesser status than men and so are open to sexual harassment in ways that men are not. Of course, the belief that it is appropriate to treat women as sexual objects in ways that men are not, such that they are sexually subordinate to men, also functions in the military, but there, I think, sexual harassment is more strongly supported by the belief that women just don't belong in the military.

Obviously, so far I have been seeking to explain the sexual harassment of ostensibly heterosexual women by ostensibly heterosexual
men, which is the dominant form of different-sex sexual harassment.
But what about same-sex and equal opportunity sexual harassment?
Same-sex and equal opportunity sexual harassment are, I believe,
best explained in a way analogous to the way I have sought to explain different-sex sexual harassment. In same-sex sexual harassment,
either the harassers believe that their victims do not belong in some
social setting, as was true in the *Oncale* case, or they believe their victims do belong but that it is still appropriate to treat them as sexual
objects in ways that others (including the harasser) are not to be
treated, as is standardly the case when the same-sex harasser is homosexual. Similarly, the same holds true of equal opportunity sexual
harassers. Either equal opportunity sexual harassers believe that their
particular victims do not belong in some social setting, or they believe that they do belong, but that it is still appropriate to treat them
as sexual objects in ways that others (including the harasser) are not
to be treated.

The Need for Positive as well as Negative Norms

Suppose then I am right, that the high incidence of different-sex sexual harassment in civilian life is explained by the belief, held by
many men and also by women, that it is appropriate to treat women
as sexual objects, and hence as sexually subordinate to men, and that
the high incidence of different-sex sexual harassment in military life
is explained by the fact that many men and women hold this same
belief, but even more so, by the fact that they also hold the belief
that women just don't belong in the military. And suppose further I
am right that same-sex and equal opportunity sexual harassment can
be similarly explained. What then can be done to rid society of the
problem of sexual harassment? Well, obviously sexual harassment
law and the moral and legal theory that supports it is an attempt to
rid society of this problem. This approach primarily tells men not to
harass women and then tries to explain what constitutes sexual harassment. However, this approach is essentially negative. It tells men
what not to do, not what to do. Of course, in most moral contexts,
it is far easier to come up with negative norms than with positive

ones—easier to tell people what they should not be doing than what they should be doing.[28] Nevertheless, when we come up with appropriate positive norms, they can be helpful in ways that merely negative ones cannot be. So what I am suggesting is that specifying some appropriate positive norms can help us to better rid ourselves of this social problem. Accordingly, I want to propose two positive norms for dealing with the problem of sexual harassment. The first is:

> THE PRINCIPLE OF ANDROGYNY (OR EQUAL OPPORTUNITY), which requires that the traits that are truly desirable and distributable in society be equally open to both women and men, or, in the case of virtues, equally expected of both women and men, other things being equal.

Why this principle? Well, we all know that when we think stereotypically about men and women at least in Western societies, we come up with different lists of desirable traits and undesirable traits such as the following:

Men	Women
Independent	**Dependent**
Competitive	Cooperative
Aggressive, assertive	Nurturant, caring
Unemotional, stoic, detached	Emotional
Active, **violent**	**passive,** nonviolent
Unconcerned with appearances	**Concerned with appearances (vain)**
Dominant	**Submissive,** self-effacing
Decisive	**Indecisive**
Seen as subject	Seen as object (of beauty or sexual attraction)
Sloppy	Neat
Sexually active	**Slut or nun**
Reasonable, rational, logical	Intuitive, **illogical**
Protective	In need of protection
Insensitive	Sensitive

And if we assume the traits in bold are undesirable ones, then in addition to having quite different stereotypical traits associated with men and women in our society, we will also have more undesirable traits on the women's list than on the men's list. Such lists clearly reflect the gender roles and traits that boys and girls, men and women are socialized into in society. In the past, the desirable gender traits stereotypically associated with men were thought to characterize mental health.[29] More recently, these same traits have been used to describe the successful corporate executive.[30] Accordingly, distinctive gender roles and traits have been used in these ways to favor men over women and heterosexuals over homosexuals. Nevertheless, there is good reason to think that the only morally defensible attitude we can take toward these gender roles and traits is expressed by the Principle of Androgyny (or Equal Opportunity). This is because for any stereotypical masculine role or trait that is desirable and distributable in society, we can always ask: why shouldn't women who have the capability to fulfill that role or acquire that trait be able to as well? And similarly, for any stereotypical feminine role or trait that is desirable and distributable in society, we can ask: why shouldn't men who have the capability to fulfill that role or acquire that trait be able to as well? And surely the answer to both of these questions is that there is no reason at all why both women and men shouldn't be able fulfill these roles and acquire these traits. This means that the Principle of Androgyny (or Equal Opportunity) is the only norm that is morally defensible in this regard. It opposes enforced gender roles and traits in favor of requiring the traits that are truly desirable and distributable in society be equally open to both women and men, or, in the case of virtues, equally expected of both women and men, other things being equal.[31]

So characterized, the Principle of Androgyny (or Equal Opportunity) represents neither a revolt against so-called feminine virtues and traits nor their exaltation over so-called masculine virtues and traits.[32] This is because it does not view women's liberation as simply the freeing of women from the confines of traditional roles, which makes it possible for them to develop in ways heretofore reserved for men. Nor does it view women's liberation as simply the reevaluation and glorification of so-called feminine activities like housekeeping or mothering or so-called feminine modes of thinking as reflected in an ethic of caring. The first perspective ignores or devalues genuine virtues and desirable traits traditionally associated with women while the second ignores or devalues genuine virtues and desirable traits traditionally associated with men. In contrast, the Principle of Androgyny (or Equal Opportunity) seeks a broader-based norm for both women and men that combines virtues and desirable traits traditionally associated with women with virtues and desirable traits traditionally associated with men. For this reason, the Principle of

Androgyny (or Equal Opportunity) is a common norm for both men (andro-) and women (-gyne).

So the Principle of Androgyny (or Equal Opportunity) by undermining enforced gender roles and traits will also be undermining those very social structures that give rise to the problem of sexual harassment. Discrimination "because of . . . sex" will be much rarer when there is very little, possibly nothing at all, that is desirable and distributable which stereotypically characterizes men over women or homosexuals over heterosexuals. When people have the chance to develop themselves in accord with their natural abilities and their free choices rather than socially imposed gender roles and traits, there will arise too many in-group differences and too many between-group similarities either with respect to women and men or with respect to homosexuals and heterosexuals to support anything like the existing practice of sexual harassment. The success of androgyny (or equal opportunity) will thus undercut the very possibility of sexual harassment.

The second positive norm I wish to propose is:

> THE PRINCIPLE OF DESERT, which requires that we treat and evaluate people on the basis of their proper role- or job-related qualifications and excellences when this is appropriate or required.

Ideally, this principle would pick up where the Principle of Androgyny (or Equal Opportunity) left off. If we have been successful in following the Principle of Androgyny (or Equal Opportunity), then we have been successful in developing ourselves on the basis of our natural abilities and free choices, and thus we have had the chance to acquire the proper role- and job-related qualifications and excellences that accord with our natural abilities and free choices. Yet whether or not the Principle of Androgyny (or Equal Opportunity) has been followed, the Principle of Desert still requires that we treat and evaluate people on the basis of their proper role- or job-related qualifications and excellences when this is appropriate or required.

Now if women in the military were treated and evaluated according to this norm, it would surely undermine the belief that they do not belong there and thus drastically reduce the sexual harassment to which this belief gives rise. What most people do not realize is that the opening up of the military to women was not embarked upon as an effort to achieve social equality. Rather the U.S. Defense

Department turned to women in order to save the all-volunteer force.[33] The women drawn to military service were smarter and better educated than the men. For example, according to one study, over 90 percent of women recruited had high school diplomas, compared to 63 percent of the men, and women also scored ten points higher on service exams.[34] In addition, proportionately more female than male cadets have been selected as Rhodes and Marshall scholars, and proportionately more women entering West Point have been National Honor Society members and high school valedictorians and salutatorians in all but two years since integration in 1976.[35] As one Defense Department report put it, "The trade off in today's recruiting market is between a high-quality female and a low-quality male."[36]

Of course, women have less upper-body strength, but 32 percent of women have met or exceeded the minimum male test scores and 78 percent of women have qualified for "very heavy" military jobs after six months of weight lifting, jogging with seventy-five-pound backpacks and performing squats with one-hundred-pound barrels on their shoulders.[37] Women's physiology also makes them more tolerant of G-force than men and so more suitable as fighter pilots, one of the most prestigious jobs in the military.[38] Interestingly, in 1961 NASA invited women civilian pilots to join the race for space against the Russians, and the women began testing out extraordinarily well. One woman Mary Wallace Funk who held several world records in flying, had beaten John Glenn on the stress tests, bicycle analysis tests, and lung power tests, and Wally Schirra on vertigo, while setting a record in the bicycle endurance and isolation tests; she lasted ten hours and thirty minutes before hallucinating. But then, without explanation, NASA canceled any further women's tests, and later in 1961, as Linda Bird Francke puts it, "Male astronauts rocketed into our history books."[39]

Of course, women are subject to pregnancy and motherhood, but statistically these have not been much of a problem in the military.[40] In fact, men suffer a higher absentee rate because of disciplinary problems and substance abuse.[41] So when women's strengths and weaknesses are taken into account compared to those of men, women turn out to be highly qualified for many combat and non-combat roles within the military, and, in fact, qualified for many more combat roles than those in which they are allowed to serve.

Accordingly, attending to women's proper role- or job-related qualifications should undermine the belief that they do not belong in the military and significantly reduce the sexual harassment to which that belief gives rise.

Similarly, attending to women's proper role- or job-related qualifications in civilian life should undermine the belief that it is appropriate to treat women as sexual objects in ways that men are not treated, such that they are sexually subordinate to men as well as significantly reduce the sexual harassment to which that belief gives rise. In fact, it will simply not be possible for men to treat and evaluate women on the basis of their proper role- or job-related qualifications and excellences when this is appropriate or required and at the same time treat women as sexual objects, and, hence, as sexually subordinate to men. Nevertheless, treating and evaluating women on the basis of their proper role- or job-related qualifications and excellences when this is appropriate or required will sometimes require a certain degree of creative imagination. For example, Lani Guinier points out that New York City once used a height requirement favoring tall men to select for police officers. When standards changed and more women became police officers, it became apparent that in some situations they were actually better at keeping the peace than were their male counterparts. For example, in New York City housing projects, black and Puerto Rican women police officers chose to mentor rather than confront teenage boys, thereby offering them respect, and the young men, grateful for the attention from adults, reciprocated by checking their own behavior. And women of all colors have been found to be better at defusing domestic violence situations.[42] Furthermore, when the Los Angeles Police Department wanted to do something about the problem of police abuse, the Christopher Commission Report told the city to hire more women. The commission found that women were not reluctant to use force, but that they were not nearly as likely to be involved in the use of excessive force. The women were also more communicative and more skillful at de-escalating potentially violent situations. The report concluded that current approaches to policing underemphasize communication skills, sensitivity to cultural differences, and courteousness.[43] What this shows is that it is not always easy to determine what are the proper role- or job-related qualifications, but assuming that these can be determined, treating and evaluating women on the basis of them when this is appropriate or required should help to undermine the belief that it is appropriate to treat women as sexual objects, and, hence, as sexually subordinate to men and also should significantly reduce the sexual harassment to which this belief gives rise.

In the case of homosexuals, because of the ability of many of them to pass as heterosexuals, they have already been able to demonstrate their ability to perform well in all sorts of social roles and jobs from which they would be excluded if they were openly homosexual. With respect to homosexuals, therefore, the Principle of Desert demands that they be given what they deserve, that is, that they be treated and evaluated according to their proper role- or job-related qualifications and excellences.

Now it is sometimes argued that discrimination can be justified against homosexuals because they engage in forms of sexual intercourse that are not open to procreation. But heterosexuals also engage in those same forms of sexual intercourse, and they are not similarly discriminated against. In fact, in the United States, heterosexuals who can reproduce are allowed to marry other heterosexuals who are sterile with the blessings of both Church and state, even though the relationships they form are no different from homosexual relationships with respect to their openness to procreation.[44] Correctly applying the Principle of Desert, therefore, should put an end to this discrimination against homosexuals.

Of course, more can and should be said about how we apply the Principle of Desert to treat and evaluate people on the basis of their proper role- or job-related qualifications and excellences when this is appropriate or required, but hopefully I have said enough to indicate how endorsing both this principle and the Principle of Androgyny (or Equal Opportunity) will, in fact, help to undermine the existing practice of sexual harassment. Summing up, in this chapter, I have first, provided:

A DEFINITION OF SEXUAL HARASSMENT. Sexual harassment is objectively unwelcome sexual advances, requests for sexual favors, and other verbal or physical conduct of a sexual nature, which are determined to be both objectionable and actionable by the standard of what is reasonable for everyone affected to accept, and which usually, but not always, impose a special burden on some individuals when there are no comparable burdens imposed on others who are similarly situated.

Second, I have shown how two fundamental beliefs help explain the high incidence of sexual harassment in military and civilian life respectively: the belief that women do not belong in the military and the belief that while women do belong in civilian life, it is still appropriate to treat them as sexual objects, and, hence, as sexually subordinate to men. Third, I have suggested two positive norms we need to attend to, in addition to the negative one prohibiting sexual harassment, if we want to better rid society of this practice. These norms are:

THE PRINCIPLE OF ANDROGYNY (OR EQUAL OPPORTUNITY), which requires that the traits that are truly desirable and distributable in society be equally open to both women and men, or, in the case of virtues, equally expected of both women and men, other things being equal.

THE PRINCIPLE OF DESERT, which requires that we treat and evaluate people on the basis of their proper role- or job-related qualifications and excellences when this is appropriate or required.[45]

Clearly, sexual harassment is a very difficult and troubling problem in our society, but dealing with it provides us with an opportunity to rethink the roles of men and women in our society, which is one of the most important moral tasks we face.

CHAPTER SIX

~

Defending Affirmative Action, Defending Preferences

Affirmative action is one of the most hotly debated issues in the United States today. This debate can only be expected to intensify now that the U.S. Supreme Court ruled on the two cases that were brought against the University of Michigan. In this essay, I hope to make a contribution to the resolution of this debate by first proposing a definition of affirmative action that should be acceptable to all sides, and then by setting out a defense of the various forms of affirmative action—outreach, remedial, and diversity affirmative action—captured by this definition.

A DEFINITION OF AFFIRMATIVE ACTION

Surprisingly, it turns out that the degree to which people in general are in favor of affirmative action depends in large measure on how that policy is described. For example, a *Los Angeles Times* poll showed that 58 percent of African Americans "opposed special preferences based on race and not merit," and another *Washington Post*/ABC poll showed that roughly two out of three women "oppose preferential treatment for women." On the other hand, according to pollster Lou Harris, every poll that has asked the simple question as to whether people "favor or oppose affirmative action—without strict quotas" has obtained a similar result: people favor affirmative action. Support runs 55 percent in favor to 40 percent against in more recent polls down from the average majority of 60 percent in favor to 38 percent against in polls taken over the past twenty-five years.

As one might expect, this lack of clarity as to how to characterize affirmative action has affected the debate over whether affirmative action can be justified. Frequently, the affirmative action that critics attack is not the affirmative action that most people defend.[1] At the same time, defenders of affirmative action need to formulate their definitions of affirmative action so as to avoid as much as possible the criticisms that have been directed against it. At least this is what I will try to do in this essay.[2]

Here I propose to define affirmative action as a policy of favoring qualified women and minority candidates over qualified men or nonminority candidates with the immediate goals of outreach, remedying discrimination, or achieving diversity, and the ultimate goals of attaining a colorblind (racially just) and a gender-free (sexually just) society (see diagram).

Affirmative Action

  Its Immediate Goals

- Outreach
- Remedying Discrimination
   Putting an End to Discrimination
   Compensating for Past Discrimination
- Diversity

  Its Ultimate Goals

- A Colorblind (Racially Just)
   and Gender-free (Sexually Just) Society

A colorblind society is a society in which race has no more significance than eye color has in most societies. A gender-free society is a society in which sex has no more significance than eye color has in most societies. It is a society in which the traits that are truly desirable and distributable in society are equally open to both women and men.[3] Alternatively, the ultimate goals can be understood to be racial justice and sexual justice. Since our society is far from being either colorblind (racially just) or gender-free (sexually just), it is generally recognized that to make the transition to a colorblind (racially just) or a gender-free (sexually just) society, we will have to take race and sex into account. For example, after the U.S. Civil War, Congress funded programs explicitly for the benefit of free blacks and former slaves, and after World War II, the West German government approved large compensations to individual Jews and to the newly created State of Israel. In addition, the U.S. government from time to time compensates American Indians for past injustices against them. For example, in 2000, the U.S. Congress approved giving an Indian tribe in New Mexico $23 million and about 4,600 acres to settle lawsuits over land claimed under a grant from the King of Spain more than 300 years ago. In general, if we want to get beyond any kind of significant wrongdoing, we need to take into account who wronged whom, and what the consequences were, and then try to set things right. There is no other morally acceptable way to get beyond significant wrongdoing.

As I define it, affirmative action can have a number of immediate goals. It can have the goal of outreach with the purpose of searching out qualified women and minority candidates who would otherwise not know about or apply for the available positions, but then hire or accept only those who are actually the most qualified. Affirmative action can also attempt to remedy discrimination. Here, there are two possibilities. (See diagram.) First, an affirmative action program can be designed simply to put an end to an existing discriminatory practice, and create, possibly for the first time in a particular setting, a truly equal opportunity environment. Second, an affirmative action program can attempt to compensate for past discrimination and the effects of that discrimination. The idea here is that stopping discrimination is one thing and making up for past discrimination and the effects of that discrimination is another, and both need to be done. Still another form of affirmative action has the goal of diversity, where the pursuit of diversity is, in turn, justified either in terms of its educational benefits or in terms of its ability to create a more effective workforce in such areas as policing or community relations.[4] Here it might even be said that the affirmative action candidates are, in fact, the most qualified candidates overall, since the less diverse candidates would not be as qualified.[5] As it turns out, all other forms of affirmative action can be understood in terms of their immediate goals to be either outreach, remedial, or diversity affirmative action, where remedial affirmative action further divides into two subtypes; one subtype simply seeks to end present discrimination and create an equal playing field, the other subtype attempts to compensate for past discrimination and its effects. (See diagram.)

Assuming that these are the basic types and subtypes of affirmative action, we need to examine them to determine when specifically they can be justified. Let us begin with outreach affirmative action.

A DEFENSE OF OUTREACH AFFIRMATIVE ACTION

Outreach affirmative action is easily the most defensible form of affirmative action. Even strong critics of affirmative action, like Louis Pojman and Thomas Sowell, defend this particular form of affirmative action. Thus, Pojman supports what he calls "weak affirmative action" which includes the "widespread advertisement to groups not previously represented in certain privileged positions." Similarly, Sowell holds that:

> Racial discrimination is [an] obvious area where merely to "cease and desist" is not enough. If a firm has engaged in racial discrimination for years and has an all-white force as a result, then simply to stop explicit discrimination will mean little as long as the firm continues to hire its current employees' friends and relatives through word of mouth referrals. . . . Clearly, the area of racial discrimination is one in which positive or affirmative steps of some kind seem reasonable.[6]

There is also considerable evidence that outreach affirmative action is needed. Social scientists have discovered that many employers tend to recruit selectively and informally, directing their efforts at neighborhoods, institutions, and media outlets that have smaller minority populations or constituencies.[7] For instance, in one study of Chicago area employers, it was found that in an effort to screen potential applicants, employers engaged in a variety of race-neutral recruitment mechanisms that had the effect of "disproportionately screen[ing] out inner-city blacks." For example, 40 percent of employers failed to advertise job openings in newspapers and relied instead on informal employee networking to generate job applicants. Of those employers who did advertise job openings, two-thirds advertised in neighborhood or "white ethnic" newspapers rather than in "black newspapers." While some employers recruited in both metropolitan and suburban schools, many of these employers gave applications from suburban schools more attention. According to another study, about 86 percent of available jobs do not appear in classified advertisements and 80 percent of executives find their jobs through networking. Thus, there is much that businesses and educational institutions can do by way of outreach affirmative action to ensure that minorities and women know about the availability of jobs and positions that in the past were foreclosed to them.

Summing up the main requirement for outreach affirmative action is the following:

> All reasonable steps must be taken to ensure that qualified minority and women candidates have available to them the same educational and job opportunities that are available to nonminority or male candidates.

A DEFENSE OF REMEDIAL AFFIRMATIVE ACTION

Virtually everyone also accepts the justification of at least some form of remedial affirmative action. Although the U.S. Supreme Court has adopted different positions at different times, it has always held that it is permissible to adopt remedial affirmative action as compensation for identifiable acts of purposeful discrimination committed by that very institution. What we need to determine, therefore, is exactly when remedial affirmative action is justified. The current legal answer in the United States, which has been defended by a number of 5 to 4 votes of the Supreme Court, is that remedial affirmative action is justified when the following two requirements are met:

1. The past discrimination that is to be remedied must be proven discrimination by the institution that is engaging in the affirmative action in question. Thus, using race-based affirmative action to remedy unproven discrimination, usually referred to as "societal discrimination," or even to remedy proven discrimination that cannot be attributed to the institution engaged in the affirmative action in question cannot be justified (first endorsed in *Bakke*, 1978; *Wygant*, 1986).[8]
2. Racial classifications must be regarded as presumptively suspect; it does not matter whether the classifications are intended to remedy the results of prior racial discrimination or whether they are intended to foster or maintain racial discrimination. Accordingly, any use of racial classifications must satisfy a strict scrutiny analysis, that is, it must be narrowly tailored to meet a compelling government interest. (first endorsed in *Korematsu*, 1944; *Bakke*, 1978; *Croson*, 1989).

Although the U.S. Supreme Court defends these two requirements as being either necessitated by or compatible with the Civil Rights Act of 1964 and/or the U.S. Constitution, particularly the 14th Amendment, most of the arguments for these two requirements are found within the Supreme Court decisions themselves, especially beginning with the *Bakke* decision in 1978. It is important, therefore, to examine the arguments the Court provides for these requirements to determine whether they are successful.

The First Requirement

Consider the first requirement—the limitation of remedial affirmative action to proven discrimination by the institution engaged in the affirmative action in question. Surely, it would be unreasonable for anyone today to deny that African Americans and other minorities suffer not only from current discrimination but also from the continuing effects of past discrimination.[9]

Evidence of Racial Discrimination

In the United States today, almost half of all black children live in poverty. Black unemployment is twice that of white, and the median net worth of white families is ten times that of black families. The infant mortality rate in many black communities is twice that of whites. Blacks are twice as likely as whites to be robbed, seven times more likely to be murdered or to die of tuberculosis. A male living in New York's Harlem is less likely to reach the age of sixty-five than a resident of Bangladesh. Blacks comprise 50 percent of the maids and garbage collectors but only 4 percent of the managers and 3 percent of the physicians and lawyers. According to a United Nations study, white Americans, when considered as a separate nation, rank first in the world in well-being (a measure that combines life expectancy, educational achievements, and income). African Americans rank twenty-seventh and Hispanic Americans even lower at thirty-second. According to the U.S. Federal Reserve Board, the loan rejection rate for blacks in the highest income bracket is identical to the rejection rate of whites in the lowest income bracket. According to another study, minority applicants are 50 percent more likely to be denied a loan than white applicants of equivalent economic status. In a study by the Urban Institute, equally qualified, identically dressed, white and African American applicants for jobs were used to test for bias in the job market for newspaper-advertised positions. White and African Americans were matched identically for age, work experience, speech patterns, personal characteristics, and physical build. The study found repeated discrimination against African American male applicants. The white men received three times as many job offers as equally qualified African Americans who interviewed for the same positions. According to a study conducted by the Fair Housing Council in Washington, D.C., minorities in the United States are discriminated against 40 percent of the time when they attempt to rent apartments or buy homes. Another study revealed that African American and Hispanic American job applicants suffer blatant and easily identifiable discrimination once in every five times they apply for a job. African American men with bachelor's degrees earn as much as $15,180 less than their white counterparts. Although native-born white males make up only 41 percent of the U.S. population, they comprise 80 percent of all tenured professors, 97 percent of all school superintendents, and 97 percent of senior managerial positions in Fortune 1000 industrial and Fortune 500 service companies. African Americans hold only 0.6 percent, Asian Americans 0.3 percent, and Hispanic Americans 0.4 percent of the senior managerial positions. For 1993, it was estimated that the failure to employ blacks in jobs using simply their *current* skills for that year represented a $137 billion loss to the U.S. economy. This means that rather than being in jobs for which they are underqualified, many blacks are actually *overqualified* for the jobs they hold. One study done in the Los Angeles area found that race and skin color affected the probability of obtaining employment by as much as 52 percent. While whites and light-skinned African Americans were relatively likely to find employment when searching for a job, dark-skinned men were not. In fact, dark-skinned men were twice as likely as others to remain unemployed. According to another study, only 10.3 percent of light-skinned African Americans men with thirteen or more years of schooling were unemployed, compared with 19.4 percent of their dark-skinned counterparts with similar education. Among men who had participated in job-training programs, light-skinned blacks actually had a lower jobless rate than their white counterparts—11.1 percent, compared with 14.5 percent. Yet the rate for dark-skinned African American men with job training was 26.8 percent. Thus, there is plenty of evidence that, at least in the United States, African Americans and other minorities not only are currently discriminated against but also currently suffer from the continuing effects of past discrimination.[10]

Given the widespread evidence of current discrimination and the continuing effects of past discrimination in the United States, no defender of affirmative action would have reason to object to restricting remedial affirmative action to discrimination that can be proven in some appropriate way. The U.S. Supreme Court itself has allowed that such discrimination can be proven by judicial, legislative, or administrative findings. The real worry here, however, is that the Court has chosen to impose too demanding a standard of proof, making it far too difficult for institutions to correct for past discrimination.

City of Richmond v. Croson

Consider the decision the U.S. Supreme Court reached in *Croson* (1989). Here the Court held that a generalized assertion of past discrimination in the entire construction industry (the basis of the federal set-aside accepted in *Fullilove,* 1980) was insufficient to justify a minority set-aside by the city of Richmond, Virginia. The Court also ruled that further evidence showing that the population of Richmond was 50 percent black while less than 1 percent of the city's construction business had been awarded to minority-owned enterprises, and that all the building trade associations in Virginia had at most one or two black members, was judged insufficient to justify the city's affirmative action program. The Court further held that the relevant comparison in this case is not between the percentage of blacks in Richmond and the percentage of the city's construction business that had been awarded to minority-owned enterprises, but rather the comparison between the number of minority-owned enterprises in Richmond and the percentage of the city's construction business that had been awarded to minority-owned enterprises. The Court's general view here was that when special qualifications are required to fill particular jobs, the relevant comparison is not to the general population, but rather to the smaller group of individuals who possess the necessary qualifications. But if discrimination was as rampant in the construction industry nationwide, and in the city of Richmond, as the evidence indicates, then, clearly not many minority-owned enterprises would have been able to survive in that environment. Thus a small number of minority-owned enterprises in the Richmond area is exactly what one would expect if there had been significant discrimination. Accordingly, we cannot use the existence of only a small number of minority-owned enterprises to indicate the absence of discrimination. In fact, without an explanation to the contrary, it would be reasonable to infer that a small number of minority-owned enterprises in the Richmond area is, in fact, evidence of discrimination. Why else would minorities in the Richmond area not have taken advantage of the construction opportunities present there if those opportunities had, in fact, been open to them? In the South, under slavery, more than 80 percent of those working as masons, blacksmiths, carpenters, and painters were slaves, according to a census taken in 1865. Even in the case at issue, Croson, the owner of the white-owned, Ohio-based enterprise, actually lost his contract with the city of Richmond because Brown, the owner of the minority-owned, Richmond-based firm that Croson tried to subcontract, astutely took advantage of the opportunity provided to bypass Croson and deal directly with the city.

In any case, the evidence of past discrimination in the *Croson* case is overwhelming. There were the numerous national studies documenting discrimination in the construction industry, some of them commissioned by Congress, none of which gave the least indication that the construction industry in Richmond was an exception to this national pattern. And then there was the particular evidence presented before the Richmond city council, all of which supported the view that discrimination in the local construction industry was widespread. In fact, no one presented any contrary evidence to the city council, although some members of the council did oppose its decision, and so they would presumably have introduced such evidence had it been available. Thus, when the U.S. Supreme Court concludes that there was insufficient evidence of discrimination to justify a five year set-aside remedial affirmative action program by the city of Richmond, they are obviously making it far too difficult to correct for past discrimination.

In addition to the U.S. Supreme Court's overdemanding standard for proof of discrimination, the Court further requires that any institution seeking to compensate for past discrimination must itself be guilty of that very discrimination. Although such a restriction might have initially seemed appropriate when it was first imposed by the Supreme Court on a race-based layoff policy in Jackson, Michigan, it is surely inappropriate when it is used to invalidate the finding of discrimination in the construction industry in the Richmond area. In *Croson,* the Court found against the city of Richmond because the city did not sufficiently implicate itself in the past discrimination that it sought to correct. But most institutions that are considering whether to engage in remedial affirmative action will understandably be quite reluctant to implicate themselves in the very discrimination they are seeking to correct because this would, in turn, open them up to further liability and censure. Moreover, once sufficient evidence of discrimination has been provided, there seems to be no reason to impose the additional requirement that the agent engaged in the affirmative action program must also be implicated in the discrimination it is seeking to correct.[11] Given these considerations, the first requirement as to when remedial affirmative action is justified should be:

> The past discrimination that is to be remedied must be proven discrimination, but the institution that is engaging in the affirmative action need not be implicated in that proven discrimination in order for the affirmative action in question to be justified.

The Second Requirement

Turning to the U.S. Supreme Court's second requirement for remedial affirmative action, we find that it begins with a reasonable assumption that racial classifications should be presumptively suspect. Surely, in the United States, there are good historical reasons to assume that racial classifications are presumptively suspect, given 250 years of slavery, 100 years of Jim Crow, plus discriminatory practices that continue right up to the present day.

A Colorblind (Racially Just) Society

Of course, if we lived in a colorblind society, racial classifications would no longer be presumptively suspect because in such a society a person's race would be no more significant than eye color is in most societies.[12] In most societies, people frequently don't even notice a person's eye color. Except for the mildest aesthetic preferences, eye color tends to be an unimportant trait. Very little turns on what eye color you have. Accordingly, if we lived in a society where a person's race was no more significant than eye color is in most societies, there would be little reason to treat race with any kind of legal scrutiny. In a colorblind society, many cultural differences would remain, but they wouldn't be based on race. As a result, the cultures that were constituted by these differences would be open to members of all races in much the same way that most religions today are open to members of all races.

But obviously we don't live in such a colorblind, or, if you prefer, a racially just society. In U.S. society, it is not at all difficult to find present discrimination as well as the continuing effects of past discrimination. U.S. society is clearly not a colorblind (racially just) society. Hence, in the United States, it is reasonable to assume that racial classifications should be presumptively suspect.

A BETTER STANDARD OF PROOF FOR REMEDIAL AFFIRMATIVE ACTION

Assuming that the standard of proof for remedial affirmative action for minorities were appropriately lowered, it would then be far easier to use race-based affirmative action to correct and compensate for widespread discriminatory practices in U.S. society. For example, it is generally recognized that in many parts of the United States there are de facto segregated primary and secondary educational systems whose existence is clearly rooted in past discrimination. In fact, U.S. primary and secondary schools are now becoming even more segregated than they were in the past.[13] In the South, the most integrated region of the country, the percentage of black students in majority white schools fell from a peak of 43.5 percent in the late 1980s to 34.7 percent in 1996, even falling below the level achieved twenty-four years earlier in 1972. National trends in the United States parallel those in the South. Nationwide, the percentage of black students in majority white schools peaked in the early 1980s and has now declined to the levels of the 1960s. Nationwide, the percentage of Hispanics in majority white schools has declined from 45 percent in 1968 to 25 percent today. Both in terms of resources and race, American schools have now become at least as segregated as they were in the 1960s. In large cities, fifteen of every sixteen black and

Hispanic students are in schools where most of the students are non-white. In medium-size cities, 63 percent of blacks and 70 percent of Hispanics attend such schools. White suburban schools have approximately twice the funds per student as do urban schools where black and Hispanic students are concentrated, although people living in urban school districts are taxed more heavily to support their poorer schools. Moreover, much of this racial segregation in primary and secondary schools in the United States can be traced to the widespread discrimination in housing we noted earlier. The financial resources that these schools currently have in the United States are primarily dependent on the wealth of the local school districts in which they are located.

Ideally, it would surely be preferable to correct for these educational disparities with an equal education opportunity program that, within a short period of time, provided every child in the United States with equally good educational opportunities, pre-school through twelfth grade for, let's say, the additional cost of $25 billion a year. Moreover, if we had to choose between existing affirmative action programs and such an equal education opportunity program—if we could not have them both—then there would be no question among defenders of affirmative action as to which one to choose.[14] If these were our options, then surely every current defender of affirmative action would favor the proposed equal education opportunity program over affirmative action. Of course, in the real world in which we live, we do not have the option of having the proposed equal education opportunity program. This alternative to maintaining and developing existing affirmative action programs is simply not a feasible option in our current social and political context, at least in the United States.

What then should we do? Recognizing that the poorer educational and residential experiences that minorities have in the United States are the result of present or past discriminatory practices, both institutions of higher education and employers could use affirmative action programs to make up for that discrimination. These affirmative action programs would favor qualified minority candidates who have been discriminated against in the past over equally or more qualified nonminority candidates who have not been similarly disadvantaged. In fact, it should be the case that those who are passed over by such programs have themselves benefited from the discrimination suffered by these affirmative action candidates, for example, the discrimination found in their unequal educational and residential opportunities.[15] Yet, to be justified, such affirmative action programs must favor only candidates whose qualifications are such that when their selection is combined with a suitably designed educational enhancement program, they will normally turn out, within a reasonably short time, to be as qualified as, or even more qualified than, their peers. Such candidates must have the potential to be as qualified as, or more qualified than, their peers, although that potential will not yet have been actualized because of past discrimination. Affirmative action of this sort, with its suitably designed educational enhancement program, purports to actualize just that potential.[16] In this way, persons who receive this form of affirmative action are like runners in a race who, for a time, are forced to compete at a disadvantage with the other runners, say, by having weights tied to their legs, but later are allowed to compete against those other runners by first having the weights removed and then receiving some special assistance for an appropriate period of time, so that the results of the race will turn out to be fair. Affirmative action of this sort, therefore, is a policy that is directed at only those minority candidates who are highly qualified, yet, because of past discrimination and prejudice, are less qualified than they would otherwise be; it seeks to provide such candidates with a benefit that will nullify the effects of past injustices by enabling them to become as qualified as, or more qualified than, their peers. Thus, once the standards of proof for race-based remedial affirmative action are suitably lowered to those that are used for sex-based remedial affirmative action, it should be possible to correct for a broad range of present and past discriminatory practices.

Summing up, then, the requirements as to when remedial affirmative action is justified should be the following:

1. The past discrimination that is to be remedied must be proven discrimination, but the institution that is engaging in the affirmative action need not be implicated in that proven discrimination in order for the affirmative action in question to be justified.
2. Although, in a colorblind (racially just) society, racial classifications would no longer be presumptively suspect, in the United States, racial classifications must be regarded as presumptively suspect because of the 250 years of slavery,

100 years of Jim Crow, plus discriminatory practices that continue right up to the present day. However, the standard of proof required to justify the use of racial classifications in remedial affirmative action should not be unreasonably high as it is in the *Croson* case. It should not be easier to correct for sexual discrimination in society than it is to correct for racial discrimination. Accordingly, remedial affirmative action still has a significant role in combating proven past and present discrimination in housing, education, and jobs, unless more broadly conceived and much better funded corrective policies are undertaken.

3. Only candidates are selected whose qualifications are such that when their selection is combined with a suitably designed educational enhancement program, they will normally turn out, within a reasonably short time, to be as qualified as, or even more qualified than, their peers.

4. Those who are passed over by such affirmative action programs would have themselves benefited from the discrimination suffered by the affirmative action candidates, for example, the discrimination found in their unequal educational and residential opportunities.[17]

A DEFENSE OF DIVERSITY AFFIRMATIVE ACTION

There is another type of affirmative action, however, that is not grounded in the ideal of remedying discrimination, whether that discrimination is present or past. The goal of this type of affirmative action is diversity, which in turn is justified either in terms of its educational benefits or its ability to create a more effective work force in such areas as policing and community relations. The legal roots of this form of affirmative action in the United States are found in *Bakke* (1978).

In *Bakke*, Justice Powell argued that the attainment of a diverse student body was clearly a constitutionally permissible goal for an institution of higher education. According to Powell, in an admissions program that aimed at diversity:

> [r]ace or ethnic background may be deemed a "plus" in a particular applicant's file, yet it does not insulate the individual from comparison with all other candidates for the available seats. . . . The applicant who

loses out in the last available seat to another candidate receiving a "plus" on the basis of ethnic background will not have been foreclosed from all consideration for that seat. . . . It will mean only that his combined qualifications. . . . did not outweigh those of the other applicant.

Furthermore, an admissions program may "pay some attention to distribution among many types and categories of students," as more than a "token number of blacks" is needed to secure the educational benefits that flow from a racially and ethnically diverse student body.

For almost twenty years, Powell's opinion in *Bakke,* supported by Justices Brennan, Marshall, Blackmun, and White, has been the rationale for the affirmative action used by most American colleges and universities. Even Justice O'Connor, who has rejected diversity as a compelling interest for the broadcasting industry in *Metro Broadcasting v. FCC* (1990), has allowed that a state interest in the promotion of diversity has been found sufficiently compelling at least in the context of higher education.[18]

In 1995, however, the U.S. Court of Appeals for the Fifth Circuit held in *Hopwood v. Texas* that Powell's opinion in *Bakke* is not binding precedent. According to the Court, the view that race may be used as a "plus" factor to obtain diversity "garnered only [Powell's] vote and has never represented the view of a majority of the Court in *Bakke* or any other case." However, it has been generally recognized that the Brennan group (which included Brennan, who wrote the opinion, and Marshall, Blackmun, and White, who endorsed it) did support Powell's view in *Bakke.* In fact, Brennan himself said as much in a subsequent decision. Moreover, the reason why no other case since *Bakke* has supported Powell's view on diversity in education is that no other case since *Bakke* has dealt with diversity in education.

The *Hopwood* court also ruled that evidence of discrimination in Texas's school system as a whole was not relevant to whether the affirmative action program of the University of Texas Law School is justified. Even though, as of May 1994, desegregation suits remained pending against more than forty Texas school districts, and at the time the *Hopwood* plaintiffs filed suit, the U.S. Office of Civil Rights had not yet determined that the state had desegregated its schools sufficiently to comply with federal civil rights laws, and, even though most of the applicants to the Law School had passed through that very same educational system with its alleged inequalities, the *Hopwood* court only allowed the Law School at the University of Texas to use evidence of its *own* discrimination to justify engaging in affirmative action.[19] But, as I have argued earlier, once sufficient evidence of discrimination has been provided, there seems to be no reason to impose the additional requirement that the agent engaged in the affirmative action program must be further implicated in the discrimination it is seeking to correct.

Interestingly, the *Hopwood* court supported its overall decision on two contradictory claims about race.[20] First, the court claimed that race does make a difference, that we can't assume there would be proportional participation in the absence of past discrimination. But then the court claimed that race does not make a difference, that race is not a good indicator of diversity. Now we might try to rescue the court from contradiction here by understanding its first claim about race to refer to an ideal society, and its second to refer to current U.S. society. So understood, the court would be claiming that in an ideal society, race would still make a difference, but in our present society, race does not make a difference. But this would only save the court from a contradiction by committing it to an absurdity. Surely, what we should believe here about actual and ideal societies is exactly the opposite of what the court appears to be claiming. What we should believe about the United States, on the basis of the evidence of past and present discrimination, is that race does make a difference in the kind of life people experience in U.S. society. And what we should believe, or at least hope for, about an ideal society is that in such a society, race will not make a difference because in such a society race will be no more significant than eye color is in most societies. Thus, the *Hopwood* court's decision, based as it is on two contradictory conceptions of race, is deeply flawed.

RECENT DECISIONS ON MICHIGAN CASES

There have also been two recent district court cases in the state of Michigan which reached diametrically opposed opinions about the legitimacy of using race as a factor to achieve diversity. In *Gratz v. Bollinger* (2000), the District Court for the Eastern District of Michigan held that under *Bakke* diversity constitutes a compelling governmental interest that, in the context of education, justifies the use of race as one factor in the admissions process. The court ruled further that the university had provided solid evidence regarding the educational benefits that flow from a racially and ethnically diverse student body.[21] By contrast, another judge from the same District Court for the Eastern District of Michigan ruled in *Grutter v. Bollinger* (2001) that using race as a factor to achieve diversity was not established as a compelling state interest in *Bakke*. The *Grutter* district court decision was reversed by the U.S. Court of Appeals for the Sixth Circuit (2002), and both decisions were decided by the U.S. Supreme Court on June 23, 2003.

In the Supreme Court's landmark *Grutter* decision, a majority held that it is constitutionally permissible to use racial preferences to achieve the educational benefits of diversity and it also approved the University of Michigan Law School's way of achieving those benefits. In *Gratz*, the majority rejected the university's way of achieving those benefits for its undergraduate program.

Yet without a doubt, the most important finding of the Court was the constitutional permissibility of using racial preferences to achieve the educational benefits of diversity. That, of course, had been the opinion of Justice Powell in *Bakke* (1978). But in recent years there had been considerable debate about whether Powell's opinion represents the holding of the Court in *Bakke,* and whether the Supreme Court's instructions in *Marks* (1977) could be applied to *Bakke* to help determine that holding. In *Grutter,* Justice O'Connor, writing for the majority, cut short the discussion by simply adopting the opinion of Powell in *Bakke* as the opinion of the majority in *Grutter.* "Today, we hold that the Law School has a compelling interest in attaining a diverse student body." In doing this, the Court also deferred to "the Law School's educational judgment that such diversity is essential to its educational mission." The grounds for this deference is the First Amendment's protection of educational autonomy, which secures the right of a university "to select those students who will contribute to the "robust exchange of ideas" (quoting Powell).[22] At the same time, the Court is moved by evidence of the educational benefits of diversity provided by the Law School and by briefs of the amici curiae (friends of the court).

> American businesses have made clear that the skills needed in today's increasingly global marketplace can only be developed through exposure to widely diverse people, cultures, ideas, and viewpoints.

What is more, high-ranking retired officers and civilian leaders of the United States military assert that "[b]ased on [their] decades of experience," a "highly qualified, racially diverse officer corps . . . is essential to the military's ability to fulfill its principle mission to provide national security."

Yet while affirming the constitutional permissibility of using racial preferences to achieve the educational benefits of diversity, the Supreme Court in *Grutter* accepted the law school's affirmative action admissions program at the same time that the Court in *Gratz* rejected the undergraduate school's program.

The difference between the two programs, according to the majority in *Grutter,* is that the undergraduate program by automatically assigning twenty points on the basis of race or ethnicity operated in a too mechanical, nonindividualized manner. If race or ethnicity is to be a factor in admissions, the majority contends, there needs to be "individualized consideration of each and every applicant." The Law School seeking to admit 350 students from 3,500 applicants had used a more individualized admissions process that the Court has now endorsed. The College of Literature, Science, and the Arts, facing the task of admitting 5,000 of 25,000 applicants, had chosen a more mechanical admissions process, still believing that it was sufficiently individualized to meet the Court's requirement of strict scrutiny. Now the Court has ruled that its requirement of strict scrutiny, which demands that any use of race or ethnicity in admissions be narrowly tailored to achieve the educational benefits of diversity, cannot be met unless each and every applicant's qualifications are individually considered. Accordingly, the University of Michigan will have to significantly increase its undergraduate admissions personnel in order to provide this individualized consideration of each and every applicant that is now required. The University of Michigan has now done this.

What appeared to particularly bother the majority in *Gratz* was that under Michigan's undergraduate affirmative action program "virtually every qualified underrepresented minority applicant is admitted." By contrast, Michigan's Law School "frequently accepts nonminority applicants with grades and test scores lower than underrepresented minority applicants (and other nonminority applicants) who are rejected." It is probably supposed that the adoption of a more individualized review process in the undergraduate admissions program will tend to eliminate this difference between the two programs. However, it may be that the difference between the two programs is due to the fact that the Law School can be more selective relative to its pool of candidates than the undergraduate school (the Law School admits 10 percent of its applicants, the undergraduate college 20 percent). On this account, the Law School may have had a comparatively larger pool of qualified minority applicants from which to choose. In any case, what the Supreme Court required in *Grutter* was a more individualized review process, not the guarantee that there will always be some nonminorities who are accepted who have grade and test scores that are lower than some underrepresented minorities who are rejected.

Of course, colleges and universities are only required to adopt this individualized approach if they seek to use race as a factor in admissions. If a college or university only takes nonracial factors into account in its admissions process, it is free to use virtually any mechanical, nonindividualized admissions procedure it wants. For example, it can give 20 or 30 points (with, say, 100 points needed for admission) to sons and daughters of those who donate a certain amount of money to the school or to sons and daughters of alumni. It is only when race is taken into account (usually to the benefit of underrepresented minorities) that the court has imposed a significant constitutional hurdle. So although the Supreme Court decision in *Grutter* is surely welcomed for permitting the individualized use of racial preferences to achieve the educational benefits of diversity, the Court's decision actually does little to achieve *real equality* of educational opportunity in higher education, which would require, among other things, significantly limiting the role of donor and legacy preferences in admissions (legacies presently constitute about 25 percent of the student body at select colleges and universities in the United States), and providing sufficient need-based support.

Objections to the *Grutter* Decision

One objection to the majority decision in *Grutter*, most forcefully stated by Chief Justice Rehnquist, was that the Law School admitted African American applicants in roughly the same proportion to their number in the applicant pool as Hispanic and American Indian applicants, even though some African American applicants had grade and test scores that were lower than some of the Hispanic applicants who were rejected. Given that the law school was looking for a critical mass of each underrepresented group, Rehnquist finds the rejection of these Hispanic applicants hard to explain, particularly since the law school admits twice as many African Americans as Hispanics, and only one-sixth as many American Indians. How could the law school be admitting a critical mass of each group?

The law school, however, never claimed to be admitting a critical mass of each group. It was only aiming at that goal, and clearly it was far from reaching it with respect to American Indians. In addition, there surely are other relevant factors, such as the quality of essays and of letters of recommendation, and maybe Michigan residency that can explain why some African Americans with lower grade and test scores were admitted while some Hispanic applicants with higher grade and test scores were rejected.[23] The objection that Rehnquist raises here had not been raised before. Nor was it raised in the oral argument before the Supreme Court. So it is not clear exactly how the Law School would respond. Still, responses of the sort I have sketched here appear to support the law school's admissions process in this regard.

Justice Thomas, in his dissent, suggested that the court's reliance on social science literature showing the benefits of diversity at Michigan might require a similar reliance on social science literature showing that black students experience superior cognitive development at historically black colleges (HBCs) and that a substantial diversity moderates the cognitive effects of attending an HBC. Yet it is surely possible for HBCs to undertake supportive measures in light of such social science literature without violating the major recent ruling of the court with regard to HBCs. That ruling, which Thomas himself cites, holds that "a State cannot maintain . . . traditions by closing particular institutions, historically white or historically black to particular racial groups."[24] Thus, there is really no conflict with the *Grutter* majority here.

Thomas also questions how the court in *Grutter* can defer to Michigan Law School's educational judgment that diversity is essential to its educational mission when it did not defer to the Virginia Military Institute's (VMI) judgment that the changes in its "adversative" method of education required for admitting women into its educational program would be too great. Thomas suggests that the reason for the difference is that Michigan Law School belongs to the elite establishment whereas VMI does not.

But there are other explanations available. At the time of the VMI case, the U.S. military academies, as well as ROTC programs around the country, had for many years been admitting women into their programs, with the major effect being that the U.S. military now has much smarter military personnel, as judged by grades, test scores, and academic honors, than it would otherwise have had.[25] So while VMI cannot draw any support from comparable institutions and programs, Michigan Law School has the overwhelming support of educational institutions across the entire country, as the briefs of the amici curiae attest. Surely this justifies a difference in deference.

Justice Scalia's main objection to the *Grutter* decision, which Justice Thomas more expansively develops, is that Michigan does not have a compelling state interest in maintaining a law school that is both elite and diverse. If it wants to have a diverse student body, it can simply lower its standards and achieve the desired diversity without using affirmative action.[26] Thomas adds to this argument by noting that while Michigan Law School accounts for nearly 30 percent of all law students graduating in Michigan, only 6 percent of its graduates take the bar exam in the state, although about 16 percent elect to stay in the state. By contrast, Wayne State University Law School is said to send "88 percent of its graduates on to serve the people of Michigan." Thomas concludes that Michigan does not even have a compelling state interest in having a law school, let alone in having one that is both elite and diverse.

Of course, percentages don't tell the whole story here, and Thomas neglects to assess how well-placed and influential that 6 or 16 percent of Michigan Law School graduates who stay or practice law in the state turn out to be. Moreover, the suggestion that Michigan does not have a compelling state interest in doing something that primarily benefits the rest of the country is extremely odd. It is like saying that Michigan does not have a compelling state interest in controlling the sulfur emissions of its power plants that cause, let's suppose, much of the acid rain that negatively affects New England states.

As to the question of whether Michigan should have to choose between having an elite law school and having the educational benefits of diversity? Unfortunately, Thomas does not provide the necessary consequentialist argument showing that the state would be better off with a law school that was diverse but not elite. And it is surely the failure of Thomas (and Scalia who endorsed the same view) to provide that argument, along with the evidence of the benefits of affirmative action that Michigan provided in its Gurin Report and the over one hundred amici curiae briefs all attesting to the benefits of affirmative action, which persuaded O'Connor to join with the more liberal side of the Court in this case.[27]

As a consequence, legally and morally, the case for diversity affirmative action is as strong as it ever was. Accordingly, diversity affirmative action should be regarded as justified when:

1. Race is used as a factor to select from the pool of applicants a sufficient number of qualified applicants to secure the educational benefits that flow from a racially and ethnically diverse student body.
2. Only candidates are selected whose qualifications are such that when their selection is combined with a suitably designed educational enhancement program, they will normally turn out, within a reasonably short time, to be as qualified as, or even more qualified than, their peers.

But, as I have argued earlier, we could also justify affirmative action in higher education on remedial grounds as well. Given that the poorer educational experiences that minorities have in the United States are the result of either present or past discriminatory practices, institutions of higher education should be able to institute affirmative action programs designed to make up for this discrimination. In addition, once the standard of proof for race-based remedial affirmative action programs is suitably lowered to that used for sex-based remedial affirmative action programs, it should be possible to correct for a broad range of present and past discriminatory practices with remedial affirmative action programs in higher education.

In response to *Grutter*, conservatives are now talking about using the affirmative action issue as a litmus test for future Supreme Court nominees, hoping thereby to overturn *Grutter*'s 5-to-4 majority when Justice O'Connor retires. In addition, there is talk of using referendums, like Proposition 209, that can frame the issue in terms of racial preferences rather than affirmative action and the benefits of diversity, as yet another way of undercutting the decision.

In the end, conservatives on this issue seem to be in the grips of an odd notion of racial equality. They seem unconcerned with the kind of evidence Justice Ruth Ginsburg cites in her dissenting opinion in *Gratz,* showing widespread discrimination against minorities in the workplace and the housing market. They do not call for increasing the meager efforts of the federal government to prosecute this sort of discrimination. Nor are they interested in overturning the more recent Supreme Court decisions that make it very difficult to prove or correct for discrimination against minorities. Nor are they generally in favor of the large increases in spending that are needed to provide all students in the United States with at least a K-through-12 quality education. Rather, they are simply focused on eliminating diversity affirmative action, which benefits underrepresented minorities by way of benefiting the student body as a whole. The goal is to benefit the student body as a whole and to achieve that we must do something that happens to benefit minorities. But this selective concern with just eliminating certain benefits to minorities is far too narrow and inadequate an ideal of racial equality. We should be very pleased, therefore, that at this moment in our history, the Supreme Court has opted for a broader and far more adequate ideal of racial equality. Much more, however, remains to be done if we are to achieve that colorblind (racially just) and gender-free (sexually just) society in which affirmative action will no longer be needed.

CHAPTER SEVEN

International Terrorism and Iraqi War II

How should we think about terrorism and Iraqi War II as a response to terrorism? To answer this question it is helpful to start with a definition of terrorism. Since 1983, the U.S. State Department has defined terrorism as follows:

> Terrorism is premeditated, politically motivated violence perpetrated against noncombatant targets by subnational groups or clandestine agents, usually intended to influence an audience.[1]

In a recent U.S. State Department document in which this definition is endorsed, there is also a section which discusses state-sponsored terrorism.[2] It is clear then that the U.S. State Department does not hold that only subnational groups or individuals can commit terrorist acts; it further recognizes that states can commit terrorist acts as well. So let me offer the following definition of terrorism, which is essentially the same as the U.S. State Department's definition once it is allowed that states too can commit terrorist acts, and once it is recognized that it is through eliciting terror (that is, intense fear, fright, or intimidation) that terrorists attempt to achieve their goals:

> DEFINITION OF TERRORISM. Terrorism is the use or threat of violence against innocent people to elicit terror in them, or in some other group of people, in order to further a political objective.

Using this definition, there is no problem seeing the attacks on New York City and Washington, D.C., particularly the attacks on the World Trade Center, as terrorist acts.[3] Likewise, the bombing of the

U.S. embassies in Kenya and Tanzania in 1998 as well as the suicide bombings directed at Israeli civilians are terrorist acts.[4]

But what about the U.S. bombing of a pharmaceutical plant in Sudan with respect to which we blocked a UN inquiry and later compensated the owner, but not the thousands of victims who were deprived of drugs,[5] or what about the U.S.-sponsored sanctions against Iraq which killed an estimated three to five thousand children in Iraq, each month,[6] or what about the $4 billion a year support the United States provides for Israel's occupation of Palestinian lands now in its thirty-sixth year, which is illegal, that is, in violation of UN resolutions specifically forbidding "the acquisition of territory by force," and which has resulted in many thousands of deaths, or if we want to go back further—what about the U.S. support for the Contras in Nicaragua, and of death squads in El Salvador, especially during the Reagan years, the U.S. use of terrorist counter-city threats of nuclear retaliation during the Cold War, and our actual use of nuclear weapons against Hiroshima and Nagasaki at the end of World War II, resulting in over 100,000 deaths.[7] Surely, all of these U.S. actions also turn out to be either terrorist acts or support for terrorist acts, according to our definition. How can we tell then, which, if any, of these terrorist acts, or support for terrorist acts, are morally justified?

THE PERSPECTIVE OF JUST-WAR THEORY AND PACIFISM

My preferred approach to addressing this question within the common ground of Kantian, utilitarian, and Aristotelian ethical theories is provided by pacifism and just-war theory, combined in a view I have called "just-war pacifism."[8] According to just-war pacifism, the just-cause and just-means requirements of just-war theory are so stringently interpreted that the few wars and large-scale conflicts that meet these requirements are the only wars and large-scale conflicts to which antiwar pacifists cannot reasonably object. Now one might think that from the perspective of just-war pacifism, acts of terrorism could never be morally justified. But this would require an absolute prohibition on intentionally harming innocents, and such a prohibition would not seem to be justified, even from the perspective of just-war pacifism.[9] Specifically, it seems, as we noted before, that harm to innocents can be justified for the sake of achieving a greater good when the harm is:

1. trivial (as in the case of stepping on someone's foot to get out of a crowded subway),
2. easily reparable (as in the case of lying to a temporarily depressed friend to keep her from committing suicide), or
3. nonreparable but greatly outweighed by the consequences of the action.

Obviously, it is this third category of harm that is relevant to the possible justification of terrorism. But when is intentional harm to innocents nonreparable yet greatly outweighed by the consequences?

Consider the following example.[10] A large person who is leading a party of spelunkers gets himself stuck in the mouth of a cave in which flood waters are rising. The trapped party of spelunkers just happens to have a stick of dynamite with which they can blast the large person out of the mouth of the cave; either they use the dynamite or they all drown, the large person with them. Now it is usually assumed in this case that it is morally permissible to dynamite the large person out of the mouth of the cave. After all, if that is not done, the whole party of spelunkers will die, the large person with them. So the sacrifice imposed on the large person in this case would not be that great.

But what if the large person's head is outside rather than inside the cave as it must have been in the previous interpretation of the case. Under these circumstances, the large person will not die when the other spelunkers drown. Presumably after slimming down a bit, he would eventually just squeeze his way out of the mouth of the cave. In this case, could the party of spelunkers trapped in the cave still legitimately use the stick of dynamite they have to save themselves rather than the large person?

Suppose there were 10, 20, 100, or whatever number you want of spelunkers trapped in the cave. At some point, won't the number be sufficiently great that it is morally acceptable for those in the cave to use the stick of dynamite to save themselves rather than the large person, even if this means that the large person is morally required to sacrifice his life? The answer has to be yes, even if you think it has to be a very unusual case when we can reasonably demand that people thus sacrifice their lives in this way.

Is it possible that some acts of terrorism are morally justified in this way? It is often argued that our dropping of atomic bombs on Hiroshima and Nagasaki was so justified. President Truman, who ordered the bombing, justified it on the grounds that it was used to shorten the war. In 1945, the United States demanded the unconditional surrender of Japan. The Japanese had by that time lost the war, but the leaders of their armed forces were by no means ready to accept unconditional surrender.[11] While the Japanese leaders expected an invasion of their mainland islands, they believed they could make that invasion so costly the United States would accept a conditional surrender. Truman's military advisors also believed the costs would be high. The capture of Okinawa had cost almost 80,000 American casualties, while almost the entire Japanese garrison of 120,000 men died in battle. If the mainland islands were defended in a similar manner, hundreds of thousands of Japanese would surely die. During that time, the bombing of Japan would continue, and perhaps intensify, resulting in casualty rates that were no different from those that were expected from the atomic attack. A massive incendiary raid on Tokyo early in March 1945 had set off a firestorm and killed an estimated 100,000 people. Accordingly, Truman's secretary of state James Byrnes admitted that the two atomic bombs did cause "many casualties, but not nearly so many as there would have been had our air force continued to drop incendiary bombs on Japan's cities."[12] Similarly, Winston Churchill wrote in support of Truman's decision "To avert a vast, indefinite butchery . . . at the cost of a few explosions seemed, after all our toils and perils, a miracle of deliverance."[13]

Yet the "vast, indefinite butchery" that the United States sought to avert by dropping atomic bombs on Hiroshima and Nagasaki was one that the United States itself was threatening, and had already started to carry out with its incendiary attack on Tokyo. And the United States itself could have easily avoided this butchery by dropping its demand for unconditional Japanese surrender. Moreover, a demand of unconditional surrender can almost never be morally justified since defeated aggressors almost always have certain rights that they are never required to surrender.[14] Hence, the U.S. terrorist acts of dropping atomic bombs on Hiroshima and Nagasaki cannot be justified on the grounds of shortening the war and avoiding a vast, indefinite butchery because the United States could have secured those results simply by giving up its unreasonable demand for unconditional surrender.

A more promising case for justified terrorism is the counter-city bombing of the British during the early stages of World War II. Early in the war, it became clear that British bombers could fly effectively only at night because too many of them were being shot down during day raids by German antiaircraft fire. In addition, a study done in 1941 showed only one-third of the planes flying at night that recorded success in attacking their targets, had actually managed to drop their bombs within five miles of what they were aiming at.[15] This meant that British bombers flying at night could reasonably aim at no target smaller than a fairly large city.[16]

Michael Walzer argues that under these conditions, British terror bombing was morally justified because at this early stage of the war, it was the only way the British had left to try to avert a Nazi victory.[17] Walzer further argues that the time period when such terror bombing was justified was relatively brief. Once the Russians began to inflict enormous casualties on the German army and the United States made available its manpower and resources, other alternatives opened up. Unfortunately, the British continued to rely heavily on terror bombing right up until the end of the war, culminating in the fire-bombing of Dresden in which something like 100,000 people were killed. However, for that relatively brief period of time when Britain had no other way to try to avert a Nazi victory, Walzer argues, its reliance on terror bombing was morally justified.

Suppose then we accept this moral justification for British terror bombing during World War II. Doesn't this suggest a comparable moral justification for Palestinian suicide bombings against Israeli civilians? Israel has been illegally occupying Palestinian land for thirty-six years now in violation of UN resolutions following the 1967 Arab-Israeli War. Even a return to those 1967 borders, which the UN resolutions require, still permits a considerable expansion of Israel's original borders as specified in the mandate of 1947.[18] Moreover, since the Oslo Peace Accords in 1993, Israeli settlements have doubled in the occupied territories. Since Sharon has been prime minister, more than thirty-five new settlements have been established in the occupied territories.[19] In Gaza, there are 1.2 million Palestinians and 4,000 Israelis, but the Israelis control 40 percent of the land and 70 percent of the water. In the West Bank, there are 1.9 million

Palestinians and 280,000 Israelis but the Israelis control 37 percent of the water.[20] In addition, Israel failed to abide by its commitments under the Oslo Peace Accords to release prisoners, to complete a third redeployment of its military forces, and to transfer three Jerusalem villages to Palestinian control.[21] Moreover, at the recent Camp David Meeting, Israeli's proposals did not provide for Palestinian control over East Jerusalem upon which 40 percent of the Palestinian economy depends.[22] Nor did Israeli's proposals provide for a right of return or compensation for the half of the Palestinian population that lives in exile (Clinton proposed that Arafat should just forget about them) most of them having been driven off their land by Israeli expansion. Nor has Bush's "Roadmap to Peace" yet offered the Paliestians a better deal. So the Palestinian cause is clearly a just one, but just as clearly the Palestinians lack the military resources to effectively resist Israeli occupation and aggression by simply directly attacking Israeli military forces. The Israelis have access to the most advanced U.S. weapons and $4 billion a year from the United States to buy whatever weapons they want. The Palestinians have no comparable support from anyone. It is under these conditions that a moral justification for Palestinian suicide bombers against Israeli civilians emerges.[23] Given that the Palestinians lack any effective means to try to end the Israeli occupation or to stop Israel's further expansion into Palestinian territories other than by using suicide bombers against Israeli civilians, why would this use of suicide bombers not be justified in much the same way that Walzer justifies the British terror bombing in the early stages of World War II?[24] If the Israelis have the ultimate goal of confining most Palestinians to a number of economically nonviable and disconnected reservations, similar to those on which the United States confines American Indian nations, then surely the Palestinians have a right to resist that conquest as best they can.[25]

Beginning with just-war pacifism, I have argued that there are morally defensible exceptions to the just-means prohibition against directly killing innocents. The cave-analogy argument aims to establish this conclusion. British terror bombing at the beginning of World War II, but not the American dropping of atomic bombs on Hiroshima and Nagasaki at the end of that war, is offered as a real-life instantiation of this argument. The Palestinian use of suicide bombers against Israeli civilians is then presented as a contemporary instantiation of that very same argument.[26]

Yet even if there is a moral justification for the Palestinian use of suicide bombers against Israeli civilians under present conditions, clearly most acts of terrorism cannot be justified, and clearly there was no moral justification for the terrorist attacks on New York City and Washington, D.C., particularly the attacks on the World Trade Center.[27]

IRAQI WAR II AS A RESPONSE TO TERRORISM

Nevertheless, the question remains as to whether the United States is morally justified in going to war against Iraq as part of a war against terrorism.

On 19 March 2003, George W. Bush ordered American forces "to disarm Iraq and depose Saddam Hussein."[28] In the course of this second war against Iraq, 138 coalition soldiers lost their lives, and an estimated 5,000 Iraqi civilians and tens of thousands of Iraqi soldiers who did not welcome the Americans as liberators also lost their lives before an end to major hostilities was declared on May 1.[29] Since then 804 coalition soldiers and an estimated 33,000 Iraqi civilians have also lost their lives in the continuing hostilities.[30] The justification for Iraqi War II was given by President Bush and by members of his administration starting in early September 2002.[31]

- On 12 September 2002, Bush declared before the United Nations General Assembly that Saddam Hussein "continues to develop weapons of mass destruction." "The first time we may be completely certain he has a nuclear weapon is when, God forbid, he uses one."
- That same month, Bush cited an International Atomic Energy Agency Report that he said showed Saddam Hussein was only months from having nuclear weapons, adding "I don't know what more evidence we need."
- In a 7 October 2002 speech, Bush declared: "In 1995, after several years of deceit by the Iraqi regime, the head of Iraq's military industries defected. It was then that the regime was forced to admit that it had produced more than 30,000 litres of anthrax and other deadly biological agents. . . . This is a massive stockpile of biological weapons that has never been accounted for, and capable of killing millions."

- On 29 January in his State of the Union message, Bush noted that the British government had learned that Saddam Hussein recently sought significant quantities of uranium from Africa.
- In his presentation to the UN Security Council on 5 February, Secretary of State Colin Powell claimed: "It took years for Iraq to finally admit that it had produced four tons of the deadly nerve agent VX. A single drop of VX on the skin will kill in minutes. Four tons. The admission only came out after inspectors collected documentation as a result of the defection of Hussein Kamel, Saddam Hussein's late son-in-law."
- In that same presentation, Powell claimed that Iraq was linked to Al Qaeda through Abu Musaab al-Zarqawi who maintained a poison and explosive training camp for Al Qaeda in northeastern Iraq.

So the main reasons offered by President Bush and members of his administration to justify going to war against Iraq were Iraq's possession of weapons of mass destruction, its continuing development of those weapons, and its connection to Al Qaeda's terrorist network.

In addition, Iraq was in a unique predicament with respect to weapons of mass destruction. Following the first war against Iraq, the UN Security Council had passed a number of resolutions (seventeen in all) some of which demanded that Iraq destroy all its weapons of mass destruction. So, unlike other nations, for Iraq to continue to possess and develop weapons of mass destruction placed it in violation of UN Security Council resolutions as well.[32] Could all these reasons taken together be thought to suffice to justify Iraqi War II?

THE APPLICATION OF JUST WAR PACIFISM TO IRAQI WAR II

To meet the requirements of just-war pacifism, there must be a just cause for Iraqi War II. This means there must be substantial aggression and the use of nonbelligerent correctives to respond to this aggression is either hopeless or too costly. It also means that the use of belligerent correctives to respond to this aggression is neither hopeless nor too costly. But what was the substantial aggression to which the U.S.-led forces were responding? Unlike Iraqi War I, Iraqi War II was not waged to oust Iraqi forces from another country. Rather, it was waged to remove weapons of mass destruction from Iraq itself. The Bush administration claimed that Iraq's possession and development of weapons of mass destruction in violation of UN Security Council Resolutions, together with its ties to Al Qaeda, constituted a threat that we were justified in going to war to eliminate.

Let us assume, for the sake of argument that a threat can be so serious that it alone can constitute an act of aggression sufficient to justify a military response.[33] For example, some have thought that the Soviet Union's deployment of missiles that could be armed with nuclear warheads in Cuba in 1962 posed such a threat to the United States.[34] So the question is whether Iraq also posed such a threat to the United States.

To answer this question, we first need to get clearer about what are weapons of mass destruction. There are three kinds of weapons of mass destruction: chemical, biological, and nuclear.[35] About all these weapons have in common is that they are illegal for at least some countries to use or even to possess. For example, while it is legal for some countries to possess nuclear weapons (including Russia, France, the United States, and the United Kingdom), it is illegal for other countries who have signed the Nuclear Nonproliferation Treaty to possess them. Certainly, these three kinds of weapons are not equally destructive, and in the case of chemical weapons, they are not really weapons of mass destruction at all.

Chemical weapons are basically battlefield artillery weapons. That is how they were used when they were first deployed in France during World War I. After the war, the Geneva Convention of 1925 outlawed their use. That neither side used them in World War II, even though they had built up enormous stocks just in case, was largely due to the fact that neither side could figure out any permanent military advantage from using them. In fact, except for a small-scale use by Soviet and Egyptian troops in the Yemeni Civil War in the 1960s, the convention was never violated until the Iran-Iraq War in the 1980s. But this is not so surprising once you consider that poison gas is really not a useful battlefield weapon, except in World War I–style circumstances, where you face an enemy with large numbers of infantry in densely populated trenches. It also helps if you face an enemy who does not have chemical weapons.

Actually, that was the situation that Saddam Hussein found himself in at the beginning of the Iran-Iraq War. Add to this that Hussein's own initial offensive into Iran had failed and that Iranian troops had advanced within a few miles of Basra, Iraq's second largest city. It was then that Iraq began using mustard gas to stop Iran's "human wave" attacks.[36] They did this with the full knowledge and substantial support of the United States. The Carter administration had in fact encouraged Iraq to go war against Iran. The Reagan administration further increased U.S. support for Iraq as the war progressed.[37]

Declassified U.S. government documents now reveal that Secretary of State George Shultz was given intelligence reports on 1 November 1983 reporting the "almost daily use of CW against Iran."[38] That same month, President Ronald Reagan signed a secret order instructing his administration to do "whatever was necessary and legal" to prevent Iraq from losing the war with Iran. On 20 December 1983, Donald Rumsfeld, then special envoy to the Middle East, now Bush's secretary of defense, traveled to Baghdad to tell Saddam Hussein personally that the U.S. government would regard "any major reversal of Iraq's fortunes as a strategic defeat for the West," and that the United States was ready for a resumption of full diplomatic relations immediately. Hussein was reportedly "extremely pleased" with Rumsfeld's visit but wanted to delay resumption of diplomatic relations until the following year.

According to a sworn affidavit prepared by Howard Teicher, a former National Security Council official, the United States, "actively supported the Iraqi war effort by supplying the Iraqis with billions of dollars in credits, by providing military intelligence and advice to the Iraqis, and by closely monitoring third country arms sales to Iraq to make sure Iraq had the military weaponry required."[39] The American government allowed vital ingredients for chemical weapons and missile components to be exported to Iraq, together with samples of all the strains of germs used by the United States to make biological weapons. The United States was also the sole country to vote against a 1986 Security Council statement condemning Iraq's use of mustard gas against Iranian troops. So when President Bush condemns Iraq for its past use of weapons of mass destruction, as he did in his 23 September 2003 speech before the United Nations, that condemnation includes this use against the Iranians, which at the time we supported.[40]

As many as 100,000 of Iran's war deaths in the Iran-Iraq War were due to Iraq's use of poison gas (which the Iranians eventually reciprocated), but delivering it on a battlefield requires thousands of poison gas shells per square mile in an artillery barrage.[41] To kill those 100,000 Iranians, Iraq probably used at least that many poison gas shells. Thus, while gas can be a useful battlefield weapon under certain conditions, it is hardly a weapon of choice for terrorists. More damage with a far higher level of confidence that your weapon would work would probably result from using a nail bomb instead of a poison gas dispenser of the same size and weight. This could be seen when the Japanese cult Aum Shinrikyo released sarin gas into the Tokyo subway system (eleven packages on five subway lines) and killed only twelve people.

So fifteen years after the Iran-Iraq War, did Saddam Hussein's regime still have poison gas weapons, even if they really aren't weapons of mass destruction, and even if they are not very useful for terrorists? It is possible that he did, although the UN arms inspectors who spent seven years in Iraq after Iraqi War I certainly found and destroyed the vast majority of Iraqi stocks. Rolf Ekeus, the chief UN inspector from 1991–1997, reported to the Security Council that 93 percent of Iraq's major weapons capacity had been destroyed.[42] Since chemical weapons degrade in five years or less, anything not destroyed by the UN inspectors would be useless by now. And new and large scale production facilities required to make chemical weapons in sufficient quantities are fairly easy to detect.[43]

But what about biological weapons? Aren't they genuinely weapons of mass destruction? According to Gwynne Dyer, the answer is that nobody really knows for sure because they have never been used in war, apart from Japanese attacks on eleven Chinese cities before and during World War II, and also during World War II by the Russians against the Germans near Stalingrad, but in each of these cases, the country using the biological weapons appeared to suffer at least as many causalities as their foes from its use.[44] Aum Shinrikyo tried to attack the Japanese parliament with botulism toxin in 1990 and in 1993 sprayed anthrax spores from the roof of a building in Tokyo, but moved on to nerve gas because these biological agents produced no discernible effect at all.[45] The only other well-known example we have of the actual use of bio-weapons is the post-9/11 anthrax attacks in the United States, in which a still-unidentified terrorist–probably a disgruntled former employee from a U.S. government lab–managed to disrupt the mail, inspire a number of hoaxes, but in the end only killed four or five people, clearly not a mass killing by anyone's measure.[46]

In order for biological weapons to qualify as genuine weapons of mass destruction, they must have the ability to be dispersed secretly and effectively so as to quickly kill a large number of people. As Dyer points out, in developed countries, this is harder to do than it seems, since the usual human immunities mean that most diseases spread relatively slowly, and that normal medical reporting procedures ensure that outbreaks will quickly be detected and contained by vaccination and quarantine measures.[47] Consider, for example, how the city of Toronto managed to effectively contain the SARS epidemic that struck the city by quarantining almost 20,000 people.

The one disease that clearly does cause a lot of worry is smallpox, given that most people now have no immunity against it because vaccinations ceased once it was eradicated over thirty years ago. The only surviving samples of the virus, as far as we know, are in government laboratories in the United States and Russia. Of course, it is possible that other countries might have found some way to acquire the virus, but, as Dyer points out, the most realistic measure of the level of threat felt in this regard is the fact that the entire population of Western countries could be protected from smallpox infection by a program of vaccination, but because the vaccine kills about one in a million of the people who take it, that risk is regarded as too high to impose on the general population.[48]

If you really want to determine what military experts think about the comparative value of the different weapons that are normally grouped together as weapons of mass destruction, consider the fact that of all the money spent on these weapons since the end of World War II, very little has been spent on chemical and biological weapons. As much as 98 percent of it has been spent on nuclear weapons. Over that period of time, the United States and Russia together have built around fifty thousand nuclear weapons—at the cost of hundreds of billions of dollars, although about half of these weapons have now been destroyed. Six other countries have followed suit—Britain, France, Israel, China, India, and Pakistan have acquired between five hundred and fifty nuclear warheads each. And still other nations are hoping to join this exclusive club. So unless the nuclear powers take credible steps toward nuclear disarmament, these numbers are likely to grow.[49]

There is also the fear that one or more of these true weapons of mass destruction might fall into the hands of terrorists. At the same time, there is a general consensus that it is unlikely that mere terrorists, lacking the resources of a state, could build such weapons themselves.[50] To make even the simplest of nuclear weapons requires an investment of hundreds of millions of dollars, a lot of electrical power, and access to strictly controlled raw materials and precision machinery. Terrorists are just not going to put a nuclear weapon together in a basement somewhere.[51] But might they not steal or be given one?

The fear that a nuclear weapon might fall into the hands of terrorists probably peaked just after the collapse of the Soviet Union in 1991.[52] At the time, there were large numbers of warheads outside of Russia in other former Soviet Republics, and even the security and accounting procedures for nuclear weapons within Russia were somewhat lax. By 1993–94, however, with American assistance to the Russian authorities, all the weapons were back on Russian soil and security measures had dramatically improved. Of course, we can't be certain that during the period of transition, one or two nuclear warheads did not end up in terrorist hands. But if they did, why would the terrorists wait over ten years to use or threaten to use them?

There is, of course, the worry that some "outlaw" state might just give a nuclear weapon to a terrorist group. Members of the Bush administration suggested that that is what Saddam Hussein would have done had he succeeded in acquiring nuclear weapons. Of course, Hussein did spend many billions of dollars over a period of more than a decade (1979–1991) in an attempt to build nuclear weapons. But if we are to understand what Hussein might have done with them if he had acquired them, we need to understand why he wanted them in the first place. During the time that Hussein was seeking nuclear weapons, he was our friend and received considerable military and diplomatic support from us. So his goal in acquiring nuclear weapons was not to threaten us but rather to deter Israel, who unlike Iraq, had never signed the Nuclear Nonproliferation Treaty and who, with the illegal help of the French, had secretly assembled about two hundred nuclear weapons.[53] Of course, Saddam Hussein would never have been able to match Israel's nuclear arsenal and means of delivery, but having just a few nuclear weapons could have constituted a sufficient deterrent; Israel most likely would never have sought to obliterate Iraq with nuclear weapons, or even threaten to do so, knowing that it might lose one or two of its own cities to a nuclear attack. In addition, Hussein may have been able to extend this deterrence to other Muslim countries as well, thereby securing considerable honor and prestige for himself and his country in the Muslim world. In any case, this was hardly the strategy of a madman. Nor was it morally appropriate for the United States to simply press Iraq to disarm, leaving Israel as the undisputed nuclear power in the Middle East. Rather, the United States should have demanded that *all* countries in the Middle East renounce nuclear weapons.

Following Iraqi War I, however, the UN inspectors were able to completely destroy Iraq's potential to make nuclear weapons, and, at the same time, the sanctions made it impossible for Iraq to import the raw materials and specialized equipment needed to re-start its nuclear program. So in the run-up to Iraqi War II, Iraq presented no nuclear threat of mass destruction to anyone, and this would have continued to be the case as long as Iraq was kept from importing certain raw materials and specialized equipment and building a large nuclear processing facility. At the same time, to remove the incentive for Muslim countries to acquire nuclear weapons, Israel should have been (and still should be) required to give up its nuclear weapons and sign the Nuclear Nonproliferation Treaty.

Given, then, that the evidence available before Iraqi War II indicated Iraq lacked any nuclear weapons, or the wherewithal to develop them, and given that the evidence showed Iraq could only have had degrading remnants of its past stockpiles of chemical and biological weapons, which in any case were not truly weapons of mass destruction, there clearly was no justification for going to war with Iraq, certainly not one based on a threat of weapons of mass destruction.

Nor was there any justification for going to war based on evidence that Iraq might pass off the small amounts of the chemical or biological weapons it might have had to Osama bin Laden and his Al Qaeda network. There was no reputable evidence at all linking Bin Laden and Al Qaeda with Iraq. In his presentation to the UN Security Council, Secretary of State Powell claimed that Iraq was linked to Al Qaeda through Abu Musaab al-Zarqawi who maintained a poison and explosive training camp for Al Qaeda in northeastern Iraq. But this supposed link was undercut by the fact that the camp was maintained in an area of Iraq that was controlled, not by Saddam Hussein, but by the Kurds. Moreover, previous attempts to find a link between Saddam Hussein and Al Qaeda had similarly failed.[54] In fact, it was recently revealed that independent interrogations of both Abu Zubaydah, Al Qaeda planner and recruiter, and Khalid Sheikh Mohamed, Al Qaeda chief of operations, both indicated no connections between Al Qaeda and Iraq. But this evidence was never made public by the Bush administration as they pressed for war with Iraq.[55] In fact, the only countries for which there is strong evidence of material support for Bin Laden and his Al Qaeda network are Saudi Arabia and Pakistan, and these countries claim to be our allies. And, for a variety of reasons, the Bush administration is currently suppressing evidence of their involvement in terrorist networks against us.[56] Interestingly, in the wake of 9/11, when all nonmilitary planes were grounded, the White House provided private planes to whisk two dozen members of the Bin Laden family out of the United States to the safety of Saudi Arabia without seriously questioning any of them.[57]

Given, then, that Iraq did not present us with a threat of weapons of mass destruction either directly, or indirectly through Al Qaeda, not even the first requirement of a just cause for Iraqi War II was met. There was simply no substantial aggression to respond to here, even when we allow that a threat of an appropriate magnitude could itself constitute substantial aggression. There just was no evidence of such a threat.

Yet maybe the evidence that the United States had before Iraq War II was inadequate, and maybe now that the U.S.-led forces are in control of Iraq, they will be able to show that Saddam Hussein really did have stockpiles of usable chemical and biological weapons and that he really was attempting to develop nuclear weapons. Of course, the justification for going to war must be based on the evidence that was available before the war. It can't be based on evidence that turns up after the war is over. After over a year in Iraq, U.S.-led coalition forces had found only two mobile labs, which may or may not have been used to produce biological weapons (weapons, I have argued, that do not really qualify as weapons of mass destruction). However, no chemical or biological weapons themselves or any precursors of such weapons have been found, except for one vial of a precursor biological agent discovered in the home of an Iraqi scientist.[58] Before the war, Bush administration officials ridiculed the inability of UN weapons inspectors to turn up evidence of chemical or biological or nuclear weapons, and now without anyone impeding the U.S. search for such weapons, the United States has not been able to uncover anything of significance other than the two mobile labs. The labs themselves show no trace of such weapons, and Iraqi scientists in custody claim that they were used legitimately to produce hydrogen for balloons to direct artillery. While the United States has not permitted any independent evaluation, many outsiders and some within the U.S. and British intelligence have concluded the vehicles are designed to do exactly what the Iraqis claimed—produce hydrogen for balloons to direct artillery.[59] In fact, the United States has a fleet of mobile labs designed exactly for the same purpose.[60] Yet even if there had been more ambiguous evidence about such mobile labs before Iraqi War II, it still would not have been enough to justify the United States going to war against Iraq. Most recently, David Kay, the head of the U.S. effort to find banned weapons in Iraq, himself a strong advocate of going to war against Iraq, resigned his position, claiming that he now believes that Iraq had no weapons of mass destruction when the United States invaded the country.[61]

THE DELIBERATE DECEPTION OF THE AMERICAN PEOPLE

Unfortunately, the situation with respect to the justification for Iraqi War II is even worse. Not only was there sufficient evidence available to show that Iraq did not threaten us with weapons of mass destruction either directly or indirectly through Al Qaeda, but there is also considerable evidence now available that President Bush and members of his administration either deliberately lied about whether Iraq presented such a threat or were grossly incompetent in using intelligence agencies to inform themselves in this regard. It is also unlikely that they were just incompetent. More likely, they deliberately lied to the American people concerning Iraq.

Consider the evidence. In September 2002, Bush cited an International Atomic Energy Report that he said showed Saddam Hussein was only months from having nuclear weapons. In fact, the report said no such thing. As Paul Krugman of the *New York Times* noted, this "discrepancy" was initially reported for a few hours as the lead story on MSNBC's Web site, which bore the headline "White House: Bush Misstated Report on Iraq." Then the story disappeared—not just from the top of the page, but from the site.[62]

In his State of the Union message, Bush claimed that the British government had learned that Saddam Hussein recently sought significant quantities of uranium from Africa. This was reported in a fifty-page document issued by the British government in September 2002. It was based on documents showing that Iraq had tried to buy uranium from Niger so it could build nuclear weapons. As it turns out, earlier, Vice President Cheney's office had asked for an investigation of the uranium deal. So a former U.S. ambassador to Africa was dispatched to Niger.[63] In February 2002, according to someone present at the meetings, that envoy reported to the CIA and State Department that the information was unequivocally wrong and that the documents had been forged. One official document was signed with the name of Allele Habibou, a Niger Minister of Foreign Affairs and Cooperation, who had been out of office for over ten years. In addition, the Niger mining program was structured so that a large diversion (five hundred tons of uranium oxide) was impossible. The envoy's debunking of the forgery was passed around the administration and seemed to be accepted—except that President Bush and members of his administration kept citing it.[64]

In February 2003, the British government issued another report presented as up-to-the-minute British intelligence on Iraq, which Secretary of State Powell praised in his presentation before the UN Security Council.[65] This report was quickly exposed as having been extensively plagiarized (eleven of nineteen pages) from three nonsecret published articles.[66] The main article, which was written by an American postgraduate student, was based on material that was over ten years old. Even typographical errors and anomalous uses of grammar from the original articles were included. The only substantial difference in the report is that the estimate of the size of the Fedayeen Saddam, given in one of the articles as between 18,000–40,000, was inflated to between 30,000–40,000. To win support for going to war, the British government needed an up-to-date report, and this unconscionable deception is what the government provided and what the U.S. government endorsed.

As we noted earlier, both Bush and Powell, as well as Cheney and other members of the U.S. government, had cited testimony provided by General Hussein Kamel, Saddam Hussein's son-in-law, who defected in 1995. Kamel testified that Iraq had produced large amounts of chemical and biological weapons, and this part of Kamel's testimony is unfailingly reported by Bush and members of his administration. But Kamel also testified in the same debriefing that Iraq had destroyed all of these weapons. How do you explain the failure to quote this part of Kamel's testimony except as an attempt to deceive the American people?

Recently Robin Cook, former Blair Cabinet Minister, revealed that Blair, at least weeks prior to the war, knew that Saddam Hussein possessed no weapons of mass destruction, and that Blair's real reason for going to war was to maintain whatever influence he had with the Bush administration.[67]

Recent attention has also been drawn to a briefing that Secretary of State Powell gave to the Egyptian Foreign Minister in February 2001. Responding to a question about the usefulness of sanctions against Iraq, Powell, had this to say:

> He (Saddam Hussein) has not developed any significant capacity with respect to weapons of mass destruction. He is unable to project conventional power against his neighbors.[68]

Since no evidence was ever offered that the sanctions had failed just in the two-year period prior to Iraqi War II, the Bush administration's real assessment of any threat from Iraq has to be the one that Powell gave to the Egyptian foreign minister, namely, that there was no threat at all. The rest is lies.

On the eve of the invasion in a nationally televised speech, President Bush told the American people: "Should Saddam Hussein choose confrontation, the American people can know that every measure was taken to avoid war." But it has now come to light that in secret talks before the war, Hassan al-Obeidi, chief of foreign operations for Iraq's intelligence service, insisted that Iraq had no weapons of mass destruction and offered to allow two thousand FBI agents "to look wherever they wanted."[69] Al-Obeidi maintained that Iraq wanted to cooperate with the Bush administration and could not understand why it was being targeted in the "war on terrorism" since it had no links to Al Qaeda. Al-Obeidi contended that if oil was the issue, Iraq would approve oil concessions to U.S. companies. If it was the peace process, Iraq would support Bush's roadmap for an Israeli-Palestinian settlement. In subsequent talks with Lt. General Tahir Jalil Habbush, the director of Iraqi intelligence service, there was even the offer to turn over Abdul Rahman Yasin, at that time in an Iraqi jail, who the United States wanted in connection with the 1993 World Trade Center bombing and had offered a $25 million reward for information leading to his capture and conviction.[70] If regime change was what was wanted, Habbush even offered to hold UN-supervised elections. The substance of these talks was conveyed to Richard Perle, an influential adviser to the administration. Perle contacted the CIA to see if he should meet directly with the Iraqis. According to Perle, the message came back: "Tell them that we will see them in Baghdad." So much for the United States exhausting nonbelligerent correctives before going to war.

A few years ago, President Bill Clinton was almost impeached by the U.S. Senate and driven from office for lying about an affair he had had with White House intern Monica Lewinsky, which was the only charge that a $40 million investigation by independent counsel Kenneth Starr was able to bring. At the time, conservative pundit, William Bennett, author the *Book of the Virtues* and the *Children's Book of Virtues,* and recently better known for his multimillion gambling losses at Las Vegas casinos, claimed that Clinton by his indiscretions had damaged the American presidency and thereby deserved impeachment.[71] For several months, the investigation into whether Clinton had lied about his relationship with Monica Lewinsky, and, if he had, whether this was an impeachable offense, virtually put a halt to any new legislative initiatives by the federal government. Yet in any fair comparison, the lying of President Bush and members of his administration is far more significant than Clinton's actions. President Bush and the members of his administration deprived the United States of the wherewithal to function as a democracy. For a democracy to function, its citizens and especially their representatives must not be deprived of the information they need to make the major decisions affecting their country. Information pertaining to whether a country should go to war is clearly information that is relevant to a major decision for any country. Information pertaining to the private sex life of one of its members, even the president of the republic, is clearly not of that sort. It was only made a topic of public concern in the United States as part of a concerted effort to keep Clinton from implementing his political agenda. By contrast, the lying of President Bush and members of his administration strikes at the heart of the republic. It is nothing less than an attempt to undermine the functioning of the American democracy, and it should be treated as such. By grossly deceiving the American people about Iraq, President Bush and the members of his administration have also undercut their own legal and moral authority for representing the American people and waging war on our behalf. For this, they should be impeached or driven from office.

OTHER POSSIBLE JUSTIFICATIONS FOR THE WAR

In the aftermath of Iraqi War II and the failure to find a nuclear weapons program or the large arsenals of chemical and biological weapons which it was claimed could be deployed within forty-five minutes,[72] some have begun to suggest that we really didn't need the threat of weapons of mass destruction to justify our going to war.[73] As Thomas Friedman, the chief foreign affairs columist for the *New York Times,* put it in a op-ed piece:

> As far as I'm concerned, we do not need to find any weapons of mass destruction to justify this war. Mr. Bush doesn't owe the world any explanation for missing chemical weapons. It is clear that ending Saddam's tyranny [is enough].[74]

In a later op-ed piece, Friedman expanded upon his view, distinguishing between the stated reason, the right reason, and the moral reason for going to war against Iraq.[75] The stated reason is, of course, that Saddam Hussein had weapons of mass destruction that posed a threat to us. The right reason was that we needed to turn back the hatred for America by doing something good for the Iraqi people—liberating them from Saddam Hussein. And the moral reason was that Saddam Hussein deserved to be overthrown because of his past atrocities. Friedman allows that Bush appealed to the "stated reason" only to get U.S. and world support. But he thinks that the "right reason" and the "moral reason" could have sufficed to justify Iraqi War II. But they could not have sufficed.

In order for reasons to justify a course of action, they must be fittingly related to the course of action; they must be the ends for which the course of action is the most appropriate and effective means. But Iraqi War II is not the most appropriate and effective means for realizing the ends that Friedman endorses. If we wanted to use $70 billion (the first installment for the war in Iraq), another $87 billion (as a second installment), and now $36 billion more (a third installment) to turn back the hate for America, we could have offered to handsomely resettle all Palestinian refugees and also made a significant dent in world hunger. That would be a far more appropriate and effective way of pursuing Friedman's "right reason." Friedman's "moral reason" could also be more appropriately and effectively pursued by first exposing and driving from power those in the United States, both inside and outside the Bush administration, who aided and supported Saddam Hussein's past atrocities, and then by terminating our economic and military support for comparable dictators and autocrats around the world. If after having thus appropriately addressed our own moral failings in this regard, we still wanted to oppose Saddam Hussein and the few other dictators and autocrats around the world that remain without U.S. support, we would still have had to exhaust the use of nonbelligerent correctives.[76] But this is not what we did at all. So we had no justification for going to war against Iraq on any conceivable grounds.

It is also important to note that the United States applied considerable pressure and offered large financial incentives in its failed attempt to gain approval from the UN Security Council for Iraqi War II. After the negative vote, the United States took whatever steps it could to punish those countries that voted against it.[77] The United States promised Turkey as much as $26 billion in economic aid to permit U.S. troops to open a northern front against Iraq, but its elected parliament voted the offer down. Subsequently, on a visit to Turkey, U.S. Deputy Secretary of Defense[78] Paul Wolfowitz openly questioned why the Turkish military did not play a stronger role in forcing its elected government to vote in favor of Iraqi War II.[79] So much for the U.S. claim to be a strong supporter of democracy in the Middle East.

CONCLUSION

When Americans reflect upon world affairs, most of them regard the two world wars as paradigms of their country's military involvement in other countries. World War I was the "War to End All Wars" and

World War II was the "War for Four Freedoms." Both wars are viewed as good wars, although, in fact, only parts of each war were good or just.[80] Most Americans do not like to think too much about other, earlier wars that pitted Americans against other nations: the conquest and extermination of American Indian nations which only ended in 1890, the Mexican-American War of 1846–48 and the Spanish-American War of 1898. Of course, today Americans might recognize these past wars as unjust, but they usually tend to identify them with a youthful, immature nation, not the America with which they identify that fought in the two world wars. However, if you reflect upon many of the more recent U.S. military interventions into other countries—for example, U.S. interventions into Chile, Nicaragua, Panama, Grenada, Lebanon, Sudan, Afghanistan, and the ten-year-long U.S. intervention into Vietnam, which left three million Vietnamese dead—these interventions do tend to resemble more those earlier wars with which we do not identify than the two world wars with which we do. At least, this is how most people in other countries have come to think about us in recent years as "the greatest threat to peace."[81] And now we have our military occupation of Iraq, the result of a blatantly unjust war that our leaders deceived us into waging. The portents are not good. Under the Bush administration, the United States has definitely begun to strongly reidentify itself with its colonial past. So unless we begin to take meaningful steps to undo the injustice of Iraqi War II and begin to take other steps to be good citizens of the world, we will soon be clearly forced to see ourselves and our country differently, the way many people of other countries already regard us, and I don't think many of us will like what we will see.

CHAPTER EIGHT

Conclusion

The conclusions I reached in this book are the result of a peacemaking way of doing philosophy. If I had adopted the standard warmaking way of doing philosophy I would have never reached the conclusions I did. Instead of trying to find common ground between Aristotelian and Kantian ethics, as I did in chapter 2, I would have focused on what appears to divide these ethical perspectives. I would not have given each perspective its most morally defensible interpretation. I would have interpreted either Aristotelian or Kantian ethics in an unsympathetic way so that it was in conflict with the other over the ideal of a morally good or virtuous person, over whether moral assessment requires a decision-procedure like Kant's Categorical Imperative, and over the importance of rules to morality, rather than finding the agreement I did in each of these areas. I would not even have looked for, and so probably never found, the justification for morality that I set out in this chapter, which both Aristotelians and Kantians can accept. If I had adopted the standard warmaking way of doing philosophy when taking up the question in chapter 3 of whether both Aristotelian and Kantian ethical theories, suitably refurbished, are in serious conflict with utilitarian ethical theories, suitably refurbished, I would have interpreted utilitarian theory in an unfavorable way, as is frequently done, so that it is incompatible with the "ought" implies "can" principle, and, therefore, in conflict with both Rawlsian welfare liberalism and libertarianism. Proceeding in this warmaking way, I would not have been able to find the common ground I did between Kantian and utilitarian theories.

In chapter 4, if I had adopted the standard warmaking way of doing philosophy instead of attempting to extend the reconciliation between Kantian and Aristotelian ethics, I would have not required each ethical theory to provide a non-question-begging justification for its stance on the moral status of nonhuman life. Accordingly, I would not have been able to derive the principles of defense, self-preservation, disproportionality, and restitution as morally appropriate conflict resolution principles that should be acceptable to both Kantians and Aristotelians. The use of a peacemaking way of doing philosophy was essential to attaining these results.

Those who engage in a peacemaking way of doing philosophy are committed to:

1. a fair-mindedness which, among other things, puts the most favorable interpretation on the views of one's opponents,
2. an openness which reaches out to understand challenging new views,
3. a self-criticalness that requires modifying or abandoning one's views should the weight of available evidence require it.[1]

In chapter 2, a fair-mindedness that puts the most favorable interpretation on the views of one's opponents was essential for reaching agreement between Kantian and Aristotelian ethics. In chapter 4, an openness that reaches out to understand challenging new views was needed in order to give a rarely considered nonanthropocentrism the chance to show its moral superiority to the commonly held anthropocentrism. And, in chapter 3, a self-criticalness that requires modifying or abandoning one's views should the weight of available evidence require it was needed because until now I had, like many others, failed to recognize that utilitarianism can be given a more morally defensible interpretation.

Now when taking up specific moral problems, as I do in chapters 5, 6, and 7, a peacemaking way of doing philosophy is especially important. Disagreements over sexual harassment, affirmative action, and international terrorism and Iraqi War II run deep in the United States and elsewhere. In the case of sexual harassment, men and women, as we noted, frequently disagree about what is sexual harassment and, therefore, about what should be prohibited. Here, it was especially important to define sexual harassment in an inclusive way that takes into account what is reasonable for everyone affected to accept and to take as one of the positive norms for ridding society of sexual harassment the inclusive ideal of androgyny, according to which the traits that are truly desirable and distributable in society should be equally open to both women and men, or in the case of virtues, equally expected of both women and men.

Affirmative action has also been subject to a warmaking way of doing philosophy. Opponents of affirmative action frequently define it in ways that defenders never accept and then go on to condemn what defenders of affirmative action never endorse. Following a peacemaking way of doing philosophy, it is important to define affirmative action in such a way that does not presuppose that it is either morally objectionable or morally acceptable. Accordingly, as I define it, affirmative action is the policy of favoring qualified woman and minority candidates over qualified men or nonminority candidates with the immediate goals of outreach, remedying discrimination, or achieving diversity, and the ultimate goals of attaining a colorblind (racially just) and a gender-free (sexually just) society. Thus, standard critics of affirmative action, like Carl Cohen and Terry Pell, will still endorse some forms of outreach and remedial affirmative action captured by the definition, while rejecting other forms, especially diversity affirmative action. In contrast, standard defenders of affirmative action will endorse all the forms of affirmative action captured by the definition.

In defending affirmative action, a peacemaking way of doing philosophy also requires facing the strongest objections head-on and responding to them fairly. Thus in working out a defense of affirmative action in chapter 6, I sought out some of the best known opponents, in particular, Carl Cohen, who used the freedom of information act to get information about the University of Michigan's affirmative action programs which he then gave to the Center for Individual Rights, and Terry Pell, under whose leadership, the Center for Individual Rights brought the lawsuits against the University of Michigan which led to the recent Supreme Court decisions, *Grutter v. Bollinger* (2003) and *Gratz v. Bollinger* (2003). Cohen and I have coauthored a point/counterpoint book, *Affirmative Action and Racial Preference* (Oxford, 2003), and Pell and I have now published two symposia on affirmative action, one just before the Michigan decisions and one just after them. In this way, as required by a peacemaking way of doing philosophy, I have tried to become as knowledgeable as I can of the strongest objections to affirmative action and I have tried to respond to them in my work.

International terrorism and Iraqi War II also presents a significant problem for a peacemaking way of doing philosophy. In the wake of 9/11, I have tried to conform to its dictates by bringing together a number of prominent scholars from a variety of perspectives to reflect on international terrorism and what should be the moral response to it. Their essays were collected together and published as *Terrorism and International Justice* (Oxford, 2003). Working on this volume and presenting to various audiences earlier versions of my own contribution to it made me aware of the different views scholars and politicians have taken on international terrorism and what seemed to me to be the most morally defensible stance to take with respect to it. The stance I take in chapter 7–that suicide bombing can be morally justified under certain conditions–is clearly not a popular one, but it is what I think results, somewhat surprisingly, from taking a peacemaking way of doing philosophy.

With regard to Iraqi War II, which still continues as of this writing, I proceeded with my discussion as I have for all the major chapters of this book. I have presented my views to as many audiences and as many scholars knowledgeable in the area as I could–just the sort of thing that is required by a peacemaking way of doing philosophy. In the process, the more I learned, it was sad to find the moral case against Iraqi War II growing stronger and stronger. However, it is important for Americans, in particular, to face up to the reality that its government is engaged in a blatantly unjust war against the Iraqi people.

Doing ethics so as resolve moral problems is never easy, but the task is far easier to carry out once we recognize the common ground that exists among the most morally defensible interpretations of Kantian, utilitarian, and Aristotelian ethics. It is this common ground, along with the merely formal tenets that are shared by contemporary defenders of Kantian, utilitarian, and Aristotelian ethical theories respectively, that help to generate the triumph of practice over theory in ethics.

NOTES

CHAPTER 1

1. Martha Nussbaum, "Recoiling from Reason," *New York Review of Books,* 36 (1989).
2. Immanuel Kant, *Observations on the Feeling of the Beautiful and the Sublime,* trans. John Goldthwait (Berkeley: University of California Press, 1960), 111. Immanuel Kant, *The Metaphysical Elements of Justice,* trans. John Ladd (New York: The Bobbs Merrill Co., 1965), Sect. 46. Kant also held that to achieve cosmopolitanism, the aim of human history, "all races, save that of the whites . . . will be exterminated." *Reflexion zur Anthropologie* note 1520 AA XV/2, 878. Kant held that the reason for this is that all races, save that of the whites, were incapable of self-governance.
3. John Stuart Mill, diary entry, 26 January 1854, in *Collected Works of John Stuart Mill,* 33 vols., ed., John Robson (Toronto: University of Toronto Press, 1962–91). Ibid. *On Liberty,* chapter 1.
4. Harriet Taylor, "The Enfranchisement of Women," in *Essays on Sex Equality,* ed. Alice S. Rossi (Chicago: University of Chicago Press, 1970), 105.
5. *The Politics of Aristotle,* trans. Ernest Barker (London: Oxford University Press, 1946), 1253b 3–4.
6. Ibid., 1253b 1–1255a 11.
7. Ibid., 1330a 14.
8. Ibid., 1259b 1–1260b 16; *The Generation of Animals,* trans. A. L. Peck (Cambridge: Harvard University Press, 1943), 737a 27–38.
9. *Generation of Animals,* 727a 3–4.
10. Ibid., 766a 17–21.
11. *Politics,* 1334 b 1–1335b 12.
12. Immanuel Kant, "What Is Enlightenment?" in *The Philosophy of Kant: Immanuel Kant's Moral and Political Writings,* trans. and ed. Carl Friedrich (New York: The Modern Library, 1949), 132–140.
13. Kant, *Observations on the Feeling of the Beautiful and the Sublime,* 78.
14. See Linda Gardiner, "Women in Science," in *French Women and the Age of Enlightenment,* ed. Samia Spenser (Bloomington: Indiana University Press,

1984), 181–197, and H. J. Mozans, *Woman in Science* (Notre Dame: University of Notre Dame Press, 1991), 151–153.

15. For further argument, see Robin May Schott, "The Gender of Enlightenment," in *What Is Enlightenment,* ed. James Schmidt (Berkley: University of California, 1996), 471–488.

16. Another way to put this point is that justice and fairness are goods within an Aristotelian perspective.

CHAPTER 2

1. For example, Alasdair MacIntyre, *After Virtue* (Notre Dame: University of Notre Dame Press, 1981); *Whose Justice? Which Rationality?* (Notre Dame: University of Notre Dame Press, 1988).

2. Philippa Foot, *Virtues and Vices* (Berkeley: University of California Press, 1978), 8–18; Rosalind Hursthouse, *On Virtue Ethics* (Oxford: Oxford University Press, 1999); Marcia Baron, Philip Pettit, and Michael Slote, *Three Methods of Ethics* (Oxford: Blackwell Publishers, 1997), 3–91.

3. Some contemporary Aristotelians still reject this view. According to Alasdair MacIntyre, if someone confronting a great danger has the right amount and kind of fear and confidence for that danger and someone else confronting a slight danger has the right amount and kind of fear and confidence for that danger, the two are equally virtuous. (e-mail to author, October 26, 2003). This would mean that someone who overcame a tremendous fear in order to rescue a small child from a burning building and someone who overcame a lesser fear to rescue a cat from a tree are equally virtuous. I have trouble understanding how this would be the case.

4. See Thomas E. Hill, *Respect, Pluralism, and Justice* (Oxford: Oxford University Press, 2000), chapter 2.

5. Now it may be possible to save Kant's ethical theory here by interpreting legislation in a universal Kingdom of Ends as choice behind the veil of ignorance in John Rawls's original position. Actually, we will take up that possibility in the next chapter.

6. Walter Schaller, "Are Virtues No More than Dispositions to Obey Moral Rules?" *Philosophy* 20 (July 1990): 195–207.

7. Rosalind Hursthouse claims "that virtue ethics not only comes up with rules (. . . couched in terms that derived from the virtues and vices) but further, does not exclude the more familiar deontological rules." *On Virtue Ethics,* 39. Rules of the first sort would be of the less informative kind we considered. Those of the second sort would be of the more informative kind we considered.

8. Hursthouse, *On Virtue Ethics,* 91.

9. Baron, Pettit, and Slote, *Three Methods,* 48.

10. On the strengths and weaknesses of Aristotle's and Kant's accounts of friendship, see Nancy Sherman, *Making a Necessity of Virtue: Aristotle and Kant on Virtue* (Cambridge: Cambridge University Press, 1997), chapter 5.

11. In subsequent chapters, I will consider still other ways to reconcile Kantian and Aristotelian ethical perspectives.
12. Although egoism is an ethical perspective because it provides norms about how one should behave, it is not a moral perspective because it never requires a person to sacrifice her overall interest for the sake of others.
13. John Rawls is typical here. See his *A Theory of Justice* (Cambridge: Harvard University Press, 1971), 136.
14. Ibid.
15. "Ought" presupposes "can" here. So unless people have the capacity to entertain and follow both self-interested and moral reasons for acting, it does not make any sense asking whether they ought or ought not to do so. Moreover, moral reasons here are understood to necessarily include (some) altruistic reasons but not necessarily to exclude (all) self-interested reasons. So the question of whether it would be rational for us to follow self-interested reasons rather than moral reasons should be understood as the question of whether it would be rational for us to follow self-interested reasons exclusively rather than some appropriate set of self-interested reasons and altruistic reasons, other things being equal.
16. I understand the pure altruist to be the mirror image of the pure egoist. Whereas the pure egoist thinks that the interests of others count for them but not for herself except instrumentally, the pure altruist thinks that her own interests count for others but not for herself except instrumentally.
17. This is one standard strategy to avoid begging the question. Another standard strategy is to assume the premises that one's opponent accepts and then argue from those premises. Still another strategy is to put the best construction on one's opponent's view and only then determine what follows from the view so construed. In the next chapter, I employ both of these other strategies.
18. Nell Nodding, *Caring: A Feminine Approach to Ethics and Moral Education* (Berkeley: University of California Press, 1984); Joyce Trebilcot, ed. *Mothering* (Totowa, N.J.: Rowman and Littlefield, 1983); Susan Brownmiller, *Femininity* (New York: Ballantine Books, 1984).
19. James Doyle, *The Male Experience* (Dubuque, Iowa: W. C. Brown & Co., 1983); Marie Richmond-Abbot, ed. *Masculine and Feminine,* 2nd ed. (New York: Random House, 1991).
20. Victor Seidler, *Rediscovering Masculinity* (New York: Routledge, 1989); Larry May and Robert Strikwerda, *Rethinking Masculinity* (Lanham, Md.: Rowman and Littlefield, 1992).
21. This is not to deny that we usually have greater knowledge and certainty about what is in our own self-interest than about what is in the interest of others, and that this difference in our knowledge and certainty can have a practical effect on what good we should do in particular contexts. It is just that, as I will point out shortly, the debate between egoism and morality gets started at the theoretical level where no assumption is made about this

difference in our knowledge and certainty, since we can, and frequently do, have adequate knowledge and certainty about both what is in our own self-interest and what is in the interest of others.

22. I am assuming that acting contrary to reason is a significant failing with respect to the requirements of reason, and that there are many ways of not acting in (perfect) accord with reason that do not constitute acting contrary to reason.

23. For a discussion of the causal links involved here, see Subcommittee of International Economic Policy and Trade of the Committee on Foreign Affairs, *Marketing and Promotion of Infant Formula in Developing Countries*, U.S. House of Representatives, 1980. See also Maggie McComas et al., *The Dilemma of Third World Nutrition* (Nestlé S.A., 1983).

24. Assume that both jobs have the same beneficial effects on the interests of others.

25. Yet it might be objected that in cases of this sort there frequently will be other reasons significantly opposed to the relevant moral reasons—reasons that you are or were able to acquire. Such reasons will be either *malevolent* reasons seeking to bring about the suffering and death of other human beings, *benevolent* reasons concerned to promote nonhuman welfare even at the expense of human welfare, or *aesthetic* reasons concerned to preserve and promote objects of aesthetic value even if those objects will not be appreciated by any living being. But assuming that such malevolent reasons are ultimately rooted in some conception of what is good for oneself or others, these reasons would have already been taken into account, and by assumption outweighed by the other relevant reasons in this case. And although benevolent reasons concerned to promote nonhuman welfare also need to be taken into account, such reasons are not directly relevant to justifying morality over egoism. They will be taken into account, however, in chapter 4. Finally, although aesthetic reasons concerned to preserve and promote aesthetic objects, even if those objects will not be appreciated by any living being, might theoretically weigh against human interests, for all practical purposes, the value of such aesthetic objects will tend to correlate with the value of the aesthetic experiences such objects provide to humans. Consequently, even with the presence of these other kinds of reasons, your acceptance of the first job can still be seen as contrary to the relevant reasons in this case.

26. This is because, as I shall argue, morality itself already represents a compromise between egoism and altruism. So to ask that moral reasons be weighed against self-interested reasons is, in effect, to count self-interested reasons twice—once in the compromise between egoism and altruism and then again when moral reasons are weighed against self-interested reasons. But to count self-interested reasons twice is clearly objectionable.

27. Of course, there are arguments for only taking self-interested reasons into account based on the assumption of psychological egoism. But this assumption is clearly false. That is why I began my argument for the justification of

morality with the assumption that we have the capacity to act upon both self-interested and altruistic reasons.

28. Assume that all these methods of waste disposal have roughly the same amount of beneficial effects on the interests of others.

29. Notice that by "egoistic perspective" here I mean the view that grants the prima facie relevance of both egoistic and altruistic reasons to rational choice and then tries to argue for the superiority of egoistic reasons. Similarly by "altruistic perspective," I mean the view that grants the prima facie relevance of both egoistic and altruistic reasons to rational choice and then tries to argue for the superiority of altruistic reasons.

30. I owe this objection to Michael Smith.

31. We are imagining that we are getting a true and accurate ranking of a person's self-interested reasons from an egoistic perspective—one that may be different from what a person thinks is his or her true and accurate ranking of such reasons, and the same holds true of a person's altruistic reasons as seen from an altruistic perspective.

32. For a response to the relativist, see my *Justice for Here and Now* (New York: Cambridge University Press, 1998), 14–17.

33. When we consider conflicts between humans and nonhumans, there are more "lifeboat situations" because, for one thing, humans need to eat something in order to live, and there are good reasons for them to generally avoid eating fellow humans.

34. See R. Duncan Luce and Howard Raiffa, *Games and Decisions* (New York: John Wiley & Sons, Inc., 1967), chapter 13.

35. I am assuming that neither of these sides has non-question-begging grounds for its assumption.

36. Actually, all of what pure altruism holds is:

1. All high-ranking altruistic reasons have priority over conflicting lower-ranking self-interested reasons, other things being equal.
2. All low-ranking altruistic reasons have priority over conflicting higher-ranking self-interested reasons, other things being equal.
3. All high-ranking altruistic reasons have priority over conflicting high-ranking self-interested reasons, other things being equal.
4. All low-ranking altruistic reasons have priority over conflicting low-ranking self-interested reasons, other things being equal.

By contrast, all of what egoism holds is:

1'. All high-ranking self-interested reasons have priority over conflicting lower-ranking altruistic reasons, other things being equal.
2'. All low-ranking self-interested reasons have priority over conflicting higher-ranking altruistic reasons, other things being equal.
3'. All high-ranking self-interested reasons have priority over conflicting high-ranking altruistic reasons, other things being equal.

4'. All low-ranking self-interested reasons have priority over conflicting high-ranking altruistic reasons, other things being equal.

And what the compromise view holds is (1) and (1') and it favors neither pure altruism nor egoism with respect to (3) and (4), (3') and (4').

37. Notice that even if one were to take this perspective, it would still follow that the egoistic and altruistic perspectives beg the question against the other to a far greater extent than the compromise view does against either of them because the whole of what egoism holds about the priority of reasons, that is, (1') and (2') are in conflict with an altruistic perspective and the whole of what altruism holds about the priority of reasons, that is, (1) and (2) are in conflict with an egoistic perspective. Consequently, even viewed this way, the compromise view, on grounds of being the least question-begging would still be the rationally preferable resolution. (As you may have suspected or may know from my previous work, this is the way I used to justify the compromise view, before I recognized that it could be given a completely non-question-begging justification.)

38. At first glance, it would seem that my defense of morality is just the sort of view that David Hume opposed. Hume had held that "reason is perfectly inert, and can never prevent or produce any action or affection." But Hume also held "reason and sentiment concur in almost all moral determinations and conclusions," and given that my own view simply attempts to apply a standard of non-question-beggingness to our self-interested and altruistic sentiments, there may be more similarity here than meets the eye.

Of course, although Hume rejected any attempt to reduce altruistic sentiments to self-interested ones, he did see a considerable compatibility between these two kinds of sentiments. He writes:

> Treating vice with the greatest candour, and making it all possible concessions, we must acknowledge that there is not, in any instance, the smallest pretext for giving it the preference above virtue, with a view of self-interest. [*An Enquiry Concerning the Principles of Morals* (La Salle, Ill.: Open Court, 1960), 122]

In contrast, the main reason that I was trying to work out a defense of morality was my belief that self-interest and morality can come into serious conflict, and so it would be helpful to have an argument that reason requires morality over self-interest in such cases. So it is possible that if Hume had come to recognize that morality and self-interest can seriously conflict, he too might have been interested in finding a role for reason in resolving that conflict.

Yet even with his belief in the compatibility of self-interested and altruistic sentiments, Hume does sometimes talk about reason having a more active role with respect to our sentiments than his general view would seem to allow. For example, he says:

> in order to pave the way for [a moral] sentiment, and give a proper discernment of its object, it is often necessary . . . that much reasoning should precede. . . .

He further argues:

> in many orders of beauty, particularly those of the finer arts, it is requisite to employ much reasoning in order to feel the proper sentiment and a false relish may frequently be corrected by argument and reflection. [And that t]here are just grounds to conclude that moral beauty partakes much of this latter species and demands the assistance of our intellectual faculty to give it a suitable influence on the human mind. (Ibid., 5–6)

Hume also hopes that his own ethical theory, his own reasoning about morality, would:

> not only stand the test of inquiry but may contribute to the amendment of men's lives and their improvement in morality and social justice. (Ibid., 118)

This would be quite an impact for the arguments of an ethical theory to have. Surely, I would rest content if my own appeal to reason, specifically a standard of non-question-beggingness, to support a moral ordering of our self-interested and altruistic sentiments would have such an impact. Overall then, despite our differences, I think Hume's ethical theory and my own justification of morality share considerable common ground.

39. It is worth pointing out here an important difference between these self-interested and altruistic reasons that constitute moral reasons. It is that the self-interested reasons render the pursuit of self-interest permissible, whereas the altruistic reasons require the pursuit of altruism. This is because it is always possible to sacrifice oneself more than morality demands and thus act supererogatorily. Yet even here there are limits and one can sacrifice oneself too much, as presumably the pure altruist does, and consequently be morally blameworthy for doing so.
40. Kai Nielsen, "Why Should I Be Moral? Revisited,"*American Philosophical Quarterly* 21 (1984): 90.
41. Thomas Scanlon discusses this problem in *What We Owe to Others* (Cambridge: Harvard University Press, 1998), chapter 3.
42. Kurt Baier, *The Moral Point of View*, abridged edition (New York: Random House, 1965), 150.
43. Henry Sidgwick, *The Methods of Ethics*, 7th ed. (London: Macmillian, 1907), concluding chapter.
44. Thomas Nagel, *Equality and Partiality* (Oxford: Oxford University Press, 1991).
45. Notice that the impersonal standpoint will coincide with the compromise view only if the impersonal standpoint is interpreted as allowing each individual to opt for a certain degree of self-preference.
46. A compromise between the personal and the impersonal would be judged too much from the personal standpoint if more consideration of others was required than the personal perspective regarded as justified. A compromise between the personal and the impersonal would be judged as not enough

from the impersonal standpoint if less consideration of others was required than the impersonal perspective regarded as justified.

47. The justification for blaming and censuring such persons is not based on any possibility for reforming them because we are assuming that they are incapable of reform. Rather, the justification is based on what the persons in question deserve because of their past behavior and on whatever usefulness blaming and censuring them would have in deterring others.

48. What constitutes rational action for those who lack even the minimal capacity for altruism is a question that I will not take up here.

49. More precisely, to say that I am morally responsible for my lack of moral reasons in this regard is to say that (a) I have or had the opportunity and capacity to acquire those reasons, and (b) I also have, had, or could have had overwhelming, good reasons of the relevant sort to utilize my capacity and opportunity to acquire those reasons.

50. Not all the reasons that people are or were able to acquire are *relevant* to an assessment of the reasonableness of their conduct. First, reasons that are evokable only from some logically possible set of opportunities are simply not relevant; the reasons must be evokable from the opportunities people actually possessed. Second, reasons that radically different people could have acquired are also not relevant. Instead, relevant reasons are those which people could have acquired without radical changes in their developing identities. Third, some reasons are not important enough to be relevant to a reasonable assessment of conduct. For example, a reason that I am able to acquire which would lead me to promote my own interests or that of a friend just slightly more than I am presently doing is hardly relevant to an assessment of the reasonableness of my conduct. Surely, I could not be judged as unreasonable for failing to acquire such a reason. Rather, relevant reasons are those which would lead one to avoid a *significant harm* to oneself (or others) or to secure a *significant benefit* to oneself (or others) at an acceptable cost to oneself (or others).

It is also worth noting that a given individual may not actually reflect on all the reasons that are relevant to deciding what she should do. In fact, one could do so only if one had already acquired all the relevant reasons. Nevertheless, reasonable conduct is ideally determined by a rational weighing of all the reasons that are relevant to deciding what one should do so that failing to accord with a rational weighing of all such reasons is to act contrary to reason.

51. Sarah Broadie, *Ethics with Aristotle* (New York: Oxford University Press, 1991); Richard Kraut, *Aristotle on the Human Good* (Princeton, N.J.: Princeton University Press, 1989); John Cooper, *Reason and Human Good in Aristotle* (Cambridge: Harvard University Press, 1975); Thomas Nagel, "Aristotle on Eudaimonia," in *Essays on Aristotle's Ethics*, ed. Amelie Rorty (Berkeley: University of California Press, 1980), 7–14; J. L. Ackrill, "Aristotle on Eudaimonia," in *Essays on Aristotle's Ethics*, 15–34; W. F. B. Hardie, "The

Final Good in Aristotle's Ethics," in *Aristotle,* ed. J. M. E. Moravcsik (New York: Anchor Books, 1967), 297–322; Kathleen Wilkes, "The Good Man and the Good for Man," in *Essays on Aristotle's Ethics,* 341–358; Amelie Rorty, "The Place of Contemplation in Aristotle's Nicomachean Ethics," in *Essays on Aristotle's Ethics,* 377–394.

52. By a viable Aristotelian account, I mean a refurbished account that can be plausibly considered morally defensible today.

53. Aristotelians who understand personal flourishing in terms of just the activity of contemplation are probably more likely to answer no to this question.

54. Kraut, *Aristotle on the Human Good,* especially chapter 2.

55. It is possible that some viable Aristotelian accounts of personal flourishing will involve both kinds of compromise: a compromise within the account of personal flourishing itself between conflicting interests of the self or between conflicting selves, or something similar, and a compromise between personal flourishing and the good of others. This will occur when the compromise within the account of human flourishing itself does not fully resolve the conflict between self and others. One might think of Nagel's attempt to reconcile the personal and impersonal standpoints as a needed "second compromise," except for the fact that if the second compromise is to be done correctly in Nagel's account, it will have to undo at least some of the compromises achieved within the personal standpoint and maybe even within the impersonal standpoint as well. With respect to the Aristotelian views requiring two compromises that I am considering here, I am assuming that there is no similar need to undo the first compromise.

56. In his comments on a version of this chapter that I presented at "Hume, Motivation, 'Is' and 'Ought,'" a conference sponsored by the Department of Philosophy of the University of Otago, Dunedin, New Zealand, 19–24 January 2003.

57. Charles Pigden, "Logic and the Autonomy of Ethics," *Australasian Journal of Philosophy* 67 (1989): 127–151.

58. For objectors to Kurt Baier's work, see *Reason, Ethics, and Society: Themes from Kurt Baier and his Responses,* ed. J. B. Schneewind. (Chicago: Open Court, 1996). For objectors to Alan Gewirth's work see *Gewirth's Ethical Rationalism,* ed. Edward Regis (Chicago: University of Chicago Press, 1984) and *Gewirth,* ed. Michael Boylan (Lanham, Md.: Rowman & Littlefield, 1999). For objectors to Christine Korsgaard's work, see her *Sources of Normativity* (Cambridge: Cambridge University Press, 1996). For objectors to my work, see my *Social and Political Philosophy: Contemporary Perspectives* (London: Routledge, 2000).

59. For a survey of the objections to Gewirth's work, see Deryck Beyleveld, *The Dialectical Necessity of Morality* (Chicago: University of Chicago Press, 1991).

60. Interestingly, there may be a way to bring Korsgaard's work in line with the defense of morality I provide in this chapter. At the very end of her responses to critics in *Sources of Normativity,* Korsgaard remarks that perhaps

the most essential rule of reflection is "that we should never stop reflecting until we have reached a satisfactory answer, one that admits of no further questioning" (258). If we interpret this rule as requiring a non-question-begging starting point, and thus taking into account the behavior of women, and focusing on altruism as well as egoism, then it may be possible to see Korsgaard's work and my own as pointing toward a common justification of morality. In a series of e-mails discussing the topic of egoism, I proposed this "reconciliation" to Korsgaard, and she replied, rightly, that e-mails were too "telegraphic" a way to resolve the issue.

61. Nevertheless, the thesis must be understood in such a way that is consistent with the principle of non-question-beggingness, and this is what I propose to do.

62. Bernard Gert, "Acting Irrationally Versus Acting Contrary to What Is Required by Reason," *Journal of Social Philosophy* (1999): 379–386; "Theoretical Versus Practical Rationality," in *Social and Political Philosophy: Contemporary Perspectives,* 71–76.

63. There are also versions of the "ought" implies "can" principle that govern egoism and altruism as well. The "ought" implies "can" principle that governs egoism prohibits an agent from unreasonably risking some of his or her (self) interests in favor of other (self) interests the agent happens to have. The "ought" implies "can" principle that governs altruism prohibits an agent from unreasonably burdening some other people to favor still others. When these two perspectives are compromised in Morality as Compromise, the standard "ought" implies "can" comes into play because self and others then need to be governed by the same principle, or, put another way, in the compromise with egoism, the "ought" implies "can" principle of altruism needs to be extended to include oneself as well as others.

CHAPTER 3

1. John Rawls, *A Theory of Justice* (Cambridge: Harvard University Press, 1971).

2. John C. Harsanyi, *Essays on Ethics, Social Behavior, and Scientific Explanation* (Dordrecht: Reidel, 1976).

3. John Rawls, *Justice as Fairness: A Restatement* (Cambridge: Harvard University Press, 2001).

4. There are moral theories, like John Finnis's, which seem to reject what I have just said about any defensible moral theory. Thus, Finnis's moral theory contains the principle that one should never do evil from which good may come. But Finnis would probably want to interpret my first two cases (stepping on people's toes to respond to an emergency and even lying (not telling the truth) to one's friend to keep her from committing suicide as not really cases of doing evil so that good may come of it. In my third case (shooting one indian to save nineteen others), Finnis would surely see this as a case of doing evil that good may come of it and so impermissible. But

what about the consequences of not doing evil in this case? Finnis contends that we need not worry about these consequences because God will take care of things. Obviously this is not a stance that a nonbeliever can take. And even for the believer, how does Finnis know that God does not want us to take consequences into account in these difficult cases?

5. There are moral requirements, such as love your neighbor as yourself (if it is a moral requirement), that violate the "ought" implies "can" principle, except when they are interpreted in an aspirational way. There are also moral requirements that give rise to residual obligations when they cannot be straightforwardly fulfilled, such as a promise to return a borrowed item one has just lost, and on that account do not really violate the "ought" implies "can" principle. There are other requirements that violate the "ought" implies "can" principle but do not appear to be moral requirements, such as that kleptomaniacs not steal, unless they are interpreted as giving rise to indirect requirements, such as that kleptomaniacs seek psychological help, in which case these requirements do not violate the "ought" implies "can" principle. See Charles Pigden, "Ought-Implies-Can: Erasmus, Luther and R. M. Hare," *Sophia* (1990): 2–30; Steve Sapontzis, "'Ought' Does Imply 'Can,'" *Southern Journal of Philosophy* (1991): 383–393; Terrance McConnell, "'Ought' Implies 'Can,'" and the Scope of Moral Requirements," *Philosophia* (1989): 437–454; Alan Montefiore, "'Ought' and 'Can,'" *Philosophical Quarterly* (1954): 24–40.

6. This link between morality and reason is expressed in the belief that (true) morality and (right) reason cannot conflict. Some supporters of this link have developed separate theories of rationality and reasonableness, contending, for example, that, while egoists are rational, those who are committed to morality are both rational and reasonable. On this interpretation, morality is rationally permissible but not rationally required, since egoism is also rationally permissible. Other supporters of the link between reason and morality reject the idea of separate theories of rationality and reasonableness, contending that morality is not just rationally permissible but also rationally required and that egoism is rationally impermissible. But despite their disagreement over whether there is a separate theory of rationality distinct from a theory of reasonableness, both groups link morality with a notion of reasonableness that incorporates a certain degree of altruism. This relates, of course, to the discussion of the justification of morality in the previous chapter.

7. It should be pointed out that the "ought" implies "can" principle primarily ranges over social and political morality, that part of morality we can justifiably enforce against others because we can reasonably expect its requirements are accessible to those to whom they apply.

8. Rawls, *Justice as Fairness*, 100.

9. Interpreting utilitarianism in this way also avoids begging the question against the utilitarian view.

10. It has also been plausibly argued on feminist grounds that greater equality in society, especially between women and men, especially in families, would actually maximize utility overall. See Maria Morales, *Perfect Equality* (Lanham, Md.: Rowman and Littlefield, 1996).

11. It is possible that a defender of utilitarianism might want to reject the "ought" implies "can" principle because of the constraint it imposes on maximization of utility. The question is whether a defender of utilitarianism could do this while still maintaining a moral perspective, that is, a perspective in which each individual counted. The utilitarian could claim that each individual did count because each individual's utility was taken into account in the maximization of utility. But it is arguable that this would not suffice to show that each individual counted whenever the "ought" implies "can" principle was violated and some individuals were required to take an enormous loss, maybe even lose their lives, in order that many more individuals could enjoy some passing pleasure, as when Christians were thrown to the lions for the pleasure of the crowds in Roman coliseums.

12. See T. M. Scanlon "Contractualism and Utilitarianism," in *Utilitarianism and Beyond*, ed. Amartya Sen and Bernard Williams (Cambridge: Cambridge University Press, 1982), 103–128. See also his *What We Owe Each Other* (Cambridge: Harvard University Press, 1998), chapter 2.

13. This does not just happen in philosophy. In a recent feature article in the *New York Times*, Lester Thurow and Paul Krugman, both at MIT and known for their opposing economic views, were said to "go at it, *never face to face* always in writing and public speaking, sometimes from the well of the same MIT lecture amphitheater, although on separate days. ..." (emphasis added) *New York Times* February 16, 1997.

14. For a more detailed discussion of a peacemaking way of doing philosophy, see my *Three Challenges to Ethics* (New York: Oxford University Press, 2001), chapter 5.

15. See Andrews Reath, Barbara Herman, and Christina Korsgaard, *Reclaiming the History of Philosophy: Essays for John Rawls* (Cambridge, Cambridge University Press, 1997), 3.

16. An internal critique of a theory if it is done right also has another advantage over an external critique in that adherents of the theory are logically required to accept the conclusions of the internal critique since it follows from the most favorable interpretation of a theory. By contrast, an external critique, issuing as it does from some external standard or ideal, can be more easily turned aside by adherents of the theory by simply rejecting that external standard or ideal from which the critique proceeds.

17. Of course, this involves rejecting John Harsanyi's interpretation of utilitarianism that we considered earlier which does not take into account the theory's implicit commitment to the "ought" implies "can" principle.

18. F. A. Hayek, *The Constitution of Liberty* (Chicago: University of Chicago Press, 1960), 11.

19. John Hospers, *Libertarianism* (Los Angeles: Nash Publishing, 1971), 5.

20. Robert Nozick, *State, Anarchy and Utopia* (New York, Basic Books, 1974), ix.

21. It is important to note that by starting with the ideal of liberty as libertarians characterize that ideal, we avoid begging the question against the libertarian view. Moreover, backing up to a more neutral starting point—the strategy used against egoism and pure altruism in the previous chapter—would not have been useful here because it would not have enabled us to reach a resolution at the practical level.

22. See John Hospers, "The Libertarian Manifesto," in *Morality in Practice*, 7th ed., ed. James P. Sterba (Belmont, Calif.: Wadsworth, 2003).

23. Basic needs, if not satisfied, lead to significant lacks or deficiencies with respect to a standard of mental and physical well-being, Thus, a person's needs for food, shelter, medical care, protection, companionship, and self-development are, at least in part, needs of this sort. For a discussion of basic needs, see my *How to Make People Just* (Totowa, N.J.: Rowman and Littlefield, 1988), 45–48.

24. See Hospers, *Libertarianism,* chapter 7, and Tibor Machan, *Human Rights and Human Liberties* (Chicago: Nelson-Hall, 1975), 231ff.

25. See James P. Sterba, "Is There a Rationale for Punishment?" *Philosophical Topics* (1990): 105–125.

26. By the liberty of the rich to meet their luxury needs, I continue to mean the liberty of the rich not to be interfered with when using their surplus possessions for luxury purposes. Similarly, by the liberty of the poor to meet their basic needs, I continue to mean the liberty of the poor not to be interfered with when taking what they require to meet their basic needs from the surplus possessions of the rich.

27. For quite different circumstances, however, I argue that a moral resolution can permit what it is not reasonable to ask and/or require everyone affected to accept. I argue for this at the end of the next chapter.

28. Under such circumstances, however, it would not be unreasonable to *ask* but not require the rich to further constrain their liberty for the sake of the poor.

29. Tibor Machan, *Individuals and Their Rights* (La Salle, Ill.: Open Court, 1989), 100–111.

30. This may be putting Machan's "concession," at least initially, too strongly. What Machan concedes is that in such circumstances the poor would be morally justified in taking from the rich what they need. In so doing, Machan says, they disregard but do not violate the rights of the rich. But I take this to be the equivalent of saying that the poor have negative right to welfare. (See the discussion of the content of such a right a few paragraphs hence.) Tibor Machan, "Sterba on Machan's 'Concession,'" *Journal of Social Philosophy* 32 (2001): 241–243. For further discussion of Machan's responses to my argument, see my "From Liberty to Welfare: An Update," *Social Theory and Practice* (2000): 465–478.

31. Machan, *Individuals and Their Rights*, 107.
32. The employment opportunities offered to the poor must be honorable and supportive of self-respect. To do otherwise would be to offer the poor the opportunity to meet some of their basic needs at the cost of denying some of their other basic needs.
33. The poor cannot, however, give up the liberty to which their children are entitled.
34. For a time, I thought so myself. See my *Justice for Here and Now*, chapter 3.
35. When the poor are acting collectively in conjunction with their agents and allies to exercise their negative welfare rights, they will want, in turn, to institute adequate positive welfare rights to secure a proper distribution of the goods and resources they are acquiring.
36. It is important to see how moral and pragmatic considerations are combined in this argument from negative welfare rights to positive welfare rights, as this will become particularly relevant when we turn to a consideration of distant peoples and future generations. What needs to be seen is that the moral consideration is primary and the pragmatic consideration secondary. The moral consideration is that, until positive welfare rights for the poor are guaranteed, any use by the rich of their surplus possessions to meet their nonbasic needs is likely to violate the negative welfare rights of the poor by preventing them from appropriating (some part of) the surplus goods and resources of the rich. The pragmatic consideration is that, in the absence of positive welfare rights, the rich would have to put up with the discretion of the poor, either acting by themselves or through their allies or agents, in choosing when and how to exercise their negative welfare rights.

Obviously peoples who are separated from the rich by significant distances will be able to exercise their negative welfare rights only either by negotiating the distances involved or by having allies or agents in the right place, willing to act on their behalf. And with respect to future generations, their rights can be exercised only if they too have allies and agents in the right place and time, willing to act on their behalf. So unless distant peoples are good at negotiating distances or unless distant peoples and future generations have ample allies and agents in the right place and time, the pragmatic consideration leading the rich to endorse positive welfare rights will diminish in importance in their regard. Fortunately, the moral consideration alone is sufficient to carry the argument here and elsewhere: Libertarians should endorse positive welfare rights because it is the only way that they can be assured of not violating the negative welfare right of the poor by preventing the poor from appropriating (some part of) the surplus goods and resources of the rich.
37. Yet even though libertarians have claimed that the rights they defend are universal rights in the manner I have just explained, it may be that they are simply mistaken in this regard. Even when universal rights are stripped of any claim to being universally recognized or unconditional, still it might be

argued that there are no such rights, that is, that there are no rights that all people ought to recognize.

But how does one argue for such a view? One cannot argue from the failure of people to recognize such rights because we have already said that such recognition is not necessary. Nor can one argue that not everyone ought to recognize such rights because some lack the capacity to do so. This is because "ought" does implies "can" here, so that the obligation to recognize certain rights only applies to those who actually have or have had at some point the capacity to do so. Thus, the existence of universal rights is not ruled out by the existence of individuals who have never had the capacity to recognize such rights. It is only ruled out by the existence of individuals who can recognize these rights but for whom it is correct to say that they ought, all things considered, not to do so. But we have just seen that even a minimal libertarian moral ideal supports a universal right to welfare. And I have also argued in the previous chapter that when "ought" is understood prudentially rather than morally, a non-question-begging conception to rationality favors morality over prudence. So for those capable of recognizing universal rights, it simply is not possible to argue that they, all things considered, ought not to do so.

38. Bob Bergland, "Attacking the Problem of World Hunger," *National Forum* 69 (1979): 4.

39. For example, see World Watch Institute, *Vital Signs 2003* (New York: W. W. Norton & Co., 2003), 28–31; http://www.bread.org/hungerbasics/international.html.

40. For example, see *Vital Signs 2003*, 30–31; Stuart Pimm, *The World According to Pimm* (New York: McGraw-Hill, 2001), chapter 2; World Watch Institute, *Vital Signs 1996* (New York: W. W. Norton & Co., 1996), 34–35; Jeremy Rifkin, *Beyond Beef* (New York: Penguin, 1992), 1.

41. For a discussion of these causal connections, see Linda Starke, ed., *State of the World 2003* (New York: W. W. Norton & Co., 2003), chapter 1; Cheryl Silver, *One Earth One Future* (Washington, D.C.: National Academy Press, 1990); Bill McKibben, *The End of Nature* (New York: Random House, 1989); Jeremy Leggett, ed., *Global Warming* (New York: Oxfort University Press, 1990); Lester Brown, ed., *The World Watch Reader* (New York: W. W. Norton & Co., 1991).

42. Charles Park, Jr., ed. *Earth Resources* (Washington D.C.: Voice of America, 1980), chapter 13; Lester Brown, *State of the World 1995* (New York: Norton, 1995), chapter 7; Brown, ed., *World Watch Reader,* 268. China currently uses more coal than the United States. See Lester Brown, *State of the World* (New York: Norton, 1997), 9.

43. Linda Starke, ed., *State of the World 2004* (New York: W. W. Norton & Co., 2004), 8.

44. See Starke, *State of the World 2004.* There is no way that the resource consumption of the U.S. can be matched by developing and underdeveloped

countries, and even if it could be matched, doing so would clearly lead to ecological disaster. See *Planet Under Stress*, ed. Constance Mungall and Digby McLaren (Oxford: Oxford University Press, 1990) and *World Hunger: Twelve Myths*, Frances Lappe and Joseph Collins (New York: Grove Press, 1986).

45. Once basic needs are met among existing generations, however, it may be that renewable resources can be used for meeting nonbasic needs in ways that do not jeopardize the meeting of the basic needs of future generations.

46. Alan Durning, "Life on the Brink," *World Watch*, 3, no. 2 (1990): 24.

47. Ibid., 29.

48. It might be thought appropriate not to rely on this argument from transitivity but to directly consider the possibility of reconciling Aristotelian and utilitarian theories, at least at the practical level. Unfortunately, I have no other arguments at the moment to directly establish this reconciliation than those I have already used.

CHAPTER 4

1. Peter Singer, *Animal Liberation*, rev. ed. (New York: Avon Books, 1992).

2. Most recently in Tom Regan, *Animal Rights, Human Wrongs* (Lanham, Md.: Rowman & Littlefield, 2004).

3. Paul Taylor, *Respect for Nature* (Princeton, N.J.: Princeton University Press, 1987).

4. James P. Sterba, "Taylor's Biocentrism and Beyond," in *Environmental Ethics*, 17 (1995): 191–208. Taylor now accepts my development of his view. See his new preface to the Chinese translation of *Respect for Nature* (Institute of Philosophy at the Chinese Academy of Social Sciences, 2004).

5. See Taylor, *Respect for Nature*, 129–135, and R. and V. Routley, "Against the Inevitability of Human Chauvinism," in *Ethics and Problems of the 21st Century*, ed. by K. E. Goodpaster and K. M. Sayre (Notre Dame: University of Notre Dame Press, 1979).

6. Assuming God exists, humans might also be better off if they could retain their distinctive traits while acquiring one or another of God's qualities, but consideration of this possibility would take us too far afield. Nonhuman animals might also be better off it they could retain their distinctive traits and acquire one or another of the distinctive traits possessed by other nonhuman animals.

7. This assumes that there is an environmental niche that cheetahs can fill.

8. Since some things that are good for some (like rationality) are not good for others, there are no universal standard of excellences that apply to all living beings, even though there are some basic goods that all living beings need (like water).

9. So far the argument for taking nonathropocentric reasons into account parallels the argument for taking altruistic reasons into account in chapter 2.

Here I go on to specify the practical consequences of the argument in terms of conflict resolution principles with respect to human and nonhuman living beings.

10. We can make this assumption here because the net effect of giving priority to high-ranking anthropocentric reasons over low-ranking nonanthropocentric reasons and giving priority to high-ranking nonanthropocentric reasons over low-ranking anthropocentric reasons, other things being equal, is to count all living beings morally.

11. For the purposes of this chapter, I will follow the convention of excluding humans from the denotation of "animals."

12. For further discussion of basic needs, see my *How to Make People Just* (Totowa, N.J.: Rowman & Littlefield, 1988), 45ff.

13. Moreover, this kind of fuzziness in the application of the distinction between basic and nonbasic needs is characteristic of the application of virtually all our classificatory concepts, and so is not an objection to its usefulness.

14. By "human ethics" I mean "an ethics that assumes without argument that only humans count morally." It should also be pointed out that the Principle of Human Preservation must be implemented in a way that causes the least harm possible, which means that, other things being equal, basic needs should be met by aggressing against nonsentient rather than against sentient living beings so as to avoid the pain and suffering that would otherwise be inflicted on sentient beings.

15. It is important to recognize here that we also have a strong obligation to prevent lifeboat cases from arising in the first place.

16. The principle just does not speak to the issue, although I do discuss in the text what is permissible and impermissible in this regard.

17. For a discussion of the "ought" implies "can" principle, see chapter 3.

18. Nevertheless, as I shall argue, this assumption does not always hold. Moral resolutions can also permit actions that they cannot require, as for example, in lifeboat cases.

19. See Holmes Rolston III, "Enforcing Environmental Ethics: Civil Law and Natural Value," in *Social and Political Philosophy: Contemporary Perspectives,* ed. James P. Sterba (London: Routledge, 2001), where Rolston uses this example to object to my Principle of Human Preservation and I respond. Rolston has also raised a further objection (e-mail 1/27/04) to which I now respond in the text.

20. This did not hold in the real-life case that Rolston actually presented. See my response in *Social and Political Philosophy*.

21. Of course, we may be required to meet our basic needs and the basic needs of other humans by aggressing against the basic needs of the members of some nonhuman species rather than others, for example, in order to protect, in this way, certain endangered species. But clearly this requirement would not undermine the present and prevailing moral acceptability of the Principle of Human Preservation understood as involving strong permissibility.

22. In the nonideal world in which we live, the Nepalese and their human allies should press rich people to acquire the available surplus to meet the basic needs of the Nepalese until their own lives are threatened. At that point, regrettably, the Nepalese would be justified in preying on endangered species as the only way for them to survive.

23. It should be pointed out that, although the Principle of Disproportionality prohibits aggressing against basic needs of nonhumans to serve nonbasic needs to humans, the Principle of Human Defense permits defense of non-basic needs of humans against aggression of nonhumans. So while we cannot legitimately aggress against nonhumans to meet our nonbasic needs, we can legitimately defend our nonbasic needs against the aggression of nonhumans seeking to meet their basic needs, although this will rarely happen for the reasons given in the text.

24. Of course, this is just how libertarians present their view. However, I have argued in chapter 3 that the view actually does entail a right to welfare, which would lead to something like the equality that socialists favor.

25. Actually, a slogan for my view, could be: Welfare Liberalism or Socialism for Humans, Libertarianism for Nonhumans! Of course, in my view, there is not a lot of difference between these perspectives.

26. For an account of what constitutes justifiably held property within human ethics, see my *Justice for Here and Now,* especially chapter 3.

27. For a detailed discussion of this argument, see chapter 3. See also my article "From Liberty to Welfare," *Ethics* (1994): 64–98, and chapter 3 of *Justice for Here and Now.*

28. For further argument of this conclusion, see chapter 3. See also *Justice for Here and Now,* chapter 3, and *How to Make People Just,* chapters 2–10.

29. Aldo Leopold's view is usually interpreted as holistic in this sense. Leopold wrote "A thing is right when it tends to preserve the integrity, stability and beauty of the biotic community. It is wrong when it tends otherwise." See his *A Sand County Almanac* (New York: Oxford University Press, 1949).

30. For a defender of this view, see Paul Taylor, *Respect for Nature* (Princeton, N.J.: Princeton University Press, 1987).

31. Of course, actions justified on holist grounds, may sometimes preclude the satisfaction of nonbasic human needs (for example, by restricting urban sprawl), but they will only rarely involve aggressing against nonbasic human needs for the reasons given earlier, except when compensation and reparation is required.

32. See, however, the last section of this chapter.

33. Peter Singer's *Animal Liberation* (New York: Avon Books, 1975) inspired this view.

34. Baird Callicott, "Animal Liberation: A Triangular Affair," *Environmental Ethics* (1980): 311–328.

35. Mark Sagoff, "Animal Liberation and Environmental Ethics: Bad Marriage, Quick Divorce," *Osgood Hall Law Journal* (1984): 297–307.

36. Mary Ann Warren, "The Rights of the Nonhuman World," in *Environmental Philosophy*, ed. by Robert Elliot and Arran Gare (New York: University of Queensland Press, 1983), 109–134, and Baird Callicott, *In Defense of the Land Ethic* (Albany: State University of New York Press, 1989), chapter 3.

37. *Realities for the 90's* (Santa Cruz, Calif.: Earth Save Foundation, 1991), 4.

38. Ibid., 5.

39. Sagoff, "Animal Liberation and Environmental Ethics," 301–305.

40. There is an analogous story to tell here about "domesticated" plants, but hopefully there is no analogous story about "extra humans" who are raised for food. Given the knowledge these "extra humans" would have of their fate, a similar use of humans would not be mutually beneficial and would most likely make their lives not worth living. But even assuming that this were not the case, with the consequence that this particular justification for domestication is ruled out because of its implications for a similar use of humans, it still would be the case that domestication is justified in a sustainable agriculture to provide fertilizer for crops to meet basic human needs.

41. To say that the proposed arrangement is in the interest of farms animals implies that the farm animals brought into existence by means of this arrangement will benefit overall, not that there are some preexistent farm animals who will benefit from the arrangement. However, the arrangement can be in the interest of some existing animals as well.

42. For a valuable discussion of this issue, see Gary Varner, *In Nature's Interests?* (New York: Oxford University Press, 1998), 100–118.

43. There are other species, such as mourning doves, cottontail rabbits, gray squirrels, bobwhite and blue quail, that each year produce more young than their habitat can support through the winter, but they usually do not degrade their environment. With respect to such species, it might be argued that hunting is morally permissible. Nevertheless, unless such hunting is either therapeutic or required to meet basic human needs, it is difficult to see how it could be permissible.

44. Regan, *Animal Rights, Human Wrongs*, chapter 8.

45. Peter Singer, *Practical Ethics*, 2nd ed. (Cambridge: Cambridge University Press, 1993), chapter 10.

46. Ibid., 274.

47. It does not even follow that what has intrinsic value in this sense is living. Works of art can be intrinsically valuable in this sense.

48. There is no opposing sense of "instrumental value" to this notion of "intrinsic value."

49. Singer, *Animal Liberation*, 170–177.

50. Ibid.

51. There even appears to be a notion of having an interest that does not presuppose sentience but only that something is for one's good.

52. There are some other arguments, but they seem far less cogent. For example, Singer claims that what distinguishes sentient living beings from nonsentient

living beings is that "a purely physical explanation is possible" for nonsentient living beings. *Practical Ethics*, 279. But how do we know that a purely physical explanation is not possible for sentient beings? At a round-table session in the World Congress of Philosophy held recently in Istanbul, Turkey, Peter Singer in responding to my objections to his criticisms of bio-centrism, raised a new objection, namely, that we cannot imaginatively put ourselves into the position of nonsentient living beings, and for that reason, he claimed, nonsentient living beings do not have moral status. I responded that although it is true that we cannot imagine ourselves consciously occupying the position of nonsentient living beings, because they have no conscious perspective for us to imagine ourselves as occupying, it is still the case that because they have a good of their own, we can imagine ourselves as being, or actually becoming, guardians of the interests of nonsentient life, and that should suffice to recognize that they have moral status.

53. Singer, *Practical Ethics*, 277ff.

54. In the first edition of *Animal Liberation*, Singer claimed that the dividing line between sentient and nonsentient living beings was somewhere between an oyster and a clam. In the second edition of the book, Singer now wants to give clams the benefit of the doubt and include them in the class of sentient beings. See the discussion in *Animal Liberation*, 2nd ed., 174ff.

55. Notice that the choice at issue is whether we should meet our basic needs by destroying a whole species or by killing individual members of some species. If the only way to preserve ourselves or defend ourselves were to destroy a whole species, that would be permitted by the Principles of Human Preservation and Defense respectively.

56. I have also argued earlier in this chapter that a mutually beneficial arrangement allows for the killing and eating of farm animals.

57. Singer, *Practical Ethics*, 279ff. See also Peter Singer, "A Response," in *Singer and His Critics*, ed. by Dale Jamieson (Oxford: Blackwell, 1999), 327–332.

58. See Frederik Kaufman, "Machines, Sentience and the Scope of Morality," *Environmental Ethics* 16 (1994): 57–70.

59. See, for example, Karen Arms and Pamela Camp, *Biology: A Journey into Life* (Philadelphia: Saunders College Publishing, 1991), 9–11.

60. David Hume, *A Treatise of Human Nature*, ed. by L. A. Selby-Bigge (Oxford: Clarendon Press, 1888), III.i.3. The discussion here relates to the justification of morality provided in chapter 2, especially my discussion of Pigden's objection.

61. One notable exception to the requirement of independence are some species and subspecies of domesticated animals who have been made into beings who are dependent for their survival on humans. I contend that because of their historic interaction with these domesticated animals, humans have acquired a positive obligation to care for these animals provided certain mutually beneficial arrangements can be maintained.

62. Moreover, to recognize a positive obligation to preserve living things, like hearts and kidneys, would also put one in conflict with one's own good, if

it was the case that one's own heart or kidney was diseased, or the good of other living beings, if their hearts or kidneys were diseased. But this only shows how granting such a positive obligation leads to a reductio ad absurdum of the biocentrist's position. The qualification "as such" is added to allow for the possibility that one may have an obligation to preserve a particular heart or kidney if one should happen to have an obligation to preserve the person whose heart or kidney it is.

63. It would be interesting to explore how this moral framework applies to disputed moral problems like abortion and euthanasia. My hope is that all disputants would find this moral framework acceptable and that the framework would also provide additional resources for resolving these problems.

64. For further discussion, see Lawrence Johnson, *A Morally Deep World* (New York: Cambridge University Press, 1991), 76ff.

65. Even the requirement that those who can be benefited or harmed in a nonderivative way must have a certain independence to their lives or a good of their own is, on my account, *derived* from what we can reasonably expect of moral agents.

66. This first premise should be understood as a biconditional. Of course, then someone might want to challenge it on the grounds that there are prudential requirements which are reasonable to impose on moral agents. To which I would counter that, for the most part, prudential requirements are not reasonable to impose on moral agents, but when they are, it is because they are also (or overlap with) moral requirements. For example, my getting a vaccination against a serious contagious disease might be something I do for my own good and for the good of others. Here it is primarily the "for the good of others" aspect that makes it a moral requirement.

67. Actually, to make this argument explicitly one from "ought" to "ought," we would need as an initial premise "We ought to abide by the requirements of morality" and as a subsequent conclusion "We ought to abide by the Principles of Human Preservation, Disproportionality, Human Defense, and Rectification."

68. Peter Singer, E-mail communications, October 19, 2003.

69. See Taylor's new preface to the Chinese translation of *Respect for Nature*.

70. See the special issue of *Philosophy in the Contemporary World* on Environmental Virtue Ethics, 8, no. 2 (2001), particularly my contribution.

71. The direct analogy is to a lifeboat case in which you try to secure a lifeboat for one person from someone else who has an equal claim to it.

72. This is what I argue presently holds with regard to the means for protecting endangered species in the Royal Chitwan National Park in Nepal, See pp. 64–65.

73. It is also possible to reformulate these principles in a more linguistically species-neutral way so that they do not make direct reference to the human species. See James P. Sterba, "A Biocentrist Fights Back," *Environmental Ethics* (1998): 361–376.

Philosophical Interlude

1. For further argument, see my article, "Is There a Rationale for Punishment?" *Philosophical Topics* (1990): 105–125.

Chapter 5

1. In 1991 in response to these Hearings of the Senate Judicial Committee, Congress amended the Civil Rights Act to allow victims to claim monetary damages in cases involving all kinds of intentional discrimination, including sexual harassment. As a result, the financial stakes in harassment cases rose dramatically. *South Bend Tribune,* April 6, 1998.
2. *Christoforou v. Ryder Truck Rental.* 668 F. Supp. 294 (S.D.N.Y. 1987).
3. *Rabidue v. Osceola Refining Co.* 805 F.2d 611, 620 (6th Cir. 1986).
4. Obviously most offers of this sort will be more subtle, but if they are going to serve their purpose their message must still be relatively easy to discern.
5. Even where there is legalized prostitution, such offers may still be objectively unwelcome, because women may want and reasonably expect a fairer, and thus better array of occupations open to them.
6. There is an analogous requirement of subjective consent in the law concerning rape that is similarly indefensible. See Susan Estrich, "Sex at Work," *Stanford Law Review* 43(1991): 813–861.
7. One should not be concerned that this suggestion would undercut an appropriate presumption of innocence. This is because the presumption of innocence is weaker for civil cases than for criminal cases. Thus, in a civil law sexual harassment case, making an objectively unwanted sexual offer and then firing the person who refused that offer should be sufficient grounds for removing that presumption.
8. Or they could simply not fire those to whom they make the offers.
9. Barbara Gutek contends that sexual harassment is caused by the fact that women are stereotypically identified as sexual objects in ways that men are not. She notes that women are stereotypically characterized as sexy, affectionate, and attractive, whereas men are stereotypically characterized as competent and active. These stereotypes, Gutek claims, spill over into the workplace, making it difficult for women to be perceived as fellow workers rather than sex objects, and it is these perceptions that foster sexual harassment. It would seem, therefore, that eliminating the problem of sexual harassment from our society will require breaking down these stereotypes. See my *Justice for Here and Now* (New York: Cambridge University Press, 1998), chapter 4.
10. *Meritor Savings Bank v. Vinson.* 477 U.S. 57 (S.C., 1986).
11. *Rabidue v. Osceola Refining Co.* 805 F.2d 611, 620 (6th Cir. 1986).
12. *Rabidue v. Osceola Refining Co.* 805 F.2d 611, 620 (6th Cir. 1986).
13. *Henson v. Dundee,* 682 F.2d 897, 904 (11th Cir. 1982).

14. *Ellison v. Brady,* 924 F.2d 872 (9th Cir. 1991).
15. As one of Gutek's studies shows, reasonable men and reasonable women can disagree over what constitutes sexual harassment in the workplace. In this study, 67.2 percent of men as compared to 16.8 percent of women would be flattered if asked to have sex, while 15 percent of the men and 62.8 percent of the women said they would be insulted by such an offer.
16. Of course, men in particular will have to make a considerable effort to arrive at this most reasonable perspective, and it certainly will not be easy for them to attain it.
17. *Robinson v. Jacksonville Shipyards,* 760 F. Supp. 1486 (M.D. Fla. 1991).
18. Nadine Strossen, "Regulating Workplace Sexual Harassment and Upholding the First Amendment—Avoiding a Collision," *Villanova Law Review* 37 (1992): 211–228.
19. It does seem reasonable to grant, however, that there is a stronger presumption of employee liability with respect to quid pro quo sexual harassment than hostile environment sexual harassment if only because a company is normally presumed to be more responsible for those who occupy positions of power within it.
20. Gomez-Preston, Cherly, *When No Means No* (New York: Carol Publishing Co., 1993), 35–36; Ellen Bravo and Ellen Cassedy, *The 9–5 Guide to Combating Sexual Harassment* (New York: John Wiley and Sons, 1992), 4–5. The problem is international as well as national. A three-year study of women in Estonia, Finland, Sweden, and the Soviet Union, showed that nearly 50 percent of all working women experience sexual harassment. A survey released in 1991 by the Santama Group to Consider Sexual Harassment at Work showed that about 70 percent of Japanese women say they have experienced some type of sexual harassment on the job. See Susan Webb, *Step Forward* (New York: Master Media, 1991), xiv, xvii.
21. *New York Times,* November 11, 1996, February 4, 1997.
22. Linda Bird Francke, *Ground Zero: The Gender Wars in the Military* (New York: Simon and Schuster, 1997), 157.
23. Ibid., 191 and Diana Schemo, "Rate of Rape at Academy Is Put at 12 Percent in Survey," *New York Times,* 29 August 2003.
24. Francke, *Ground Zero,* 187.
25. Ibid., 232.
26. Marysia Zalewski and Jane Parpart, *The "Man" Question in International Relations* (Boulder, Colo.: Westview, 1998), 1.
27. *Time,* March 23, 1998, 49.
28. See the discussion in chapter 3.
29. Beverly Walker, "Psychology and Feminism—If You Can't Beat Them, Join Them," in *Men's Studies Modified,* ed. by Dale Spender (Oxford: Pergamen Press, 1981), 112–114.
30. Debra Renee Kaufman, "Professional Women: How Real Are the Recent Gains?" in *Feminist Philosophies,* 2nd ed., ed. by Janet A. Kourany, James

P. Sterba, and Rosemarie Tong (Upper Saddle River, N.J.: Prentice-Hall, 1999), 189–202.

31. To distinguish traits of character that are virtues from those that are just desirable traits, we can define the class of virtues as those desirable and distributable traits which can be reasonably expected of both women and men. Admittedly, this is a restrictive use of the term "virtue." In normal usage, the term "virtue" is almost synonymous with the term "desirable trait." But there is good reason to focus on those desirable traits that can be justifiably inculcated in both women and men, and so for our purposes let us refer to this class of desirable traits as virtues.

32. For a valuable discussion and critique of these two viewpoints, see Iris Young, "Humanism, Gynocentrism and Feminist Politics," *Women's Studies International Forum* 8 (1985): 173–183.

33. Francke, *Ground Zero,* 16.

34. Ibid.

35. Ibid., 198.

36. Ibid., 16.

37. Ibid., 248.

38. Ibid., 236.

39. Ibid., 226; see also Martha Ackmann, *The Mercury 13* (New York: Random House, 2003).

40. Ibid., 18.

41. Ibid., 16.

42. Lane Guinier, *Becoming Gentleman* (Boston: Beacon, 1997), 18–19.

43. Christopher Commission, *Report of the Independent Commission of the Los Angeles Police Department* (1991).

44. John Corvino, *Same Sex* (Lanham, Md.: Rowman & Littlefield, 1997), 6.

45. These two norms, of course, are not the only positive norms that are relevant to sexual harassment cases, although they are probably the most important ones. Other norms would provide guidance as to how romantic overtures should be made so as to avoid sexual harassment.

CHAPTER 6

1. For example, what I defend as affirmative action is not captured by what Louis Pojman calls strong affirmative action. Yet, it should also be noted that Pojman combines his opposition to affirmative action with support of a range of more radical welfare and environmental programs, which I too support, but, which, unlike affirmative action, are politically unfeasible at the present time. See, in particular, his "Straw Man or Straw Theory: A Reply to Mosley," *International Journal of Applied Philosophy* (1998): 169–180, and his "Pedaling Power: Sustainable Transportation," in his *Environmental Ethics,* 3rd ed. (Belmont, Calif.: Wadsworth Publishing, 2001), 549–551.

2. According to my definition, whether particular affirmative action programs are justified or not depends on how well they instantiate the goals of affirmative action or how one understands both the immediate and ultimate goals. Some might even want to argue that one or more of these immediate goals—most likely the goal of diversity—can never serve the ultimate goals of affirmative action.

3. For further discussion of the ideal of a gender-free society, which I also call an androgynous society, see my books *Justice for Here and Now* and *Three Challenges to Ethics*.

4. I am defining affirmative action for a context where the benefits of diversity can serve the ultimate goal of colorblindness (racial justice) rather than just being compatible with it as would obtain in a colorblind or racially just society.

5. One might wonder how diversity affirmative action candidates can be the most qualified, given that, as I will argue later, they may still need remedial help for a certain period of time. The reason this is the case is that the qualifications that affirmative action candidates lack can be remedied, whereas the qualification that nonaffirmative action candidates clearly lack—diversity—usually cannot be remedied. It is in this sense that nonaffirmative action candidates are not the most qualified.

6. Thomas Sowell, *Affirmative Action Reconsidered* (Washington, D.C.: The American Enterprise Institute for Public Policy Research, 1975), 3. Likewise, Supreme Court Justice Clarence Thomas at his confirmation hearings spoke passionately of his support for outreach affirmative action.

7. Kathryn M. Neckerman & Joleen Kirschenman, "Hiring Strategies, Racial Bias and Inner-City Workers," 38 *Social Problems*, (1991): 433, 437–41.

8. It is important to note here that societal discrimination is simply unproven discrimination. If discrimination can be proven then it is not societal discrimination in this sense even if it can be proven to be caused by society as a whole.

9. See *New York Times* July 12, 1994; Gerald Jaynes and Robin Williams, eds. *A Common Destiny* (Washington, D.C.: National Academy Press, 1989); Andrew Hacker, *Two Nations* (New York: Ballantine Books, 1992); Gertrude Ezorsky, *Racism and Justice* (Ithaca: Cornell University Press, 1991); *Hunger 1995: Fifth Annual Report on the State of World Hunger* (Silver Spring, Md.: Bread for the World Institute, 1995); Todd Michael Furman, "A Dialogue Concerning Claim Jumping and Compensatory Justice," *Teaching Philosophy* 21 (1998): 131–151; Deborah Jones, "The Future of Bakke: Will Social Science Matter?" *Ohio State Law Journal* 59 (1998): 1054–1067; George Curry, ed., *The Affirmative Action Debate* (Reading, Mass.: Perseus Books, 1996); Tom L. Beauchamp and Norman Bowie, *Ethical Theory and Business*, 5th ed. (Upper Saddle River, N.J.: Prentice-Hall, 1996); Bryan Grapes, ed. *Affirmative Action* (San Diego: Greenhaven Press, 2000), Introduction; Robert Weiss, *We Want Jobs* (New York: Garland Publishers, 1997); M. V. Lee

Badgett. *Economic Perspectives on Affirmative Action* (Washington, D.C.: Joint Center for Political and Economic Studies, 1995).

10. In a recent undergraduate class, most of my white students regarded discrimination against minorities as so severe that they would not agree to change their skin color, even if it were possible, for a half million dollars! I didn't try to see if they would accept a higher sum.

11. The Hopwood Court has further restricted the scope of the discrimination for which an institution can claim to be responsible. Thus, the court held that the Law School at the University of Texas could only seek to correct discrimination engaged in by its own Law School and so could not justify its affirmative action program as a partial attempt to remedy discrimination in Texas's educational system as a whole, even though that system was still under desegregation orders when the Hopwood case was being tried. By contrast, the Sixth Circuit (Hopwood was tried in the Fifth Circuit) upheld a district court ruling that refused to limit its review of Tennessee's professional schools to past discrimination at each individual school but also took into account discrimination in Tennessee's educational system as a whole. The Sixth Circuit reasoned that "applicants do not arrive at the admissions office of a professional school in a vacuum. To be admitted they ordinarily must have been students for sixteen years." *Geier v. Alexander,* 801F. 2d 799 (6th Cir. 1986).

12. For further development of this idea, see Richard Wasserstrom, "Racism, Sexism and Preferential Treatment," *UCLA Law Review* 24 (1977).

13. See Paul Wellstone and Jonathan Kozol, "What Tests Can't Fix," *New York Times*, March 13, 2001; Gary Orfield and John Yun, "Resegregation in American Schools," *The Civil Rights Project*, Harvard University, 1999; Gary Orfield, "The Resegregation of Our Nation's School," *Civil Rights Journal* 5 (Fall 1999); William Celis, "Study Finds Rising Concentration of Blacks and Hispanic Students," *New York Times*, December 14, 1993; Micaela di Leonardo, "White Lies, Black Myths," *Voice*, September 22, 1992.

14. Of course, if these were our options, it may turn out that some current critics of affirmative action would favor retaining affirmative action over such a radical equal educational opportunity alternative. But my point here is simply that current defenders of affirmative action would not favor retaining affirmative action if these were the options.

15. Of course, if someone passed over by an affirmative action program could make the case that he or she had not benefited from the discrimination suffered by the relevant affirmative action candidates (something it would be very difficult to do in the United States given its level of racial and sexual discrimination) that would have to be taken into account.

16. The question arises as to how we might implement such an affirmative action program. But clearly there are ways to do so. At Georgia Tech, the performance gap between white and minority first-year engineering students was eliminated by instituting an intensive five-week summer course

for the minority students. See Susan Strom and Lani Guinier, "The Future of Affirmative Action: The Innovative Ideal," *California Law Review* (1996): 10.

17. Of course, if someone passed over by an affirmative action program made the case that he or she had not benefited from the discrimination suffered by the relevant affirmative action candidates (something it would be very difficult to do in the United States given its level of racial and sexual discrimination) this would have to be taken into account.

18. The diversity at issue here is not identical with racial or ethnic diversity, although the latter is an important element in the diversity that is sought. Moreover, as Justice Powell recognized, achieving the educational benefits of a racially and ethnically diverse student body requires a critical mass of underrepresented minority students.

19. Actually, the University of Texas Law School, like most state law schools, does "discriminate" against nonresidents; it reserves 80 percent of its seats for Texas residents.

20. For a discussion of this point, see Reva Siegel, "The Racial Rhetorics of Colorblind Constitutionalism: The Case of *Hopwood v. Texas,*" in *Race and Representation: Affirmative Action,* ed. by Robert Post and Michael Rogin (New York: Zone Books, 1998), 29–72.

21. Patricia Gurin, "The Compelling Need for Diversity in Higher Education." *Gratz v. Bollinger* (2000) 122 F. Supp. 2nd 811. For additional evidence, see Thomas Weisskoff, "Consequences of Affirmative Action in U.S. Higher Education: A Review of Recent Empirical Studies," *Economic and Political Weekly,* December 22, 2001.

22. I will not take up this aspect of the majority's defense of affirmative action because I am inclined to agree with Justice Thomas that the First Amendment cannot permit what the Fourteenth Amendment forbids.

23. The relevancy of Michigan residency is that most of the Hispanics who applied were not Michigan residents.

24. *United States v. Fordice* (1992) 505 U.S. 717.

25. Franke, *Ground Zero,* 16, 198.

26. Actually, the desired diversity is not thereby guaranteed, as my discussion of the lottery alternative in my main essay and response shows.

27. The majority in *Grutter v. Bollinger* (2003) 539 U.S. 982 also granted a certain deference to the Law School with respect to its judgment concerning the educational importance of diversity, which I too would grant although I wouldn't try to ground it in the First Amendment as the Court does.

CHAPTER 7

1. Office of the Coordinator for Counterterrorism. *Patterns of Global Terrorism–2000.* April 2001.

2. Ibid.

3. If we use the just-war distinction between combatants and noncombatants, those killed at the Pentagon might be viewed as combatants in some undeclared war.

4. Since the bombings in Kenya and Tanzania were of U.S. government installations, they are only classified as terrorist acts in virtue of the fact that they were intended to maximize civilian casualties.

5. Phyllis Bennis, *Z magazine*, September 12, 2001. Although the bombing of the pharmaceutical plant may have involved unintentional harm to innocents, refusing to compensate the thousands of victims who were deprived of the drugs they needed is to intentionally harm innocents.

6. "Life and Death in Iraq," *Seattle-Post-Intelligencer*, May 11, 1999. See also Jeff Indemyer, "Iraqi Sanctions: Myth and Fact," *Swans Commentary*, September 3, 2002.

7. During the Reagan years and after, there was also support for Jonas Savimbi—Reagan referred to Savimbi as Angola's Abraham Lincoln. Savimbi personally beat to death a rival's wife and children. He also shelled civilians and bombed a Red Cross factory. From 1975 until his recent death, he refused to give up a struggle for power in a civil war that resulted in more than 500,000 deaths. See Nicholas Kristof, "Our Own Terrorist," *New York Times*, March 5, 2002, 23.

8. For the defense of just-war pacifism, see my *Justice for Here and Now*, chapter 7.

9. This is because the requirements of just-war pacifism do not directly address the question of whether there are exceptions to the prohibition on intentionally harming innocents. Moreover, when that question is taken up by means of the same case by case analysis with which I defended the earlier stated requirements of just-war pacifism (see my *Justice for Here and Now*, chapter 7), certain exceptions to the prohibition on intentionally harming innocents turn out to be morally justified, as I go on to show.

10. See Philippa Foot, "The Problem of Abortion and the Doctrine of Double Effect," *Oxford Review* 5 (1967): 5–15. This example is quite similar in its implications to the example of Sonya and the indians discussed in chapter 3.

11. See Michael Walzer, *Just and Unjust Wars*, 2nd ed. (New York: Basic Books, 1992), 263–268.

12. James Byrnes, *Speaking Frankly* (New York: Harper, 1947), 264.

13. Winston Churchill, *Triumph and Tragedy* (New York, 1962), 639.

14. Another way to put this is to claim that a right not to have to unconditionally surrender is one of our basic universal human rights.

15. Noble Frankland, *Bomber Offensive* (New York: Ballantine Books, 1970), 38–39.

16. As examples of how inaccurate night bombing was at the time, one oil installation was attacked by 162 aircraft carrying 159 tons of bombs, another by 134 aircraft carrying 103 tons of bombs, but neither suffered any major damage. See Charles Webster and Noble Frankland, *The Strategic Air Offensive Against Germany 1939–45* (London: HMSO, 1961), vol. I, 164.

17. Walzer, *Just and Unjust Wars,* 255–262.
18. The Palestinians made a big concession to Israel in the Olso Peace Accords by accepting this expansion (23 percent more than Israel was granted according to the 1947 UN partition plan) hoping thereby to gain Palestinian control of the remaining 23 percent of historic Palestine.
19. *New York Times,* April 26, 2002.
20. Avishai Margalit, "Settling Scores," *New York Review,* August 22, 2001.
21. See Robert Malley and Hussein, "Camp David: The Tragedy of Errors, *New York Review,* August 9, 2001 and "A Reply to Ehud Barak," *New York Review,* June 11, 2002; "A Reply," *New York Review,* June 27, 2002. See also Benny Morris and Ehud Barak, "Camp David and After: An Exchange," *New York Review,* June 13, 2002; "Camp David and After–Continued," *New York Review,* June 27, 2002.
22. Jeff Halper, The Israeli Committee Against House Demolitions, http://www.icahd.org
23. There is a further requirement that must be met here. It is that the Palestinians must have exhausted nonbelligerent correctives. The evidence that this is the case can, I believe, be found in the numerous Palestinian peace initiatives especially from the early 1970s on, when the Palestinians had acquired political standing in the international community. In 1976 the United States vetoed a UN Security Council Resolution calling for a settlement on the 1967 borders, with "appropriate arrangements . . . to guarantee . . . the sovereignty, territorial integrity and political independence of all states in the area and their right to live in peace within secure and recognized boundaries," including Israel and a new Palestinian state in the occupied territories. The resolution was backed by Egypt, Syria, Jordan, the PLO, and the USSR. See Noam Chomsky, *The Fateful Triangle* (Cambridge, Mass.: South End Press, 1999), 64ff. Israel has rejected every peace plan put forward by the Arabs and the United States except for the bilateral treaty with Egypt and the Olso Peace Accords, and these accords have now been, in effect, abandoned by the current Israeli government. See Paul Finlay, *Deliberate Deceptions* (Brooklyn, N.Y.: Lawrence Hill Books, 1993), 201ff.
24. Nor will it do to distinguish British terror bombing from Palestinian suicide bombing on the grounds that the Nazis represented an unprecedented evil in human history because at the early stage of World War II the British could not have known the full character of the Nazi regime.
25. Some will contest whether this correctly represents Israeli intentions. But even in its best offer at Camp David, Israel proposed dividing Palestine into four separate cantons: the Northern West Bank, the Central West Bank, the Southern West Bank, and Gaza. Going from any one area to another would require crossing Israeli sovereign territory and consequently subject movements of Palestinians within their own country to Israeli control. Restrictions would also apply to the movements of goods, thus subjecting the Palestinian economy to Israeli control. In addition, the Camp David

proposal would have left Israel in control of all Palestinian borders, thereby giving Israel control not only of the internal movement of people and goods but international movement as well. Such a Palestinian state would have had less sovereignty and viability than the Bantustans created by the South African apartheid government, which both Israel and the United States once supported. The Camp David proposal also required Palestinians to give up any claim to the occupied portion of Jerusalem. The proposal would have forced recognition of Israel's annexation of all of Arab East Jerusalem. Talks after Camp David in Egypt suggested that Israel was prepared to allow Palestinian sovereignty over isolated Palestinian neighborhoods in the heart of East Jerusalem. However, these neighborhoods would have remained surrounded by Israeli colonies and separated not only from each other but also from the rest of the Palestinian State. See http://www.nad-plo.org. For a map of the Camp David proposal with its partition of Palestine into four cantons see http://www.nad-plo-org/maps/map13.html. Although Yāsir Arafāt and the Palestinians were roundly condemned in the U.S. media for rejecting the Camp David offer, to my knowledge no maps of the U.S.-Israeli proposal, which would have undercut the claim that it was a reasonable offer, were published in the United States, although they were widely published elsewhere. In my searching, the closest any U.S. media source came to acknowledging these facts, was Anthony Lewis, "Waiting for America," *New York Times,* November 17, 2001.

26. Still, one might think that Palestinian suicide-bombing is not morally justified on the grounds that it is unlikely to be successful, unlikely, that is, to stop the oppression of the Palestinian people. But even if this is the case, suicide bombing can still be morally justified, as was terror-bombing by the British at the beginning of World War II, if it is the best means available for resisting oppression. Of course, when such suicide-bombing is morally justified, it is as an exception to the requirements of just-war pacifism.

27. Al Qaeda have shown themselves capable of inflicting significant damage on both military (the Cole) and diplomatic targets (the U.S. embassies in Kenya and Tanzania). So their opposition to the United States could have continued in just this fashion. Moreover, the attack on the Pentagon differs morally from the attack on the World Trade Center, although the deaths of innocent airline hostages is objectionable in both cases. So, Al Qaeda could still have effectively waged its war against the United States without attacking the World Trade Center. With respect to the possibility of effectively attacking military or governmental targets, Al Qaeda is much better situated vis-à-vis the United States and its allies than the Palestinians are vis-à-vis Israel. This is because Al Qaeda can target the far-flung military and governmental outposts of the United States all around the world, and through such attacks it has effectively brought the United States and its allies to withdraw their military forces from such places as Somalia, Yemen, and even, in terms of effective use, from Saudi Arabia.

Of course, it might be questioned whether Al Qaeda effectively exhausted nonbelligerent corrections before it resorted to belligerent ones. If we take Al Qaeda's grounds for just cause to be U.S. support for the Israeli occupation, the U.S. stance against Iraq, U.S. bases in Saudi Arabia, and U.S. support for repressive governments in the Middle East, then I think we can say that in each case Al Qaeda gave nonbelligerent correctives some chance to work.

28. It is worth noting that at the time that the United States launched its war against Iraq, no public in the world but the Israeli one supported the war under the conditions in which it was launched—that is, without UN support. Jonathan Shell, "The World's Other Superpower," *Nation*, April 14, 2003.

29. http://www.cdi.org/iraq/casualties.cfm, and http://www.wsws.org/articles/2003/may2003/iraq-m05.shtml, http://www.wsws.org/articles/2003/aug2003/iraq-a21.shtml

30. Associated Press, "A Daily Look at U.S. Military Deaths in Iraq," June 26, 2004. http://www.wsws.org/articles/2004/aug2004/civi-a05.shtml. "Three GI's are Killed," *New York Times,* September 22, 2003; *New York Times,* January 4, 2004.

31. As for why the campaign for Iraqi War II began in early September 2002, Andrew H. Card, the White House chief of staff explained, "From a marketing point of view, you don't introduce new products in August . . ." Quoted in Chalmers Johnson, "The Sorrows of Empire," http://www.antiwar.com/orig/johnson1.html

32. It is worth noting here that the United States has not been equally concerned with enforcing other Security Council Resolutions. There are about thirty-one UN Security Council Resolutions against Israel, mostly in connection with the West Bank and the Gaza strip, land that Israel occupied after the Arab-Israel War in 1967, and twenty-three resolutions against Turkey in connection with its occupation of Cyprus. Yet both of these countries receive vast amounts of U.S. aid and weaponry, even though they are in blatant violation of UN Security Council Resolutions. Given that the United States supports the violation of some UN Security Council Resolutions, while opposing the violation of others, it is clear that its opposition to Iraq has little to do with the mere fact that Iraq is in violation of UN Security Council Resolutions.

33. This way of thinking about the issue cuts across the distinction between preemptive and preventive war suggesting that the key question to be assessed is not whether the war is preemptive or preventive but how serious the threat is.

34. See Graham Allison, *Essence of Decision* (Boston: Little, Brown and Co., 1971) and Robert F. Kennedy, *Thirteen Days: A Memoir of the Cuban Missile Crisis* (New York: W. W. Norton & Co., 1969).

35. In what follows, I rely on Gwynne Dyer's account of the differences between these weapons. See his *Ignorant Armies* (Toronto: The Canadian Publishers, 2003), 22ff.

36. Michael Dobbs, "U.S. Had a Key Role in Iraq Buildup," *Washington Post,* December 30, 2002; Christopher Dickey and Evan Thomas, "How Saddam Happened," in Said Aburish, et al., *Inside Iraq* (New York: Marlow and Company, 2002), 211–224.

37. See William Rivers Pitt with Scott Ritter, *War on Iraq: What Team Bush Doesn't Want You to Know* (New York: Context Books, 2002), 20ff.

38. Dobbs, "U.S. Had a Key Role in Iraq Buildup"; Research Unit for Political Economy, "Behind the War on Iraq," *Monthly Review* 55 (2003).

39. Ibid.

40. "The Struggle for Iraq," *New York Times* September 23, 2003.

41. Dyer, *Ignorant Armies;* Bruce Hoffman, "Terrorism and Weapons of Mass Destruction," (Washington, D.C.: Rand 1999).

42. Research Unit for Political Economy, "Behind the War on Iraq."

43. Pitt and Ritter, *War on Iraq.*

44. Dyer, *Ignorant Armies,* 27–8; http://www.precision.rotor.com/trailpgs/reconn-BioTerror.shtml

45. Richard Falkenrath et al., *America's Achilles' Heel* (Cambridge: MIT, 1998), 19–26.

46. In 1984 there was a use of a biological weapon—salmonella—in rural Oregon by a religious cult in an effort to try to sicken enough people to effect the results of a local election. Seven hundred fifty-one people became sick from salmonella, but no one died and the election was not effected.

47. Dyer, *Ignorant Armies,* 22ff.

48. Ibid.

49. Unfortunately, recent actions by the U.S. government are only likely to increase the danger from nuclear weapons. After a self-imposed decade-long ban on the research and development of low-yield nuclear weapons, the U.S. Senate Armed Service Committee voted to lift the ban and push ahead with the production of nuclear weapons that would be more useable. Surely other nuclear powers will feel impelled to follow our example. See http://www.wsws.org/articles/2003/may2003/nuci-m14.shtml, and *New York Times,* July 19, 2003.

50. Dyer, *Ignorant Armies,* 22ff.

51. Of course, there is the possibility that terrorists might use radiological weapons, that is they might combine nuclear waste, say from a hospital, with conventional explosives.

52. Dyer, *Ignorant Armies,* 22ff.

53. France had violated the Nuclear Nonproliferation Treaty in helping the Israelis develop nuclear weapons, and Mordechai Vanunu who exposed Israel's secret acquisition of nuclear weapons in 1986 was kidnapped by Israeli agents in Rome that same year and was released just this year after completing his entire eighteen year sentence, more than eleven years of which was in solitary confinement.

54. David Cortright et al., *Contested Case,* A Report of the Fourth Freedom Foundation and the Joan B. Kroc Institute for International Peace Studies, Policy Brief F8 February 6, 2003.

55. James Risen, "Captives Deny Qaeda Worked with Baghdad," *New York Times,* June 9, 2003. German officials who had been investigating Al Zarqawi for some time have found no evidence of a direct link between Al Zarqawi and Baghdad. Don Van Natta Jr. with David Johnson, "A Terror Lieutenant with a Deadly Past," *New York Times,* February 10, 2003.

56. See Robert Baer, *Sleeping with the Devil: How Washington Sold Our Soul for Saudi Crude* (New York: Crown, 2003) and "Pakistan, A Troubled Ally," *New York Times,* September 9, 2003.

57. See http://www.wsws.org/articles/2003/sept2003/sll.shtml

58. Judith Miller and James Risen, "No Illicit Arms Found in Iraq," *New York Times,* October 3, 2003.

59. Bill Vann, "*New York Times* Reporter Judith Miller Accused of "Hijacking" Military Unit in Iraq," http://www.wsws.org/articles/2003/jun2003/mill-j27.shtml. See also Judith Miller and William J. Broad, "Some Analysts of Iraq Trailers Reject Germ Use," *New York Times,* June 7, 2003, and Greg Miller, "2 Suspect Labs Could Have Produced Hydrogen," *Los Angeles Times,* June 21, 2003, Douglas, Jehl, "Iraqi Trailers Said To Make Hydrogen, Not Biological Arms." *New York Times,* August 8, 2003.

60. Greg Miller, "2 Suspect Labs Could Have Produced Hydrogen."

61. Richard Stevenson, "Iraq Illicit Arms Gone Before War, Inspector Insists," *New York Times,* January 24, 2004.

62. Paul Krugman, "Matters of Emphasis," *New York Times,* April 29, 2003.

63. See Nicholas Kristoff, "Missing in Action," *New York Times,* May 6, 2003; Seymour Hersh, "Who Lied to Whom? Why Did the Administration Endorse a Forgery About Iraq's Nuclear Program?" *The New Yorker,* March 31, 2003, 41.

64. In fact, the CIA recommended its deletion from a speech Bush gave in Cincinnati, only to have it reinserted into Bush's State of the Union address.

65. See "Iraq–Its Infrastructure of Concealment, Deception and Intimidation," http://www.pm.gov.uk

66. Glen Rangwala, "Intelligence? The British Dossier on Iraq's Security Infrastucture," February 5, 2003. http://casi.org.uk/discuss/2003/msg00457.html; Toby Helm, "Fiasco over the Saddam Dossier," February 8, 2003, http://www.telegraph.co.uk

67. http://www.wsws.org/articles/2003/oct2003/cook-o08.shtml

68. http://www.informationclearinghouse.info/article4810.htm

69. James Risen, "Iraq Said to Have Tried to Reach Last-Minute Deal to Avert War," *New York Times,* November 6, 2003. http://www.wsws.org/articles/2003/nov2003/Iraq-n07.shtml

70. Yasin has since disappeared, and some U.S. officials are suggesting he is active with Islamic forces in the Iraqi resistance.

71. See Sidney Blumenthal, *The Clinton Wars* (New York: Farrar, Straus and Giroux, 2003), 491 and Jonathan Alter and Joshua Green, "Gambling: Bennett: Virtue Is as Virtue Does?" *Newsweek*, May 12, 2003.

72. It is interesting that the claim about the forty-five minutes that it would take for Iraq to deploy weapons of mass destruction turns out to be based on a statement that one Iraqi general was overheard making. But that statement was not made about weapons of mass destruction at all, but only about ordinary conventional weapons. So a relatively innocuous statement by an Iraqi general about conventional weapons was distorted by the United Kingdom, and accepted by the United States, to be a threatening statement about weapons of mass destruction. See http://www.wsws.org/articles/2003/aug2003/hurt-a28.shtml

73. In addition to Thomas Friedman (cited below), see Michael Schrage, "No Weapons, No Matter," *Washington Post*, May 11, 2003. Interestingly, with respect to the claim that Iraq could have deployed weapons of mass destruction within forty-five minutes—the claim that has been the focus of much of Lord Hutton's inquiry in the United Kingdom—it turns out that the evidence behind this claim was a hearsay comment of an Iraqi general that related not to weapons of mass destruction but to ordinary battlefield weaponry. See http://www.wsws.org/articles/2003/aug2003/blai-a30.shtml

74. Thomas Friedman, "The Meaning of a Skull," *New York Times,* April 27, 2003.

75. Thomas Friedman, "Because We Could," *New York Times,* June 4, 2003.

76. To simplify this argument a bit: Morality requires that you first punish murderers in your own country and stop supporting murderers in other countries before you think about punishing murderers you once supported but who have turned on you and you now no longer support. Otherwise, your opposition to murderers will be thought (quite rightly) to have little to do with the fact that they are murderers and everything to do with the fact that they no longer support you and you them.

77. In 1990, when Yemen voted against a UN Security Council resolution to militarily oust Iraq from Kuwait, a senior American diplomat told the Yemeni ambassador: "That was the most expensive No vote you ever cast." Three days later, a U.S. aid program of $70 million to one of the world's poorest countries was stopped. Yemen began to have problems with the IMF and World Bank, and Saudi Arabia expelled 800,000 Yemeni workers, Later, when the United States sought another resolution to blockade Iraq, two other rotating members of the Security Council were duly coerced. Ecuador was warned about the "devastating economic consequences of a No vote," and Zimbabwe was threatened with new IMF conditions for its debt. Norman Solomon and Reese Erlich, *Target Iraq: What the New Media Didn't Tell You* (New York: Context Books, 2003), 69–70.

78. Dexter Filkins with Eric Schmitt, "Demands $32 Billion U.S. Aid Package if It Is to Take Part in a War on Iraq," *New York Times*, February 19, 2003.

79. http://www.wsws.org/articles/2003/turk-m24.shtml

80. The firebombing of Dresden and Hamburg and dropping atomic bombs on Hiroshima and Nagasaki were neither good nor just. For an argument to this effect, see my article "Terrorism and International Justice," in my collection *Terrorism and International Justice* (New York: Oxford University Press, 2003), 212–213.

81. According to a *Time* (Europe) poll, 87 percent of respondents regarded the United States as the greatest threat to peace in 2003. http://www.time.com/time/europe/gdml/peace2003.html

CHAPTER 8

1. For a more detailed discussion of a peacemaking way of doing philosophy, see my *Three Challenges to Ethics*, chapter 5.

SELECTED BIBLIOGRAPHY

Ackmann, Martha. *The Mercury 13*. New York: Random House, 2003.

Ackrill, J. L. "Aristotle on Eudaimonia." In *Essays on Aristotle's Ethics*, edited by Amelie Rorty, 15–34. Berkeley: University of California Press, 1980.

Allison, Graham. *Essence of Decision*. Boston: Little, Brown and Co., 1971.

Aristotle. *The Generation of Animals*. Translated by A. L. Peck. Cambridge: Harvard University Press, 1943.

Aristotle. *The Politics of Aristotle*. Translated by Ernest Barker. London: Oxford University Press, 1946.

Badgett, M. V. Lee. *Economic Perspectives on Affirmative Action*. Washington, D.C.: Joint Center for Political and Economic Studies, 1995.

Baer, Robert. *Sleeping with the Devil: How Washington Sold Our Soul for Saudi Crude*. New York: Crown, 2003.

Baier, Kurt. *The Moral Point of View*. Abridged ed. New York: Random House, 1965.

Baron, Marcia, Philip Pettit, and Michael Slote. *Three Methods of Ethics*. Oxford: Blackwell Publishers, 1997.

Beauchamp, Tom L., and Norman Bowie. *Ethical Theory and Business*, 5th ed. Upper Saddle River, N.J.: Prentice-Hall, 1996.

Beyleveld, Deryck. *The Dialectical Necessity of Morality*. Chicago: University of Chicago Press, 1991.

Blumenthal, Sidney. *The Clinton Wars*. New York: Farrar, Straus and Giroux, 2003.

Boylan, Michael, ed. *Gewirth*. Lanham, Md.: Rowman & Littlefield, 1999.

Bravo, Ellen, and Ellen Cassedy. *The 9–5 Guide to Combating Sexual Harassment*. New York: John Wiley and Sons, 1992.

Broadie, Sarah. *Ethics with Aristotle*. New York: Oxford University Press, 1991.

Brownmiller, Susan. *Femininity*. New York: Ballantine Books, 1984.

Byrnes, James. *Speaking Frankly*. New York: Harper, 1947.

Callicott, Baird. "Animal Liberation: A Triangular Affair." *Environmental Ethics* 2(1980): 311–328.

Callicott, Baird. *In Defense of the Land Ethic*. Albany: State University of New York Press, 1989.

Churchill, Winston. *Triumph and Tragedy*. New York, 1962.

Cooper, John. *Reason and Human Good in Aristotle*. Cambridge: Harvard University Press, 1975.

Corthright, David, et al. *Contested Case*. A Report of the Fourth Freedom Foundation and the Joan B. Kroc Institute for International Peace Studies, Policy Brief F8 6 February 2003.

Corvino, John. *Same Sex*. Lanham, Md.: Rowman & Littlefield, 1997.

Curry, George, ed. *The Affirmative Action Debate*. Reading, Mass.: Perseus Books, 1996.

Dickey, Christopher, and Evan Thomas. "How Saddam Happened." In *Inside Iraq*, edited by Said Aburish et al., 211–224. New York: Marlow and Company, 2002.

Dobbs, Michael. "U.S. Had a Key Role in Iraq Buildup." *Washington Post*, December 30, 2002.

Doyle, James. *The Male Experience*. Dubuque, Iowa: W.C. Brown & Co., 1983.

Dyer, Gwynne. *Ignorant Armies*. Toronto: The Canadian Publishers, 2003.

Estrich, Susan. "Sex at Work," *Stanford Law Review* 43 (1991): 813–861.

Ezorsky, Gertrude. *Racism and Justice*. Ithaca: Cornell University Press, 1991.

Falkenrath, Richard, et al. *America's Achilles' Heel*. Cambridge: MIT, 1998.

Finlay, Paul. *Deliberate Deceptions*. Brooklyn, N.Y.: Lawrence Hill Books, 1993.

Foot, Philippa. "The Problem of Abortion and the Doctrine of Double Effect." *Oxford Review* 5 (1967): 5–15.

Foot, Philippa. *Virtues and Vices*. Berkeley: University of California Press, 1978.

Francke, Linda Bird. *Ground Zero*. New York: Simon and Schuster, 1997.

Frankland, Noble. *Bomber Offensive*. New York: Ballantine Books, 1970.

Furman, Todd Michael. "A Dialogue Concerning Claim Jumping and Compensatory Justice." *Teaching Philosophy* 21 (1998): 131–151.

Gert, Bernard. "Acting Irrationally Versus Acting Contrary to What Is Required by Reason." *Journal of Social Philosophy* 30, no. 3 (1999): 379–386.

Gert, Bernard. "Theoretical Versus Practical Rationality." In Sterba, *Social and Political Philosophy*, 71–76.

Gomez-Preston, Cherly. *When No Means No*. New York: Carol Publishing Co., 1993.

Grapes, Bryan, ed. Introduction to *Affirmative Action*. San Diego: Greenhaven Press, 2000.

Guinier, Lani. *Becoming Gentleman*. Boston: Beacon, 1997.

Gurin, Patricia. "The Compelling Need for Diversity in Higher Education." *Gratz v. Bollinger* (2000). 122 F. Supp. 2nd 811.

Hacker, Andrew. *Two Nations*. New York: Ballantine Books, 1992.

Hardie, W. F. B. "The Final Good in Aristotle's Ethics." In *Aristotle*, edited by J. M. E. Moravcsik, 297–322. New York: Anchor Books, 1967.

Harsanyi, John C. *Essays on Ethics, Social Behavior, and Scientific Explanation*. Dordrecht: D. Reidel, 1976.

Hayek, F. A. *The Constitution of Liberty*. Chicago: University of Chicago Press, 1960.

Hersh, Seymour. "Who Lied to Whom? Why Did the Administration Endorse a Forgery About Iraq's Nuclear Program?" *The New Yorker,* March 31, 2003, 41.

Hill, Thomas E. *Respect, Pluralism, and Justice.* Oxford: Oxford University Press, 2000.

Hospers, John. *Libertarianism.* Los Angeles: Nash Publishing, 1971.

Hospers, John. "The Libertarian Manifesto." In *Morality in Practice,* 7th ed., edited by James P. Sterba, 23–31. Belmont, Calif.: Wadsworth, 2003.

Hume, David. *An Enquiry Concerning the Principles of Morals.* La Salle, Ill: Open Court, 1960.

Hume, David. *A Treatise of Human Nature.* Edited by L. A. Selby-Bigge. Oxford: Clarendon Press, 1888.

Hursthouse, Rosalind. *On Virtue Ethics.* Oxford: Oxford University Press, 1999.

Jamieson, Dale, ed. *Singer and His Critics.* Oxford: Blackwell, 1999.

Jaynes, Gerald, and Robin Williams, eds. *A Common Destiny.* Washington, D.C.: National Academy Press, 1989.

Johnson, Lawrence. *A Morally Deep World.* New York: Cambridge University Press, 1991.

Jones, Deborah. "The Future of Bakke: Will Social Science Matter?" *Ohio State Law Journal* 59 (1998): 1054–1067.

Kant, Immanuel. *Observations on the Feeling of the Beautiful and the Sublime.* Translated by John Goldthwait. Berkeley: University of California Press, 1960.

Kant, Immanuel. "What Is Enlightenment?" In *The Philosophy of Kant: Immanuel Kant's Moral and Political Writings,* translated and edited by Carl Friedrich. New York: The Modern Library, 1949.

Kaufman, Debra Renee. "Professional Women: How Real Are the Recent Gains?" In *Feminist Philosophies,* 2nd ed., edited by Janet A. Kourany, James P. Sterba, and Rosemarie Tong, 189–202. Upper Saddle River, N.J.: Prentice-Hall, 1999.

Kaufman, Frederik. "Machines, Sentience and the Scope of Morality." *Environmental Ethics* 16 (1994): 57–70.

Kennedy, Robert F. *Thirteen Days: A Memoir of the Cuban Missile Crisis.* New York: W. W. Norton & Co., 1969.

Korsgaard, Christine. *Sources of Normativity.* Cambridge: Cambridge University Press, 1996.

Kraut, Richard. *Aristotle on the Human Good.* Princeton, N.J.: Princeton University Press, 1989.

Leopold, Aldo. *A Sand County Almanac.* New York: Oxford University Press, 1949.

Luce, Duncan R., and Howard Raiffa. *Games and Decisions.* New York: John Wiley & Sons, Inc., 1967.

Machan, Tibor. *Human Rights and Human Liberties.* Chicago: Nelson-Hall, 1975.

Machan, Tibor. *Individuals and Their Rights.* La Salle, Ill.: Open Court, 1989.

Machan, Tibor. "Sterba on Machan's 'Concession.'" *Journal of Social Philosophy* 32 (2001): 241–243.

MacIntyre, Alasdair. *After Virtue.* Notre Dame: University of Notre Dame Press, 1981.

MacIntyre, Alasdair. *Whose Justice? Which Rationality?* Notre Dame: University of Notre Dame Press, 1988.

Malley, Robert, and Hussein Agha. "Camp David: The Tragedy of Errors." *New York Review of Books,* August 9, 2001.

Malley, Robert, and Hussein Agha. "A Reply." *New York Review of Books,* June 27, 2002.

Malley, Robert, and Hussein Agha. "A Reply to Ehud Barak." *New York Review of Books,* June 11, 2002.

Margalit, Avishai. "Settling Scores." *New York Review of Books,* August 22, 2002.

May, Larry, and Robert Strikwerda. *Rethinking Masculinity.* Lanham, Md.: Rowman and Littlefield, 1992.

McConnell, Terrance. "'Ought' Implies 'Can,' and the Scope of Moral Requirements." *Philosophia* (1989): 437–454.

Montefiore, Alan. "'Ought' and 'Can.'" *Philosophical Quarterly* (1954): 24–40.

Morales, Maria. *Perfect Equality.* Lanham, Md.: Rowman and Littlefield, 1996.

Morris, Benny, and Ehud Barak. "Camp David and After: An Exchange." *New York Review of Books,* June 13, 2002.

Morris, Benny, and Ehud Barak. "Camp David and After–Continued." *New York Review of Books,* June 27, 2002.

Nagel, Thomas. "Aristotle on Eudaimonia." In *Essays on Aristotle's Ethics,* edited by Amelie Rorty, 7–14. Berkeley: University of California Press, 1980.

Nagel, Thomas. *Equality and Partiality.* Oxford: Oxford University Press, 1991.

Neckerman, Kathryn M., and Joleen Kirschenman. "Hiring Strategies, Racial Bias and Inner-City Workers." *Social Problems* 38 (1991): 433, 437–441.

Nodding, Nell. *Caring: A Feminine Approach to Ethics and Moral Education.* Berkeley: University of California Press, 1984.

Nussbaum, Martha. "Recoiling from Reason." *New York Review of Books,* vol. 36. December 7, 1989.

Office of the Coordinator for Counterterrorism. *Patterns of Global Terrorism– 2000.* April 2001.

Orfield, Gary, and John Yun. "Resegregation in American Schools." *The Civil Rights Project,* Harvard University, 1999.

Orfield, Gary. "The Resegregation of Our Nation's Schools." *Civil Rights Journal* (Fall 1999).

Pigden, Charles. "Logic and the Autonomy of Ethics." *Australasian Journal of Philosophy* (1989): 127–151.

Pigden, Charles. "Ought-Implies-Can: Erasmus, Luther and R. M. Hare." *Sophia* (1990): 2–30.

Pitt, William Rivers, with Scott Ritter. *War on Iraq: What Team Bush Doesn't Want You to Know.* New York: Context Books, 2002.

Pojman, Louis P. "Pedaling Power: Sustainable Transportation." In *Environmental Ethics*, 3rd ed., edited by Louis P. Pojman, 549–551. Belmont, Calif.: Wadsworth Publishing, 2001.

Pojman, Louis P. "Straw Man or Straw Theory: A Reply to Mosley." *International Journal of Applied Philosophy* (1998): 169–180.

Rawls, John. *A Theory of Justice*. Cambridge: Harvard University Press, 1971.

Reath, Andrews, Barbara Herman, and Christine Korsgaard. *Reclaiming the History of Philosophy: Essays for John Rawls*. Cambridge: Cambridge University Press, 1997.

Regan, Tom. *Animal Rights, Human Wrongs*. Lanham, Md.: Rowman & Littlefield, 2004.

Regis, Edward, ed. *Gewirth's Ethical Rationalism*. Chicago: University of Chicago Press, 1984.

Richmond-Abbot, Marie, ed. *Masculine and Feminine*. 2nd ed. New York: Random House, 1991.

Rolston, Holmes III. "Enforcing Environmental Ethics: Civil Law and Natural Value." In *Social and Political Philosophy*, 349–369.

Rorty, Amelie. "The Place of Contemplation in Aristotle's Nicomachean Ethics." In *Essays on Aristotle's Ethics*, edited by Amelie Rorty, 377–394. Berkeley: University of California Press, 1980.

Routley, R., and V. Routley. "Against the Inevitability of Human Chauvinism." In *Ethics and Problems of the 21st Century*, edited by K. E. Goodpaster and K. M. Sayre. Notre Dame: University of Notre Dame Press, 1979.

Sagoff, Mark. "Animal Liberation and Environmental Ethics: Bad Marriage, Quick Divorce." *Osgood Hall Law Journal* (1984): 297–307.

Sapontzis, Steve. "'Ought' Does Imply 'Can.'" *Southern Journal of Philosophy* (1991): 383–393.

Scanlon, Thomas. *What We Owe to Others*. Cambridge, Harvard University Press, 1998.

Scanlon, T. M. "Contractualism and Utilitarianism." In *Utilitarianism and Beyond*, edited by Amartya Sen and Bernard Williams, 103–128. Cambridge: Cambridge University Press, 1982.

Schaller, Walter. "Are Virtues No More Than Dispositions to Obey Moral Rules?" *Philosophy* 20 (July, 1990): 195–207.

Schneewind, J. B., ed. *Reason, Ethics and Society: Themes from Kurt Baier and His Responses*. Peru, Ill.: Open Court, 1996.

Schott, Robin May. "The Gender of Enlightenment." In *What Is Enlightenment*, edited by James Schmidt. Berkeley: University of California Press, 1996.

Seidler, Victor. *Rediscovering Masculinity*. New York: Routledge, 1989.

Shell, Jonathan. "The World's Other Superpower." *Nation*, April 14, 2003.

Sherman, Nancy. *Making a Necessity of Virtue: Aristotle and Kant on Virtue*. Cambridge: Cambridge University Press, 1997.

Sidgwick, Henry. *The Methods of Ethics*. 7th ed. London: Macmillian, 1907.

Siegel, Reva. "The Racial Rhetorics of Colorblind Constitutionalism: The Case of *Hopwood v. Texas*." In *Race and Representation: Affirmative Action*, edited by Robert Post and Michael Rogin, 29–72. New York: Zone Books, 1998.

Singer, Peter. *Animal Liberation.* Rev. ed. New York: Avon Books, 1992.

Singer, Peter. *Practical Ethics.* 2nd ed. Cambridge: Cambridge University Press, 1993.

Solomon, Norman, and Reese Erlich. *Target Iraq: What the New Media Didn't Tell You.* New York: Context Books, 2003, 69–70.

Sowell, Thomas. *Affirmative Action Reconsidered.* Washington, D.C.: The American Enterprise Institute for Public Policy Research, 1975.

Sterba, James P. "A Biocentrist Fights Back," *Environmental Ethics* 20 (Winter 1998): 361–376.

Sterba, James P. "From Liberty to Welfare: An Update," *Social Theory and Practice* (2000): 465–478.

Sterba, James P. *How to Make People Just.* Totowa, N.J.: Rowman and Littlefield, 1988.

Sterba, James P. "Is There a Rationale for Punishment?" *Philosophical Topics* 18 (1990): 105–125.

Sterba, James P. *Justice for Here and Now.* New York: Cambridge University Press, 1998.

Sterba, James P. "Taylor's Biocentricism and Beyond." *Environmental Ethics* 17 (1995): 191–208.

Sterba, James P. *Three Challenges to Ethics.* New York: Oxford University Press, 2001.

Sterba, James P., ed. *Social and Political Philosophy: Contemporary Perspectives.* London: Routledge, 2001.

Strom, Susan, and Lani Guinier. "The Future of Affirmative Action: The Innovative Ideal." *California Law Review* (1996): 10.

Strossen, Nadine. "Regulating Workplace Sexual Harassment and Upholding the First Amendment—Avoiding a Collision," *Villanova Law Review,* 37 (1992): 211–228.

Taylor, Harriet. "The Enfranchisement of Women." In *Essays on Sex Equality,* edited by Alice S. Rossi. Chicago: University of Chicago Press, 1970.

Taylor, Paul. *Respect for Nature.* Princeton, N.J.: Princeton University Press, 1987.

Trebiloct, Joyce, ed. *Mothering.* Totowa, N.J.: Rowman and Littlefield, 1983.

Varner, Gary. *In Nature's Interests?* Oxford: Oxford University Press, 1998.

Walker, Beverly. "Psychology and Feminism—If You Can't Beat Them, Join Them." In *Men's Studies Modified,* edited by Dale Spender, 112–114. Oxford: Pergamon Press, 1981.

Walzer, Michael. *Just and Unjust Wars.* 2nd ed. New York: Basic Books, 1992.

Warren, Mary Ann. "The Rights of the Nonhuman World." In *Environmental Philosophy,* edited by Robert Elliot and Arran Gare, 109–134. New York: University of Queensland Press, 1983.

Wasserstrom, Richard. "Racism, Sexism and Preferential Treatment. *UCLA Law Review* (1977).

Webb, Susan. *Step Forward.* New York: Master Media, 1991.

Webster, Charles, and Noble Frankland. *The Strategic Air Offensive Against Germany 1939–45.* London: HMSO, 1961, vol. I, 164.

Weiss, Robert. *We Want Jobs.* New York: Garland Publishers, 1997.

Weisskoff, Thomas. "Consequences of Affirmative Action in U.S. Higher Education: A Review of Recent Empirical Studies." *Economic and Political Weekly* December 22, 2001.

Wilkes, Kathleen. "The Good Man and the Good for Man." In *Essays on Aristotle's Ethics,* edited by Amelie Rorty, 341–358. Berkeley: University of California Press, 1980.

Young, Iris. "Humanism, Gynocentrism and Feminist Politics." *Women's Studies International Forum* 8 (1985): 173–183.

Zalewski, Marysia, and Jane Parpart. *The "Man" Question in International Relations.* Boulder, Colo.: Westview, 1998.

INDEX

A

Affirmative action
  definition of, 110–13
  diversity, 123–32
  outreach, 113
  remedial, 114–23
Affirmative Action and Racial
  Preference, 157
Aliens, 81–84
al-Obeidi, Hassan, 150
Al Qaeda, 8, 140, 141, 146–47,
  148, 188n27
Al-Sarqawi, Abu Mussaab, 140, 146
Altruism, 15, 24–26, 32–33, 36,
  162n26, 169n6
Animal liberationists, objections
  from, 73–81
Animals
  farm, 72–73, 177n41
  wild, 73
Anthropocentrism, 6, 58, 60
Aristotle, 1–4, 9–11
Aum Skinrikyo, 143

B

Baier, Kurt, 25, 33
Bakke, 123–24, 126
Baron, Marcia, 13
Basic needs
  and environmental ethics,
    61–73, 83–86, 175n13

and the libertarian ideal of
  liberty, 47–57, 174n45
Bennett, William, 151
Biocentrism, 75–81, 84
Biological weapons, 143–44
Burington Industries v. Ellerth, 99
Bush, George W., 8, 138, 139–40,
  142, 148–52

C

Callicott, Baird, 71
Cannibalism, 63
Categorical Imperative, 6, 9–11
Chemical weapons, 141–43
China, 55
Christoforou v. Ryder Truck
  Rental, 92
City of Richmond v. Croson, 117–19
Civil Rights Act of 1964, Title VII
  of, 91, 93, 98
Clinton, Bill, 90, 138, 151–52
Cohen, Carl, 157
Colorblind society, 119–20, 132
Conflict Resolution Principles,
  61–70

D

Distant peoples and future
  generations, 54–56
Dyer, Gwynne, 143, 144